DARLING CHILD

Private Correspondence of
Queen Victoria and the Crown Princess of Prussia

1871–1878

Darling Child,

Just two words
to say that affairs
looks better - an
armistice
of 6 Months &c
Servia & Jrvvnce
do well. - But
Turn is always a

DARLING CHILD

Private Correspondence of
Queen Victoria and the Crown Princess of Prussia

1871–1878

Edited by
ROGER FULFORD

Evans Brothers Limited London

Published by
EVANS BROTHERS LIMITED
Montague House, Russell Square, London WCiB 5BX

This selection © Roger Fulford 1976

First published 1976

Set in 11 on 12 point Bembo
and printed in Great Britain by
Butler and Tanner Limited, Frome and London
ISBN 0 237 44857 2   PRA 4894

CONTENTS

ILLUSTRATIONS

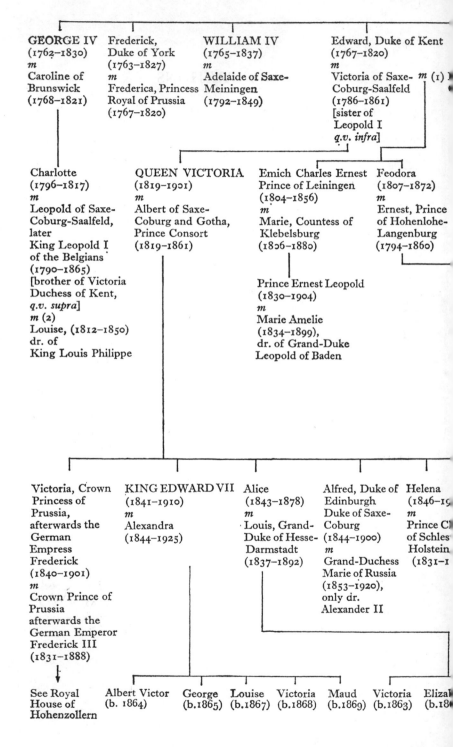

GEORGE IV
(1762–1830)
m
Caroline of
Brunswick
(1768–1821)

Frederick,
Duke of York
(1763–1827)
m
Frederica, Princess
Royal of Prussia
(1767–1820)

WILLIAM IV
(1765–1837)
m
Adelaide of Saxe-
Meiningen
(1792–1849)

Edward, Duke of Kent
(1767–1820)
m
Victoria of Saxe- m (1)
Coburg-Saalfeld
(1786–1861)
[sister of
Leopold I
q.v. infra]

Charlotte
(1796–1817)
m
Leopold of Saxe-
Coburg-Saalfeld,
later
King Leopold I
of the Belgians
(1790–1865)
[brother of Victoria
Duchess of Kent,
q.v. supra]
m (2)
Louise, (1812–1850)
dr. of
King Louis Philippe

QUEEN VICTORIA
(1819–1901)
m
Albert of Saxe-
Coburg and Gotha,
Prince Consort
(1819–1861)

Emich Charles Ernest
Prince of Leiningen
(1804–1856)
m
Marie, Countess of
Klebelsburg
(1806–1880)

Prince Ernest Leopold
(1830–1904)
m
Marie Amelie
(1834–1899),
dr. of Grand-Duke
Leopold of Baden

Feodora
(1807–1872)
m
Ernest, Prince
of Hohenlohe-
Langenburg
(1794–1860)

Victoria, Crown
Princess of
Prussia,
afterwards the
German
Empress
Frederick
(1840–1901)
m
Crown Prince of
Prussia
afterwards the
German Emperor
Frederick III
(1831–1888)

KING EDWARD VII
(1841–1910)
m
Alexandra
(1844–1925)

Alice
(1843–1878)
m
Louis, Grand-
Duke of Hesse-
Darmstadt
(1837–1892)

Alfred, Duke of
Edinburgh
Duke of Saxe-
Coburg
(1844–1900)
m
Grand-Duchess
Marie of Russia
(1853–1920),
only dr.
Alexander II

Helena
(1846–19
m
Prince C
of Schles
Holstein
(1831–1

See Royal
House of
Hohenzollern

Albert Victor
(b. 1864)

George
(b.1865)

Louise
(b.1867)

Victoria
(b.1868)

Maud
(b.1869)

Victoria
(b.1863)

Eliza
(b.18

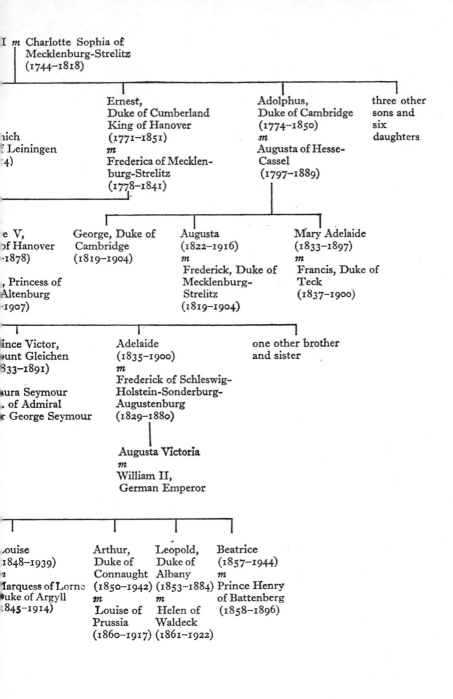

I *m* Charlotte Sophia of
   Mecklenburg-Strelitz
   (1744–1818)

Ernest,
Duke of Cumberland
King of Hanover
(1771–1851)
m
Frederica of Mecklen-
burg-Strelitz
(1778–1841)

Adolphus,
Duke of Cambridge
(1774–1850)
m
Augusta of Hesse-
Cassel
(1797–1889)

three other
sons and
six
daughters

ich
Leiningen
4)

e V,
of Hanover
-1878)

, Princess of
Altenburg
-1907)

George, Duke of
Cambridge
(1819–1904)

Augusta
(1822–1916)
m
Frederick, Duke of
Mecklenburg-
Strelitz
(1819–1904)

Mary Adelaide
(1833–1897)
m
Francis, Duke of
Teck
(1837–1900)

ince Victor,
unt Gleichen
833–1891)

ura Seymour
. of Admiral
r George Seymour

Adelaide
(1835–1900)
m
Frederick of Schleswig-
Holstein-Sonderburg-
Augustenburg
(1829–1880)

Augusta Victoria
m
William II,
German Emperor

one other brother
and sister

ouise
1848–1939)
1
larquess of Lorne
uke of Argyll
845–1914)

Arthur,
Duke of
Connaught
(1850–1942)
m
Louise of
Prussia
(1860–1917)

Leopold,
Duke of
Albany
(1853–1884)
m
Helen of
Waldeck
(1861–1922)

Beatrice
(1857–1944)
m
Prince Henry
of Battenberg
(1858–1896)

THE ROYAL FAMILY TREE

ne
1866)

Ernest
(b.1868)

Frederick William
(b.1870)

2 others

PREFACE

I express the deep sense of my gratitude to Her Majesty the Queen for her gracious permission to publish this further volume of the correspondence between Queen Victoria and her eldest daughter, the German Crown Princess, who was subsequently the Empress Frederick. The letters from the Empress are in the Royal Archives at Windsor, and the letters from Queen Victoria are in the Empress's old home at Friedrichshof in the Taunus mountains.

I should not have been able to edit these letters without the help and encouragement of the Landgrave of Hesse and his brother Prince Wolfgang, the Empress's grandsons, who live at Friedrichshof and most generously allowed me to work in this country on the relevant volumes of Queen Victoria's letters. I thank them. The guidance and sympathetic understanding of Prince Wolfgang have saved me from many blunders and, in countless ways, have greatly added to the enjoyment of my task.

The Queen's librarian, Sir Robin Mackworth Young, and his staff have given me ungrudging help over the difficulties which arise in explaining and collating a double correspondence of this nature. I would particularly thank Miss Cuthbert who transcribed many of the Empress's letters for me, and adjusted my reading of both sides of the correspondence from material in the Royal Archives. The Empress's handwriting is admirably clear, influenced by the scrupulous style of her father, the Prince Consort, but Queen Victoria's writing presents the editor with anxious problems, which do not grow less as she grows older. Many is the time I have puzzled over the possible English of words and phrases only to realise that they were in French or German. To give an example at random, I decided that she described one of her sons as "wayward and ungrateful": in fact she had written "wayward and *ungeratheuen*" (undutiful). Editing her letters has something in common with attempting a crossword puzzle, knowing that the solution is possibly—though not certainly—correct. I make no claim that the letters in this book are free from slips and mis-readings, but I can claim that my approach to the Queen's handwriting has never been confident—always cautious. No doubt the letters of Queen Victoria will give posterity plenty of opportunity for editions "cum notis variorum".

I thank Mrs. Rogers of Kendal who tackled the difficult job of typing from dictaphone belts my original reading of the letters. My relative, Mrs. Willy Rous, sought change from the life of an army officer's wife in Northern Ireland, by typing a faultless final draft of the book. I am deeply grateful to her.

The illustration of members of the Royal Family between pages 188 and 189 has a curious history. It is the work of Lachlan McLachlan (1825–91); he was one of the pioneers of photography in Manchester and his large group of the Famine Relief Committee is well-known. In the early 1870's he received permission to do a somewhat similar picture of the Royal Family. For this he employed the artist Frederick Shields to paint the Green Drawing Room at Windsor and arrange the members of the Family—who were all photographed separately—in a convenient montage in his painting. It was the Queen's wish that her grand-children—at least one from each married child—should be included. The finished picture was intended for the Town Hall at Manchester and the Town Clerk did many of the negotiations with the Queen. There were however various legal difficulties and the original picture would seem to have disappeared, but I was fortunate to find a photograph of the original.

I am particularly grateful to Mr. Francis Hawcroft, the Keeper of the Whitworth, who helped my original enquiry. Mr. Harry Milligan, the honorary Assistant Keeper of Photographs at the North West Museum of Science and Industry, gave me valuable details of McLachlan's work, and Mr. Julian Treuherz, the Assistant Keeper of Paintings at the City Art Gallery, encouraged me to pursue my enquiries. He took me out to the Queens Park Art Gallery, that huge treasure store of Victorian and later pictures, where we found the photograph of McLachlan's work.

I acknowledge my debt to the *Book of Kings*, edited by Mr. Arnold McNaughton and published by the Garnstone Press in 1973. As always the London Library and Mr Hobbs, who looks after the concerns of country members, have been infinitely resourceful and helpful. Finally I record my gratitude to my publishers, Evans Brothers Limited, and the director concerned, Audrey White, whose interest in the personalities in the book and whose encouragement to me over many years is remembered with affectionate gratitude.

INTRODUCTION

The method which I have followed in editing these letters follows that which I have used in earlier volumes. People mentioned in the text are identified in the index: the reason for this is to avoid cluttering the pages with footnotes. There are a few exceptions where I felt that the reader would be helped by an immediate identification, but I have tried to keep the footnotes to explain passages which might puzzle the reader or to give a short historical background to points raised by either writer. The Christian or nicknames used are explained in the table on page 8.

I here add a word about the title of this volume. I had originally thought of using the phrase "Kissing Your Dear Hand" a form of respectful endearment with which the Crown Princess invariably ends her letters but it was pointed out to me that this would not explain the contents of the book. In the opening volume of this series the letters from the Queen always began "Dearest Child" or "My Dearest Child". "Darling" was just occasionally used in the body of the letters or in references to the Prince Consort after his death. It would not seem that the word "Darling" was used as a term of endearment in the Royal Family before the end of the 1860's. It was, for example, not used by King George IV whose family letters are masterpieces of flamboyant affection. But in this volume of the correspondence the Queen's letters invariably begin "Darling Child" though on a few occasions when she was vexed with her daughter "Darling" rather noticeably drops to "Dearest". However, "Darling" as the general usage in this volume makes the title for it.

In editing family letters of this kind an editor is faced by one recurring problem. What shall be left out? There could be no question of publishing the letters in their entirety because we should feel, with King Solomon, that they would make many books to which there is no end. More than a half has had to be excluded. Some of the cuts are easy—the weather, family ailments, repetitions, recollections of anniversaries, grave or gay. No doubt a different editor would have reached different decisions and I feel that the reader is entitled to know what were the influences which guided my choice of what should be included. The first consideration was obviously the importance of the public or family matter about which the Queen and her daughter are writing. The second point was the style in which even quite trivial things are expressed. The Queen's descriptive powers and the cut and thrust of one ever accustomed to say exactly what she thought obviously play a large part here, and now that the Crown Princess is older her letters show something of the assurance of her mother. She never, I think, returns fire but on occasions she stands her ground. There was a somewhat serious disagreement in the summer of 1872: on such rare occasions the letters are generally destroyed; but for some weeks "Darling Child" drops to "Dearest Child". The dispute almost certainly concerned the marriage of Princess Louise to Lord Lorne. (The Crown Princess had been an advocate of Abbat—Prince Albrecht of Prussia—being chosen.) The Crown Princess's closing letter on the disagreement has survived. "It pains me much to see how my letter has been misconstrued—and that you should think its tone wanting in respect or affection when you must know, dearest Mama, that nothing in the world can be further from my intentions. . . . As I see I have so utterly failed I will not attempt it again or refer to the subject any more —though I can not help feeling much aggrieved at a reproach I hardly feel I deserved." (7 August 1872.)

The third influence which governed my selection was the desire that private and personal matters should not be used to crowd out the comments and feelings of both correspondents on matters of public policy. I remember that in a letter which the last Czar wrote to his wife on the eve of the Revolution he said "I greatly miss my half-hourly game of patience every evening. I shall take up dominoes again in my spare time." The incongruity of those two sentences with the thunderous events taking place in St. Petersburg gives a totally unfair impression of the preoccupations of the Czar and Czarina at the time. In a different but not wholly dissimilar way the publication of the Queen's Highland Journal in 1868 emphasises domestic and holiday affairs at the expense of more serious concerns. Indeed that is probably why the Queen's children thought the publication unwise. I was therefore particularly anxious that as domestic and family preoccupations naturally appear in almost every letter they should be kept in balance with more serious things.

I had originally intended that the selection of letters for this book should begin in 1871 and end in 1876, but when I had finished I was not satisfied that this particular period brought out the political importance of the correspondence. In this connexion a point deserves to be noticed. In the middle years of the nineteenth century the nations of Europe were securely attached at the top not only through Royal Families but through leading aristocratic families, known to students of the Almanac de Gotha and through thinkers, artists and writers with European reputations. The fact is well developed in a recent book about Sir Robert Morier, who was a diplomat and a close friend of both the Queen and the Crown Princess. (*Sir Robert Morier* by Agatha Ramm, Oxford, 1973.) This kind of arching at the top meant that great attention was paid to persons and their influence over events—more possibly than to movements. It explains why it could seriously be considered that the Duke of Edinburgh, whose marriage with the Russian Grand-Duchess is covered by letters in this book, would make a sovereign of the Ottoman Empire acceptable to the Powers. Both the Queen and her daughter (though neither refers to the possibility of the Duke reigning in Constantinople) show that they were fully alive to the play of personality on European politics. In order to bring this out fully it seemed sensible to enlarge the present selection to the middle of 1878 and the Treaty of Berlin. In order to fit this in I decided to start this volume with the illness of the Prince of Wales in November 1871. This was made easier because the Crown Princess was in England for much of the summer, and for a few weeks after she got back to Germany the Queen's letters are somewhat muted owing to her serious illness. I have made a very few extracts, so as not to break the sequence, at the beginning of this volume.

I thought it would help the reader if I set out the background to the lives of the Queen and the Crown Princess as the 1870's began. Outwardly Queen Victoria's life followed an unchanging routine. Christmas and the beginning of the year at Osborne, then Windsor and a few days in London before a visit to Balmoral to include her birthday (24 May). Then she came back to Windsor and, to escape the heat, she went to Osborne for high summer. Here is an account of her life there in July 1871. "You will always find me out either sitting or walking by $\frac{1}{2}$ p 10 and that I remain out till $\frac{1}{2}$ p 12. Also in the afternoon after luncheon I am generally disengaged [at home]. I take my tea out at 5 or $\frac{1}{4}$ p 5—and remain sitting out till $\frac{1}{2}$ p 6 or $\frac{1}{4}$ to 7—when I do not take a very long drive. I generally write and read when I sit out." She went to Balmoral towards the end of August staying there till November. She was then at Windsor always leaving just before Christmas to escape the memories of "former, happy times".

Yet if the outward life was unchanging, inwardly a change is apparent. We may assume that scarcely an hour in any day passed without her thinking of the Prince but she became reconciled to existence without him. Indeed she felt, on occasions, almost thankful that he had been spared knowing about the somewhat frivolous lives of his elder sons and about political developments which, she thought, he would have tried to resist, and which might have made him unpopular.

Her family troubled her. She never fails in this correspondence to express vehemently those passing irritations of family life which are common to all human beings. The Prince of Wales and at this time his wife (to whom the Queen was most warmly attached) led a restless, peripatetic existence characterised by the Queen as "this senseless life" (19 April 1871). In this book—although there are several outbursts of indignation against the Prince—she shows her real feeling for him. "Towards Bertie they [the country] are very unjust. No doubt he leads too *remuant* and frivolous a life but he is a very good and affectionate son to me, and so kind to people, so true a friend that he should be shown indulgence" (30 May 1871).

The Queen's comments on her second son, the Duke of Edinburgh, are unfavourable chiefly because he treated her with reserve. Their relations improve slightly after the Duke's marriage to the Grand-Duchess Marie of Russia in 1874. The Queen's second daughter, Princess Alice, had married Prince Louis of Hesse-Darmstadt in 1862; she is sometimes criticised for being extravagant and fashionable but she and her children—she had five when this book starts—were obviously close to the Queen's heart. Her third daughter, Princess Helena "Lenchen" has somewhat slipped from favour. She has misfortunes with her babies, and the Queen complains of her minor ailments—"cold upon cold, and unbecoming stoutness". Her husband, Prince Christian of Schleswig-Holstein, pampered her "and does not understand in the least how to manage her" (6 May 1871). She was perhaps the least vital of the Queen's children, and was now quietly settled at Cumberland Lodge close to Windsor Castle. The fourth daughter, Princess Louise, was married at St. George's on 21 March 1871, to Lord Lorne, heir to the Duke of Argyll. When they drove away after the ceremony they received "showers of shoes and a broom into the open carriage" (22 March 1871). Though rapturously received by the public, especially in Scotland, the marriage was not happy. This probably explains the Queen's recurring indignation with the Crown Princess for having tried to arrange a different husband for her sister.

Of the three younger children Prince Arthur, the Duke of Connaught, was 21 on 1 May 1871. He caused his mother no anxiety.

Princess Beatrice, the youngest of the family, was 14 when the book begins, and receives from her mother praise without alloy. The Queen was determined that this daughter should be her constant companion and never marry. This was a not unusual fate for younger daughters in the nineteenth century, and the Queen's desire that Princess Beatrice should not marry is the explanation of her outpourings against marriage. Prince Leopold, who was 19 at the beginning of the book, was the intellectual member of the family—the friend in later years of Ruskin, President of the Royal Society of Literature and a constant advocate of university extension. His health was more precarious than is often supposed: he was an epileptic and afflicted by haemophilia—the blood disease inherent in the Royal Family.

In Germany the setting is scarcely changed: the Crown Princess's family was completed in 1872 by the birth of her youngest daughter, Princess Margaret. Prince William, the future Kaiser, was 13 when the book starts. The Prussian Royal Family continues on its unchanging course—as it was in the days of King Frederick William III so shall it ever be. The Crown Princess's parents-in-law, uncles- and aunts-in-law and their children clustered in Berlin from November for the winter. The only gaiety was the Carnival, which was a series of festivities held for several days before Ash Wednesday; these derived from the Roman Saturnalia and it is clear from her letters that the Crown Princess would have agreed that both ceremonies demanded human sacrifice—the Roman one by slaughter and the Berlin one by exhaustion. When the weather improved the whole Prussian Royal Family moved off to Potsdam.

In this correspondence we see the Prussian family through the eyes of the Princess: we see her explanation for what she and the Crown Prince felt and did. We should not be excessively English or unfair if we said that after reading her letters we feel that this highly gifted woman was condemned to incarceration in Berlin and Potsdam with that peculiar brand of conservative-philistinism which flourished in the Prussian family at that time. But to see the picture which she painted, in all lights, two points must be remembered.

Unfortunately the Crown Princess completely failed to establish a reasonable relationship with her mother-in-law, the Empress. It is true that the Empress revelled in formality, the Carnival and all the social functions of the wife of the head of a state. But she was very intelligent, influenced by Goethe and other members of the Weimar circle among whom she had been brought up, loathed Bismarck and all his ways, shared very largely the liberal outlook of the Crown Princess and feared the consequences of her husband's surrender to the Right. She was on terms of close private friendship with Queen Victoria and after her visit to the Queen in 1872 she wrote "It is a rare blessing to possess a real bond of friendship in our high station—which so many are inclined to envy but the burden of which we know! To be able to speak openly and feel ourselves bound to each other by mutual confidence. This blessing has fallen to my lot, and I recognise it with sincere gratitude." (*Letters of Queen Victoria*, Second Series, II, p. 204.) When the Empress died the Crown Princess wrote "I will try not to remember all I had to endure in thirty years". (*The Empress Frederick writes to Sophie* by A. Gould Lee, Faber, p. 55.) No one would blame the Crown Princess for failing to adapt herself to the Empress, but it was unlucky that she failed to get on with the one member of the family with whom she had most in common.

The other point to remember is that she dominated the Crown Prince. The Germans might have forgiven her liberal politics, her unorthodoxy in religion, her longing for domestic seclusion, and her too flamboyant love of all things English but to the German mind at that time the idea of comradeship in marriage was inconceivable. It was her influence over her husband and to an extent over the Royal Family which they disliked and feared. We see this in the view formed of her by an extremely intelligent European—the Archduke Albrecht. A soldier, and not unsuccessful in his country's disastrous war with Prussia in 1866, he was no blind admirer of the Prussian Royal Family or of Prussia. Writing to his cousin the Emperor of Austria in 1875 he says "the better you get to know the Crown Princess the more puzzling she appears to be." He emphasises that she was a good mother and that she had "true womanly feelings." He adds—though this is certainly not borne out by the correspondence—that she had an "inordinate lust for power." He goes on that she was "spoiled in England as Princess Royal". That is not true, but it could be paraphrased as meaning that, through the influence of her father, she had absorbed certain liberal ideals about the true place for monarchy in nineteenth-century Europe which were anathema to her husband's family. The Archduke added "she needed an iron hand to control her: instead she completely dominates her husband" adding that "her parents-in-law had no idea how to manage her." (*The English Empress* by Count Corti, Cassell, 1957, pp. 195–6.)

No doubt she made mistakes, but we can see that with her fearless, straight-forward character she could not accommodate herself to the prevailing harshness of Bismarck's Germany but she would have argued —and there are signs of this in her letters—that when her husband became Emperor all would change "some future day when what is now is not." But for her alas! and perhaps alas! also for Europe when the future day dawned it revealed her husband mortally ill. After reigning for 100 days he died ten years after the last letter in this book.

FAMILIAR NAMES USED IN THE
CORRESPONDENCE

In this list of names, the Queen is Queen Victoria, and the Emperor is William I, German Emperor.

ALBRECHT or POOR OLD PRINCE ALBERT. Brother of the Emperor.

ABBAT. Son of the above.

ADA and FRITZ. Duke and Duchess of Schleswig-Holstein. Daughter and son-in-law of Princess Feodora q.v.

ADDY. Princess Alexandrine of Prussia, sister of Abbat, married Duke William of Mecklenburg-Schwerin.

AUNT ADELAIDE. Wife of the English king William IV.

ADOLPHUS. Prince of Mecklenburg-Strelitz, son of Fritz Strelitz q.v.

AFFIE. Prince Alfred, Duke of Edinburgh.

ALBERT. Son of the Count of Flanders, later King of the Belgians.

ALBERT V. Eldest son of the Prince of Wales.

ALICE. The Queen's second daughter, married to Prince Louis of Hesse-Darmstadt.

ALIX. The Princess of Wales.

ALPHONSE. Count von Mensdorff-Pouilly, first cousin to the Queen and Prince Consort.

AMALIE COBURG. Daughter of Augustus of Saxe-Coburg, married the Duke in Bavaria.

ARTHUR. The Queen's third son, afterwards Duke of Connaught.

AUGUSTA or COUSIN AUGUSTA or AUGUSTA STRELITZ. See FRITZ STRELITZ

AUGUSTA. More usually Lady Augusta Stanley, wife of Arthur Stanley Dean of Westminster, and Woman of the Bedchamber to the Queen.

AUGUSTUS. Prince Augustus of Saxe-Coburg, first cousin of the Queen.

AUGUSTUS OF PORTUGAL. Son of Maria II and Prince Ferdinand of Saxe-Coburg.

BABY. Princess Beatrice, the youngest daughter of the Queen.

THE BAD MAN or THE GREAT BAD MAN or THE ALL POWERFUL B. Bismarck.

THE OLD or THE GOOD or THE BELOVED BARON. Christian Frederick Stockmar.

THE YOUNG BARON. Ernest Stockmar, son of above.

BERNARD. Hereditary Prince of Saxe-Meiningen, married the Crown Princess's eldest daughter.

BERTIE or B. The Prince of Wales.

JOHN BROWN. The Queen's personal servant.

CAMBRIDGES. Children of the 1st Duke of Cambridge.

AUNT CAMBRIDGE. Princess Augusta of Hesse, widow of the 1st Duke.

LADY CAROLINE or LADY CAR. Widow of Captain George Barrington, R.N. Woman of the Bedchamber to the Queen.

CHRISTIAN. Prince Christian of Schleswig-Holstein, husband of the Queen's third daughter.

PRINCE CHARLES. The Emperor's brother.

AUNT or PRINCESS CHARLES. Wife of the above and sister of the Empress.

CHARLOTTE. The Crown Princess's eldest daughter.

CHARLOTTE OF MEXICO. Daughter of King Leopold I, and widow of the Emperor Maximilian.

AUNT CLEMENTINE. Daughter of Louis Philippe and wife of Prince Augustus of Coburg.

CLOTILDE. Sister to Prince Augustus and married to the Archduke Joseph.

CESAREVITCH. Afterwards the Emperor Alexander III.

DAGMAR. Wife of above and sister of the Princess of Wales.

ELISA HOHENLOHE. Daughter of the Queen's half-sister. Died young.

ELLA. Princess Elizabeth, second daughter of Princess Alice.

THE EMPEROR. William I, King of Prussia and German Emperor.

THE EMPRESS. Augusta, Princess of Saxe-Weimar, wife of above.

UNCLE ERNEST or UNCLE E. or DARLING UNCLE. Ernest II, Duke of Saxe-Coburg and brother of the Prince Consort.

ERNEST or ERNEST L. The Prince of Leiningen, son of the Queen's half-brother.

ERNIE. Prince of Hesse-Darmstadt, son of Princess Alice.

FANNY B. Lady Frances Baillie, sister of Lady Augusta Stanley.

AUNT or AUNT FEODORA. The Queen's half-sister, Princess of Hohenlohe-Langenburg.

FRITZ. The Crown Prince and only son of the Emperor.

FRITZ AUGUSTENBURG. Prince Frederick of Schleswig-Holstein-Sonderburg-Augustenburg, married to the Queen's niece, Princess Adelaide of Hohenlohe-Langenburg.

FRITZ OF BADEN. The Grand Duke of Baden, married to the Emperor's only daughter.

FRITZ CARL. Prince Frederick Charles of Prussia, nephew of the Emperor.

FRITZ LEOPOLD. Son of above.

FRITZ SCHLESWIG-HOLSTEIN. See Fritz Augustenburg.

FRITZ or FRITZ STRELITZ or FRITZ AND AUGUSTA. The Grand Duke of Mecklenburg-Strelitz, married to Princess Augusta of Cambridge.

FRITZIE. Princess Alice's second son.

UNCLE GEORGE. The 2nd Duke of Cambridge, first cousin to the Queen.

GEORGE OF M. The Duke of Saxe-Meiningen. He had made a morganatic marriage.

GEORGIE OF WALES. The second son of the Prince of Wales, afterwards George V.

GRANDMAMA. The Queen's mother.

HENNY AUGUSTENBURG. Princess Henriette of Schleswig-Holstein, sister of Fritz Augustenburg.

HENRY. Prince Henry of Prussia, second son of the Crown Princess.

SIR JAMES. Sir James Clark, the Queen's doctor.

LENCHEN. Princess Helena, the Queen's third daughter.

LEOPOLD or LEO. Prince Leopold, afterwards Duke of Albany, youngest son of the Queen.

LEOPOLD. Leopold II, King of the Belgians.

LITTLE ALICE. Daughter of Princess Alice, the future Czarina.

LORNE. Lord Lorne, husband of Princess Louise.

LOUIS. Prince of Hesse-Darmstadt, husband of Princess Alice.

LOUISE. Princess, the Queen's fourth daughter and married to Lord Lorne.

LITTLE LOUISE OF WALES. The eldest daughter of the Prince of Wales, afterwards Duchess of Fife.

LOUISE. Princess Louise, also in context daughter of Prince Fritz Carl and afterwards Duchess of Connaught.

LOUISE OF BADEN. Sister of the Crown Prince.

QUEEN LOUISE. The courageous Queen of Prussia and mother of the Emperor.

MARIANNE. Princess Marie Anne of Anhalt, wife of Prince Fritz Carl.

MARIE or MARIE A. Daughter of the Czar and wife of the Duke of Edinburgh.

MARIE BRABANT. Archduchess of Austria, married to King Leopold II of the Belgians.

MARIE or MARIE L. Sister of the Grand Duke of Baden and married to Ernest, Prince of Leiningen.

MARIE OF MEININGEN. Daughter of George Duke of Saxe-Meiningen and grand-daughter of Prince Albrecht. She never married.

QUEEN MARIE AMALIE. Wife of Louis Philippe.

MARIECHEN. According to context Princess Marie of the Netherlands, niece of the Emperor, the Queen of Bavaria or the daughter of Prince Fritz Carl.

MARY. Princess Mary of Cambridge, Duchess of Teck and 1st cousin to the Queen.

MINNIE. See Dagmar.

MOSSIE. Princess Margaret, the Crown Princess's youngest daughter.

PHILIPPE and MARIE. Count and Countess of Flanders, younger son of King Leopold I.

THE QUEEN DOWAGER. Elizabeth, widow of Frederick William IV of Prussia.

SANNY. Princess Alexandra of Saxe-Altenberg, wife of the Grand-Duke Constantine.

OLD GRAND DUCHESS OF SCHWERIN. Grand-Duchess of Mecklenburg-Schwerin, sister of the Emperor.

OLD SKERRETT. Principal Dresser to the Queen.

SOPHIE. Third daughter of the Crown Princess.

THYRA. Youngest sister of the Princess of Wales, afterwards Duchess of Cumberland.

TIS. Charles, son of the Grand-Duke of Saxe Weimar.

UNCLE or UNCLE LEOPOLD. Leopold I, King of the Belgians.

VICKY. The Crown Princess's second daughter.

VICTORIA. Eldest daughter of Princess Alice.

VICTOR. Count Gleichen, son of the Queen's half-sister.

LITTLE VICTORIA. Second daughter of the Prince of Wales.

WALDY. Prince Waldemar, youngest son of the Crown Princess.

WILLY or occasionally WILLIAM. Eldest child of the Crown Princess. The future Kaiser.

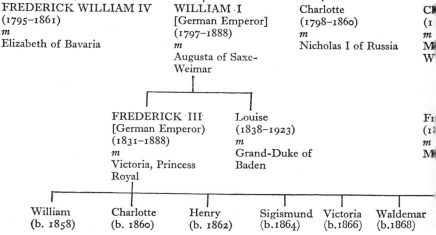

FREDERICK WILLIA
(1770–1840)

FREDERICK WILLIAM IV	WILLIAM I	Charlotte	C
(1795–1861)	[German Emperor]	(1798–1860)	(1
m	(1797–1888)	m	m
Elizabeth of Bavaria	m	Nicholas I of Russia	M
	Augusta of Saxe-Weimar		W

FREDERICK III·
[German Emperor)
(1831–1888)
m
Victoria, Princess
Royal

Louise
(1838–1923)
m
Grand-Duke of
Baden

Fı
(1
m
M

William	Charlotte	Henry	Sigismund	Victoria	Waldemar
(b. 1858)	(b. 1860)	(b. 1862)	(b.1864)	(b.1866)	(b.1868)

THE ROYAL HOUSE OF HOHENZOLLERN

Louise of Mecklenburg-Strelitz
(1776–1810)

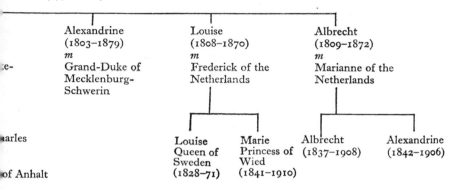

Alexandrine (1803–1879)	Louise (1808–1870)	Albrecht (1809–1872)
m	m	m
Grand-Duke of Mecklenburg-Schwerin	Frederick of the Netherlands	Marianne of the Netherlands

:e-

arles

of Anhalt

Louise Queen of Sweden (1828–71)

Marie Princess of Wied (1841–1910)

Albrecht (1837–1908)

Alexandrine (1842–1906)

Margaret
(b.1872)

THE CORRESPONDENCE

The last volume closed with the signs of ill-feeling between England and Germany engendered by the Franco-Prussian war. Opinion in England which had started strongly in favour of Prussia veered against Germany—especially after the fall of Metz, which was the largest capitulation known in military history. What may have been sentimental sympathy for the losing side was given a keener edge by "the violent laceration"—the phrase is Gladstone's—of Alsace-Lorraine. The Crown Princess suggested that she should pay back the £40,000 voted to her on marriage by the English Parliament.

The Crown Prince and his father, the Emperor, returned from the battles in France in triumph on 17 March 1871. "I think beloved Fritz in good spirits and not altered and aged as I feared he would be, as little taken up with himself as usual and never boasting of all he has done, without hatred or undue contempt of the French and without bitterness against England" (24 March). A few days earlier the Queen had seen Lord Odo Russell, a diplomat who was the embodiment of sense and fair-mindedness. He had been sent by the Foreign Office on a special mission to the German headquarters at Versailles and was shortly to be British Ambassador in Berlin. The Queen writes "I have seen and talked very confidentially to Odo Russell (who I need not praise to you as you know how clever and very charming he is) and I must say I found him most truly impressed with all that you and I can wish—completely understanding and appreciating Germany—not blinded by Bismarck's charm of conversation, and much attached to the Emperor and beloved Fritz. He is full of the noble conduct and aspirations of the Germans for he has a good deal of the outlook of the Germans which is totally unappreciated and misunderstood in Old England. I understand both countries as I have always lived in intimacy with Germans and those who do not cannot really comprehend all that moves and affects them. He is so shocked and grieved at the feeling here—but he says it has already improved and will come right with patience and by letting the people here learn all Germany has really done" (15 March 1871).

In May the Commune, which had controlled Paris for several weeks, ended in blood and flame. On 22 April the Queen had written "How dreadful the state of Paris is! Surely that Sodom and Gomorrah as

Papa called it deserves to be crushed." On 7 June the Crown Princess writes "I thought the Emperor looking ill and tired. He talked politics with me—and said that he was sure the Emperor Napoleon had not wished for this war. The rest of what the Emperor said was the usual Conservative banalities which one is tired of hearing—but which of course is in greater force than ever since the horrors of Paris; as it is an easy and convenient explanation of all that has happened there to say it is the consequences of Liberal ideas and of the concessions the Emperor Napoleon had allowed himself to be forced into making to the Liberal party. Despotism and Militarism are uplifted by people of this short-sighted creed as the only two safeguards against revolutions and communism. What nonsense!"

The Crown Princess contrasted such opinions, which she felt were a barrier between England and Germany, with those of a young Englishman whom she had met earlier.

"I have made the acquaintance of a Mr. Cartwright* (a friend of Morier's and Lady William Russell's sons) a very agreeable and intellectual man with a touch of singularity in his appearance. He understands Germany thoroughly and is very well calculated to clear away the heap of prejudice and nonsense which has gathered in German heads about England" (14 April 1871). She made it clear that the prejudice and nonsense were not shared by her.

Writing on the Queen's birthday she says: "A glorious summer's day—our garden and house decorated with flags and flowers hail your dear birthday in honour of which a Royal salute has just been given. May God bless you and send every blessing that our hearts can wish—power and peace to our beloved England the first among the nations of the world as you are the first among sovereigns. The words of our National Anthem—common-place to say—always fill my eyes with tears and make me wish to sing with a thousand voices 'God Save the Queen'; it sends an electric thrill through one—and when one is in a foreign country it makes one feel an inch taller. I have never felt the 'John Bull' so strong in me as in these last twelve months though you know I never lacked the spirit when I was a child."

On 5 July the Crown Prince and Princess landed at Gravesend and were in England for several weeks. When the Queen reached Balmoral she developed a serious illness, and it was not until 22 November that she could write "felt I was returning to ordinary life" (*Letters*, Second Series, II, p. 169). The Crown Princess had written of the irksomeness of illness for one so active as her mother. The Queen evidently thought

---

William Cornwallis Cartwright (1825–1915). At this time Liberal member for Oxford.

the comment inadequate and answered on 27 October "You speak of the irksomeness of helplessness for one as active as me—but I can't help thinking that anyone, even inactive, would not like (which you hardly seem to take in) to be fed like a baby which lasted three days and a half —the food being put into your mouth, your nose blown and everything done for you. Would you enjoy that?"

But such things were forgotten in the anxiety over the Prince of Wales's illness, which opens the interchange of letters in this book.

1871

From the Queen

WINDSOR CASTLE, NOVEMBER 25, 1871

I received your dear letter of the 21st yesterday morning before leaving my beloved Balmoral. You did not then know that our dear Bertie was ill. Thank God! he is going on so far well, but still it is a great anxiety, and for 10 or 12 days more we can not feel he is safe. This, at this time of the year is indeed a great anxiety and brings most painfully back all the recollections of 10 years ago.[1]

From the Crown Princess

BERLIN, DECEMBER 9, 1871

I hardly know how to write—I am in such a state of mind between grief—anxiety—hope and fear—thinking of you, of darling Alix of them all—and of the darling boy himself. . . . I cannot fancy him ill—he who is always so gay and strong and active, so full of life and vigour, always on the move and never ill or cast down.

From the Queen

SANDRINGHAM, DECEMBER 16, 1871

This morning all is much the same and we would like to say it was a marked improvement but it is not yet that. I am pretty well though of course I feel not being at home and living such an altered life of anxiety. Only Alice and Louis (who arrived unexpectedly and suddenly) and Louise remaining here now. All the rest are gone this morning. I hope to be able to return on Monday or Tuesday—but this must be uncertain. I must I fear remain at Windsor for Christmas which I never have done since '60 and which will be painful. But it is unavoidable this year. I do not think this place wholesome and the drainage is defective —though he did not catch the fever here but at Scarborough. The poor groom is very ill, I went to see him on Thursday.

---

[1] At the end of October the Prince had stayed with Lord Londesborough near Scarborough. After the visit he, his fellow-guest Lord Chesterfield and his groom Blegge were attacked by typhoid fever. Lord Chesterfield and Blegge both died.

From the Queen

Doctor Gull is a very clever, and the fashionable, doctor; but he is a very clever man besides, and a good, religious, courageous one—who is as anxious for dear Bertie's moral welfare as for his physical well doing. We all feel that if God has spared his life it is to enable him to lead a new life—and if this great warning is not taken, and the wonderful sympathy and devotion of the whole nation does not make a great change in him, it will be worse than before and his utter ruin. All the papers and the many sermons all tend to show the same feeling; there is one of a Mr. Holland which is peculiarly striking—an extract of which is in Monday's *Times*. You should read it. The loyalty shown, is most striking. Beloved Alix I can never praise enough. Her devotion, calmness and simple, strong religious faith were touching and beautiful to see. She is dearer to me than I can say—and so true, so discreet, so kind to all. It was a great lesson to *all*—to see the highest surrounded by every luxury which human mortal can wish for—lying low and as helpless and miserable as the poorest peasant. How utterly nothing are we poor mortals—and how it ought to humble pride, and haughtiness to those below us. In one minute the humblest may be above us in another world! Bertie is adored by his people for his frank, kind, hearty manner to them all—and the same by all my people. They all showed the deepest feeling which is most gratifying.

From the Queen

His progress is terribly slow. Broken sleep—wandering (yesterday morning a great deal) and great prostration. The nerves have received a terrible shock and will take long recovering. Another person, a woman who helped in the kitchen has now got the fever. I think the house very unhealthy—drainage and ventilation—bad; bad smells in some rooms —of gas and drains. It would never do to let the children go back there. We shall spend it [Christmas] quite quietly having only a tree for ourselves and no *élatage* of dishes etc. Sant[1] has painted a most lovely head of little Ernie—partly from a photograph. It is a pity he did not do Waldy. He paints children beautifully. He is now to do Albert V. and little Louise who is a very pretty little thing, though little Victoria has

---

[1] James Sant (1820-1916). Painter-in-Ordinary to Queen Victoria.

the sweetest expression and prettiest nose. They are all five sweet, dear, merry, simple, little things.

From the Queen

WINDSOR CASTLE, DECEMBER 27, 1871

Alas, dear Bertie is far less well again and we feel very anxious. I go to Sandringham this afternoon and will telegraph. We have felt anxious about the hip since a week and more, but since the last three days the temperature has risen to 100 and since yesterday to above 101; added to this there are spasms with great difficulty of breathing since yesterday—and the pulse is 112 and respiration at 28. This is very anxious. Sir William[1] went down yesterday which had been decided on already on Sunday and he considered the state "not satisfactory". I go with an anxious heart—but it is a great relief to me to be there for I get so dreadfully anxious away from them and feel I am of use and a comfort to them.

From the Queen

SANDRINGHAM, DECEMBER 30, 1871

These lines are to wish you both most warmly every blessing for the New Year. I pray that all may be peace, and that God in His mercy will protect and bless you, and keep us free from illness.

I wish I could give you a really satisfactory report of dear Bertie— but I cannot. He has the most dreadful pain in his leg which comes on in violent spasms—and the temperature is very high which if it were merely pain would not be the case. There is, as Sir William Jenner (who has been here since the 26th) says, no cause of alarm but for anxiety. The breathing is not good—and always hurried when he talks or moves. The leg can hardly be moved and he had a most restless night. I saw him on Thursday and yesterday each day twice—and thought him quite clear and talking about everything. But I thought his speaking was breathless—rather. They fear some deep seated inflammation somewhere and certainly it is very anxious. I give you these details but beg you not to repeat them to anyone but Fritz. You can merely generally say that the recovery is very slow—and not as satisfactory as could be wished.

No one is to see Bertie today.

---

[1] Sir William Jenner, the Queen's doctor.

From the Crown Princess

BERLIN, DECEMBER 30, 1871

I have just received a lovely book from [of] a "Landseer Album", and a pocket book and 2 Letts' Diaries for which many tender and affectionate thanks.

Those who have returned from Petersburg are shocked at the manners and morals of the young Grand-Dukes (with the exception of Minnie's husband) but all join in the praise of the young Grand-Duchess Marie; I thought it might be interesting to you to hear this.

1872

From the Crown Princess

BERLIN, JANUARY 1, 1872

I am in great pain this evening from neuralgia in my face, my right cheek and ear. I had not got rid of my cold and having to go twice today to the Emperor's Palace, which was so fearfully hot that I had not a dry thread upon me and then coming out into the cold air, has brought this on.

From the Queen

WINDSOR CASTLE, JANUARY 3, 1872

I returned yesterday evening or afternoon with Alice from Sandringham where I left dear Bertie with comparative ease. He has had three good nights and though the temperature and pulse still quicken every evening, they do so less than they did. They cannot find any outer swelling to cause the dreadful pain in his poor leg—and they do not find any active disease in the lung though it is not right yet and the air does not pass through the left one as it ought yet. He himself ordered and gave me a nosegay on New Year's Day and it is difficult to keep him from knowing things—as he is naturally so anxious to know all, especially in his own house. The pain was fearful at times and the difficulty to move him from one bed to another very great.

You will have seen my letter and the articles on it. There were great crowds and great loyalty on my way back from Sandringham. How is the great bad man going on? As rude as ever to you both?

From the Crown Princess

BERLIN, JANUARY 6, 1872

You ask how the all-powerful B. is getting on and whether he is still rude? I am happy to say we have not seen him once—he was unwell—and in mourning for his father-in-law—so we have never come across him since our return. As for politics I am thankful to say we have not heard much of them lately, the time when everybody is periodically seized with a fever of politics here is the spring; for the last four years there has always been something up and brewing in March, April and May.

From the Queen

Dear Bertie seems, though of course very weak and obliged to take great care, to go on well and steadily though slowly. The rise of temperature, which still occurs every afternoon, lessens each day a little; the pain in the leg is also much better and the lung likewise improved. One only trembles lest he should commit any imprudence—which will become more likely when once he is no longer entirely under the care of the doctors. This, and the necessity of his being well and deeply impressed with the necessity of entirely changing his present life are what make me most anxious. If this lesson and opportunity are lost I know not what is to happen.

From the Queen

The poor Emperor Napoleon is undergoing operations more serious and painful than those which poor dear Uncle Leopold had to undergo even! I never knew of it till about three weeks ago Bertie told me it was likely to come to this and then I was startled by the accounts in the papers. It is too disgusting to see every detail, with dissertations in *The Times* daily on the poor sufferer. The poor Empress must be in great anxiety!

You will be interested and I am sure pleased to hear that I mean to put up in St. George's a Monument to my dear father, as I feel it is not right that there is nothing to my father,[1] who would have been King had he not been cut off in health and strength! A recumbent figure on a tomb which is what I always like best. I think it is but a loving and dutiful tribute to his memory from his only child.

From the Queen

Dear Bertie is going on quite well. You ask me several questions all of which I can't answer—
1. His appetite—it is good but I don't think so very large.
2. He is grown very thin—and his weight has lessened immensely.
3. His hair comes off dreadfully and has been cut quite short.

---

[1] Edward, Duke of Kent (1767–1820). This is now in the Royal Mausoleum at Frogmore.

From the Queen

I fear that I have been long without writing but I wrote to dear Fritz through Arthur and I have just heard that he is safely arrived. He is not *en beauté* and dresses and *coiffés* himself so badly, I hope you and Fritz may get him to change that frightful division down the middle, and those monstrous stick-ups.

From the Crown Princess

I ought to have written yesterday but we were engaged in showing as much of Potsdam to Arthur as could be squeezed into a few hours. He went out shooting with Fritz and afterwards we showed him Bornstädt. He dined with the Garde du Corps and went to a soirée given by the First Guards Regiment. He pleases everyone so much and is so amiable, civil and unaffected. I think there are moments when Arthur reminds one very much of dear Papa—without there being as much likeness as Affie has. The collars you object to so much seem to have grown much smaller and I do not think he wears his hair in an unbecoming fashion though it is cut very short.

From the Queen

Let me begin by wishing you warmly joy of this dear day, your dear eldest child's birthday and his first entering his teens as they used to call it here. May God bless and protect him and fit him for his fearfully difficult position. May he grow up good, honest, straightforward, humble and simple minded—and religious without which no one can be happy and no one can really be successful in what he undertakes in this world! I chose the shell links[1] in recollection of Osborne. Unfortunately the last fortnight's recollections of Osborne and last summer are most painful to me—for I did feel so ill. I am very grateful that I am as well as I am now—though I am not strong—and often have rheumatic pains—but nothing thank God! to prevent my walking or going out in all weathers.

---

[1] "Oyster-shell sleeve buttons" as the Crown Princess called them.

From the Queen

OSBORNE, JANUARY 31, 1872

Mr. Sant, who is now my painter-in-ordinary since Sir G. Hayter's death—is going to paint a full length picture of me with little Victoria on my lap and the two boys near me.[1] I feel as if those little children were almost my own, they have been so often with me and also through this anxious time, and belong to the Country, and are as it were our children over again.

From the Crown Princess

BERLIN, JANUARY 31, 1872

Many affectionate thanks for your kind wishes for Willy's birthday. His future is indeed a great anxiety—I only trust he may be fit for it in every way. His poor arm is a sad disadvantage to him—a hindrance to his education—and will not be without influence on the development of his character—he will never be manly and independent like other boys—and never feel at his ease, he cannot do any single thing in the way of amusement or bodily exercise that they can. It always was and continues to me a great grief—those who only see him occasionally have not an idea how it affects everything. I cannot help thinking it very hard and very cruel. His appearance seems to me to grow more awkward as the limb gets stiffer—but that is not of vital importance, though it makes his manner shy and sheepish and all his movements so awkward. He is really a good boy on the whole—and can be so pleasant and amiable; he is lazy as all boys are, more or less, but takes a great deal of interest in many things—it is such a pity that neither he nor any of them have a shadow of taste for music or drawing, they dislike it particularly. Willy is very fond of reading and being read to. If any of my boys grow up as nice as dear Arthur I shall be very proud and happy— they will not be as good looking but that does not matter, if they are only as good and as gentleman-like.

Have you heard that Henny Augustenburg is engaged to the Doctor Professor Esmarch of Kiel? I should think it would be a good thing as there would be an old maid less in the family.

---

[1] Princess Victoria of Wales and her brothers.

From the Crown Princess

Alas! dear Arthur is gone, and of course I was very sorry to part with the dear boy—who is so good and amiable and has gained friends and admirers everywhere, winning all hearts by his charm of manner and civility. I hope and trust he was pleased with his visit and not too much bored. I fear I was a very dull companion for him as I have plenty to do in the house, and was often so tired that I could hardly hold up my head. Fritz took him about everywhere, and had the greatest pleasure in showing him what little we have worth seeing, compared with larger and richer capitals.

Have you read *Shut up in Paris* by Nathan Sheppard[1]—and the *Member for Paris* by ***[2]—they are very good.

From the Queen

I have desired an official Despatch to be written expressing my deep sense of the very kind and gracious reception given to Arthur which I am sure will have a very good effect. Uncle Ernest forbid his going to Coburg which I am shocked and pained at as I wish dear Papa's children to go and see dear old Coburg—the cradle of our family— often. He was so anxious for that.

From the Queen

I was bound till now not to speak of Henny's marriage but I think if she loves the Professor as she does and wishes to marry she is quite right to do it.

From the Queen

Another dreadful event has occurred—and I got the news just as I was waiting to receive dear Bertie—the awful assassination of poor Lord Mayo, my admirable Viceroy of India. He was so energetic, such

---

[1] A vivid account of conditions in Paris during the siege: the author was an American businessman.
[2] Grenville Murray (1821–81), a forceful if unscrupulous journalist. In 1869 he was horse-whipped by Lord Carrington and thereafter lived in Paris.

a fine, noble creature and such a devoted, loyal subject—universally beloved—that it has cast a general gloom over everyone besides being a terrible loss!

Dear Bertie looks very delicate, very pale and thin and drawn—walks slowly, still a little lame, but is very cheerful and quite himself, only gentler and kinder than ever, and there is something different which I can't exactly express. It is like a new life—all the trees and flowers give him pleasure as they never used to do—and he was quite pathetic over his small wheelbarrow and little tools at the Swiss cottage. He is constantly with Alix and they seem hardly ever apart! I am sure he is less strong than he likes to appear.

From the Crown Princess

BERLIN, FEBRUARY 14, 1872

We are rather anxious about the Emperor, but pray don't telegraph to ask, as every appearance of alarm must be avoided—both for his sake and the public. His Doctor is anxious but not alarmed. Just at present there are political complications which agitate the King very much (the laws for school supervision, which are the chief tool of the Catholics, are going to be revised and the right of the Catholic clergy going to be curtailed as much as possible). The Empress takes the opposite view to the Emperor and Ministers and is very violent on the subject. She hardly likes our going near him as she is so afraid he might mention the subject to us—and we are always being kept away.—I cannot help thinking she commits a most dangerous mistake, makes the Emperor quite unhappy, and does herself and the good cause the greatest mischief—however she is in such a state of irritation and excitement that one dare not discuss any thing with her or cross her in any way. All this is not very comfortable as you can imagine, and torments Fritz very much.[1]

From the Queen

OSBORNE, FEBRUARY 17, 1872

I am sorry to hear about the Emperor. I am very sorry too to hear of

---

[1] The Catholics were a strong minority in Prussia—particularly in the Rhineland, Westphalia and East Prussia. After the creation of the Empire the Catholics of Southern Germany made the minority formidable. The Empress, though she was not a Catholic herself, was an ardent advocate of their rights. When the Crown Princess writes of the position of the Catholic clergy being "curtailed" she means over education. It marked the beginning of the policy, put forward by Bismarck, of establishing the sovereignty of the state over all the churches.

the worries and disagreements which are always distressing. Anything of this kind is very painful. Our Government here does not get on very well. They have contrived to get so very unpopular. Mr. Gladstone is a very dangerous Minister—and so wonderfully unsympathetic. I have felt this very much, but find his own followers and colleagues complain fully as much. An excellent and most kind hearted man who is really devoted to me is Mr. Forster. This dreadful death of excellent Lord Mayo is a terrible loss and I never saw such universal praise of anyone both publicly and privately. His family adored him and his friends loved him most dearly. He had quite a chivalrous loyalty and devotion for his Sovereign. And there he is—cut off in the prime of life by the hand of an assassin.

From the Crown Princess

BERLIN, FEBRUARY 20, 1872

What you say about your Ministry I can perfectly understand. The government is composed of very clever, talented, eminent, and highly cultivated men—who hold all the principles which seem philosophically to be the undoubtedly right ones for the present day, but they seem to lack that tact and *savoir faire* which is the essence of statesmanship and which does not depend upon knowledge alone, at any rate one has seen it oftenest in the highest—but not in the most highly educated and learned men. Consequently the present government have made themselves unpopular and have made many blunders which must rob them of the confidence of the people. As for Mr. Gladstone he seems to be most uncertain and incomprehensible—clever as he is—strangely made up of contradictions. It is very bold of me to speak of your Ministers at all, and it is only in answer to your remarks that I ventured to do so and because I have profound sympathy with their principles, and devoutly hoped—the first great Liberal, modern middle-class government in England would be the greatest success. That it is not so, only proves to me, that one may be very clever, very learned, understand all the requirements of a modern state in their most Liberal sense, and yet not be a good statesman or a good man of business. The best professors do not make the best doctors always. Being enthusiastically liberal myself —I always regret when those professing this highest creed make mistakes—still even those mistakes are useful as they throw light on that most difficult of trades the art how to govern, and what are the dangers to be avoided. They are further useful as they may prevent public opinion from rushing headlong into new ideas which require long preparation and careful assimilation before they modify all our time-honoured and excellent institutions.

From the Queen

Our dear Bertie is not as well as was supposed. His leg is swelled (not painful) from a stoppage and thickening of the veins—and he must not walk and must be very careful to keep it up a great deal. It is still uncertain if Bertie can go on the 27th to this dreadful affair at St. Paul's.[1] It will be a great, great trial and what I don't like is religion being made a vehicle for a great show!! However, that could not it seems be avoided.

From the Queen

I am so much pleased with what you say about governments and people and certain people in particular. It is most true and I have continually observed it—that the highest and the best educated and the cleverest may be totally wanting in tact and judgment and thus do great harm. Whereas the lowest and least educated may have inborn tact and good sense which the others will never get. Mr. G. is a misfortune—that is all that I can say.

A dreadful thing has happened near here. Poor Lady Charles Ker, daughter-in-law to the Duchess of Roxburghe, one of those great riding, hunting ladies, one of whom is Lady Dangan—had a frightful fall taking a fence on Monday last—fractured her skull and is still alive but that is all![2] She is lying in a small farmhouse near Langley where my poor Duchess is nursing her—but can only last a few hours more. I drove over yesterday to inquire after her. It was a sad sight—to see all the family about and this poor cottage in which she lies—such an end for a young wife and mother of the highest rank. May it be a warning to many of those fast, wild young women who are really unsexed. And to the husbands, fathers and brothers too who allow their wives, daughters and sisters to expose themselves in such an unfeminine way. In other respects this poor young thing was very quiet and not very strong—but imagine her going down alone to hunt while her husband was walking about in London!

---

[1] The Thanksgiving Service for his recovery.
[2] Lady Charles Ker and Lady Dangan, afterwards Lady Cowley, were sisters.

From the Crown Princess

BERLIN, FEBRUARY 27, 1872

We have just returned from Monbijou where we had a short special service, and the form of prayer used which will be read at St. Paul's before you. I need hardly say how much I thought of you, with how many fervent prayers, and of dearest Bertie nor how much touched I felt, in spite of the anything but eloquent or touching address the clergyman delivered in the worst English. What did it matter? I felt so thankful to join my prayers to those of many thousand beloved countrymen at home—for you and dearest Bertie. There is nothing like being abroad to make one feel how deep and almost passionate one's attachment is to our proud and great country, nor how profoundly the ties of child to parent, sister to brother, and subject to Sovereign are grafted in one's heart! The Empress, the children, and all our household were there.

From the Queen

BUCKINGHAM PALACE, FEBRUARY 28, 1872

I am thankful to say that yesterday was a day of triumph—really most marvellous! Such touching affection and loyalty cannot be seen anywhere I think. It was as much when I went to open Blackfriars Bridge and the Viaduct—but then we did not go into the very heart of the City or then near so many streets. Millions must have been out and the decorations were really beautiful—the cheering deafening. It was the first time since Bertie was a boy that he had ever been with me on a great public occasion—and such an occasion—even in former happier days—perhaps there never has been; he looked ill and was very lame but was touched by the immense loyalty and really touching affection shown. From the highest to the poorest "rags" there was but one and the same feeling! It was of course very fatiguing—bowing all this time but still it was so very gratifying that one could not feel tired. My head aches rather but not very much today. We left the Palace at twelve and reached St. Paul's at 15 minutes to 1. The Lord Mayor actually rode from Temple Bar—on a white horse—with a long crimson cloak, his hat off and the great sword in his other hand. "God Bless the Prince of Wales" was always played after "God Save the Queen" and when we were stopping at Temple Bar amid deafening cheers I took dear Bertie's hand and pressed it—people cried. Indeed he had tears in his eyes and I often felt a lump in my throat.

The Church part was the least elevating excepting the concluding

hymn. St. Paul's is a most dreary, gloomy place, so dingy and bare—
and one could hear very little of the good Archbishop's address—.
Though the anthem[1] and the Te Deum were pretty—the old Hallelujah
Chorus would have been much more effective. I took Bertie's arm but
he was terribly lame and had to walk very slow. Alix went on my other
side and the two little boys—Albert V. with Bertie and Georgie with
Alix. We had some sandwiches, wine, biscuits etc., in a little room
arranged at the entrance which was very necessary for us all. Going back
was even finer than going, the decorations in Oxford Street were so
tasteful, the inscriptions very pretty. You will see very good accounts in
today's *Times*. Our open carriage was drawn by six handsomely
harnessed bays with many crimson bows and ridden by postilions in
state liveries. Brown in his very fullest and very handsome full dress—
and Collins in his state livery sat behind. The other three brothers went
also in an open carriage and four bays—with the Master of the Horse.
The seven others were open (but they open very little) dress coaches
and pairs driven from the box. Dear Alix was not looking well. "Baby"
looked very sweet and pretty in mauve trimmed with swansdown. She
was of course with us in our carriage. We left St. Paul's at a quarter
past 2 and came back here at 20 minutes to 4. The day was fine. The
poor Emperor and Empress came to see us go and witnessed it from the
very room from which we saw them go in State in '55 to the City![2]
Dear Bertie is not really the worse. I send you a photograph of him as
he is now. It will make you sad to see it. So far I wrote this morning
and have that part copied for the three sisters.

I now wish to give you the following message. Only on Friday did
I know whether I could manage to run over to Baden during the
Easter Recess to see poor dear Aunt.[3] I have very little time and must go
quite incognito and on account of the much easier embarkation at
Gosport and disembarkation at Cherbourg I shall go through France.
Now I cannot of course go anywhere else—and the journey will be very
fatiguing and I must refuse all visits and sightseeing etc., etc., and mean

---

[1] The Anthem, "The Lord is my Strength" and the Te Deum were composed by John
Goss, the organist at St. Paul's.
[2] They came out and stood on the balcony.
[3] The Queen's half-sister Feodora, Princess of Hohenlohe-Langenburg. When Princess
Feodora was widowed she built herself an "oak and pine" house in Baden-Baden. This
town was the most fashionable and raffish of the European resorts at that time. It had much
in common with Thackeray's Rougetnoirbourg. Both the Queen and the Crown Princess
were not quite at ease if they heard that the Prince of Wales was staying at Baden. But it
was also a centre for the two families. The Empress's only daughter had married the
Grand-Duke of Baden, and the Empress was frequently there and had her own house
in the town (Miramar).

to remain perfectly quiet in a small villa outside Baden which I have hired for the ten to twelve days I can stay—but I wish the Emperor should know this and of course if he should be near there—for I can't expect him to come from Berlin—it would give me the greatest pleasure to see him—though I shall only be there as Countess of Kent with a very small suite—solely to see my poor, sick sister who is in deep mourning.[1] As regards the Empress of course it would be the same for her, but you can say that I meant to ask her to come at the very beginning of May to Windsor when I could see her till the 14th or 15th when I should have to go to Scotland but she could if she liked stay a few days longer at Buckingham Palace.

I am very tired and I must end. I have just been at Marlborough House. Dear Bertie is very lame, in short he cannot put his foot to the ground but is not otherwise ill.

From the Queen

WINDSOR CASTLE, MARCH 4, 1872

You will have seen by Jane Ely's note and by the papers and the evidence what a horrid, daring thing this was![2] I never saw the pistol—because when I saw a strange face and heard a strange voice at my own door, where surely everyone thought I must be safe—I threw myself over Jane,—who had never seen the man. But it is entirely owing to good Brown's great presence of mind and quickness that he was seized (he held him by the throat) before he could touch me and dropped his pistol. Arthur and Leopold both saw him point it at my face! But it was not loaded, still I think his original intention was to shoot me but that his ignorance and folly prevented it. But he is not the least mad. Old Fuller, who is rather past work—saw him run past him, but did not or could not stop him and Lord Charles thought he was a garden boy—(rather strange too!) Brown alone saw him spring round and suspected him. It is sad that this blot should come to spoil or at least mar and cloud over the splendid day of Tuesday February 27. It makes people so angry. I received the most enthusiastic ovation on Friday on driving from the Palace to the Station! Everybody was out and the carriage could hardly get through the Park.—Strange to say my head and health have not suffered from this dreadful fright, but I know I shall feel it when I go out as I always have done in London. There was certainly not sufficient vigilance on the part of the police or rather more

---

[1] For her daughter, the Duchess of Saxe-Meiningen. The Crown Princess could not go as she was expecting the birth of her child.
[2] The attempt on the Queen's life as she drove into Buckingham Palace.

not enough police. We shall have three inside the gardens. The "Boy" is not the least mad and looks clever.[1] It does not so far appear to be more than an isolated act. But these Fenians are horrid reckless people.

From the Queen

His [Lord Mayo's] successor, Lord Northbrook, is said to be very clever but he is not near so amiable or popular. Lord Mayo had the Irish joviality about him, and was free and hearty, yet had a fine presence.

My good Brown is far too simple and modest ever to think much of any service he has rendered me—and this only one of many, many for which I can never be grateful enough. I was therefore only too pleased to be able to reward him publicly. This Gold Medal is to be for any very special act of devotion to the Sovereign—and is to be given in addition to the silver one which is to be for long and faithful service. It (the silver one) will only be given to those who have in any way personally served me, and not merely for length of service.[2] It is to be called the "Victoria Faithful Service Medal" and on one side will be my head and on the other the person's name. Instead of a ribbon and to make it unlike Military Medals there will be a V.R. surmounted with a crown in the same metal as the medal. I shall probably give a few of them on an occasion like my birthday. Pray tell all this to Fritz who I know kindly interests himself in such things.

From the Queen

I am sorry that the education measures have produced such excitement. But these Catholic priests must really be checked. I am feeling tired. There has been so much to try and tire me.—Great crowds in London which make going out very trying and the great precautions taken make one think continuously of what has passed. Do tell me who told you about Beatrice? Because I do want to know who does write these inventions abroad. She is not 15 and I shall certainly not have her confirmed till after she is 16 for all of you sisters have come out too early and been made grown up too soon. I mean to keep her back much

---

[1] Arthur O'Connor, aged 17; great-nephew of Feargus O'Connor.
[2] John Brown's medal was struck from the same die as the silver one and was engraved round the edge "Victoria Devoted Service Medal". No other Devoted Service Medal was awarded. See Appendix to *Royal Family Orders* by G. P. L. James, 1951.

more—for her own good as well as for my comfort. She only came to the Drawing-room and the Court as a child and because at the Court she was the only princess in the country able to appear! But she did not come to the Levée nor will she appear at the next Drawing-room after Easter. She hardly ever dines of an evening; except on birthdays.

From the Crown Princess

Today's sad anniversary is not forgotten with us.[1] It seems strange to mix up sad and joyful subjects still I will add my congratulations for Louise's birthday to my letter and also those for the approaching first anniversary of her wedding day. I hope that the first year of her married life has been a happy one—and that she will always like to look back upon it as such. I do not know whether she regrets not having any children at present, perhaps not—no doubt in time they will make their appearance, and I suppose she is in no hurry, and that you are best pleased as it is for her.

From the Queen

Two words to thank for your letter of the 19th and to say that I shall burn it and not forget the contents. You need be under no apprehension. I shall just see him once and not again.[2] Only Lady Churchill, Colonel Ponsonby, Sir William Jenner and William Collins go with us. Lady Ely joins us at Baden.

From the Crown Princess

I wonder how you will like Baden, now when all the *beau monde*— the fashionable and the bad society are not there. You will see dear Countess Blücher's little home—and her faithful Fanny and perhaps in some of your walks pass by the churchyard where her daughter and her husband are buried.

---

[1] The death of the Duchess of Kent in 1861.
[2] Almost certainly Princess Feodora's eldest son, Prince Charles, whose private life was unsatisfactory.

From the Queen

We had a good though excessively cold passage and journey. We embarked on Saturday at 6¼; the evening was then fine but it snowed heavily when we left Windsor and had done so all the morning; we started at 9 on Sunday morning and were at Cherbourg at half past 2. There was a good deal of rolling but I kept well and so did the brother and sister. We landed quite quietly at the dockyard—and started off by rail at 6 in a comfortable carriage and had also a comfortable sleeping salon. We stopped only so very often and the noise was very great; the people talk so much and so loud. We saw nothing of Paris. But it was very strange to see Prussian soldiers at Bar le Duc, Commercy and Nancy. We got out at Oos where Ada and Fritz met us and drove by carriage to Baden. How very pretty it is! The house here is prettily situated, and very private but not comfortable. Four salons for show with not one door which shuts—and only means to have fire in one. The moment the stove is lit in the house the heat is stifling. I have a very nice bedroom and a little dressing room where there is also an open fireplace. You can walk about everywhere now without meeting a soul hardly. I drove up yesterday morning to see dearest Aunt (who is at her pretty little villa) whom I find much better than I expected though looking pale and her poor dear eyes very red having had an inflammation in them. She is however more cheerful than I expected. In the afternoon I walked up to dear Aunt and took tea with her. It is barely twenty minutes fast walk but it is half an hour if you walk slowly as it is all up hill. Today I have been again up to dear Aunt and been sitting with her. It is beautiful again today and the country lovely. This afternoon I mean to take a longer drive. Pray tell the Empress all about where I have been. Her house is to me in a most extraordinary position I must say for a Queen.[1]

From the Crown Princess

I am so glad to see you think Baden pretty. How nice it must be to move unmolested from place to place at Baden. I only know it is the most odious haunt I know, with two Courts one up at the Schloss and the other in that wretched Miramar House—between which I am

---

[1] "I am not astonished at your not understanding the Empress's taste in choosing that nasty house of Miramar to live in year after year. Fritz is always in despair about it." The Crown Princess, April 1, 1872.

perpetually going up and down.—Swarms of people and a very uninteresting society. More fatiguing than Paris during the Exhibition, more tiring than the London Season—an excessive bore besides— seasoned with the most charming "scenes" at the Emperor's; this is my fourteen years' experience of Baden! Apart from all this I think the country charming and enjoyed the short visits I paid dearest Aunt up in her dear little villa very much indeed.

From the Queen

THE VILLA DELMAR, BADEN, MARCH 31, 1872

I am anxious to explain that I can offer dear Fritz no *pied-à-terre*, there is not one spare room, or even any room for anyone to wait in. I would expect him for luncheon and he would perhaps like to remain after luncheon a little while and return to dine should he like, or would that make him too late? We dine at ¼ past or ½ past eight. I hope to persuade dear Aunt to come to luncheon here too.

Certainly nothing can be quieter or, to other people who like much amusement, duller than Baden is now.

I do indeed understand your wish that I should be once under your dear roof, and wish earnestly it might be possible. But even now, quiet though I am, I am not well—and feeling the few visits I receive too much. I have never yet been able to thoroughly recruit myself after all I went through! I look to my spring visit to dear Balmoral as the only means of doing so.

From the Crown Princess

BERLIN, APRIL 8, 1872

You have heard of the engagement of the Emperor of Austria's daughter to Prince Leopold of Bavaria? It is a very poor match in every way, though politically in the Austrian interest.

From the Queen

WINDSOR CASTLE, APRIL 10, 1872

I am sorry to see you are not well. But I am not surprised at it. I only hope and pray you will be satisfied when you have seven—and not go on exhausting your health and strength so precious to all you belong to and so necessary to your husband and children and your adopted country.

D C—D

I can really not imagine how the Empress Queen could possibly choose such a house in such a position!

From the Queen

WINDSOR CASTLE, APRIL 13, 1872

The Judge[1] who tried O'Connor (who pleaded guilty) behaved very stupidly and has shocked everyone—giving him the lightest sentence possible! Only one flogging with merely a year's imprisonment and hard labour! But he must be got out of the country as soon as possible.

We heard that Fritz was going to Rome. Is that true? Also that there was an idea of Fritz Carl's daughter marrying the King of Bavaria? I told Fritz I had also heard that Fritz Carl wished to get a divorce. All these reports come from trustworthy sources.

From the Crown Princess

NEUES PALAIS, APRIL 16, 1872

I took leave of the Empress yesterday, who is very kind, in fact the whole winter through she has been most kind to me, and we have got on very well—in spite of little rubs—you know she has many trials besides the one of her own "unquiet and restless disposition"; it is not in her nature to enter much into the feelings of others or show any consideration for their necessities,—so life can never be easy either to her or with her but I am always most thankful when we are on loving and cordial terms, delighted when I can be of use to her and grateful for any kindness she shows me. No one appreciates her great and good qualities more than I do or understands the difficulties of her position more than I do. I think she knows and feels this. Unfortunately she is a little impatient with her son, and often expects things of him which he cannot do from the best of reasons. These reasons she does not quite see and then is displeased and dissatisfied with him, which of course he feels. Usually these are only little misunderstandings which a word would clear up, but the Queen is then in a state of nervous excitement and irritation, so that to explain anything which is contrary to what she wishes is only to add fuel to the flames.

The most ridiculous fable of Fritz intending a journey to Rome made us laugh, such a thing was never contemplated or spoken of. No more than Mariechen's marriage to the King of Bavaria which the newspapers kept repeating Heaven knows why. Fritz Carl is not meditating

---

[1] Anthony Cleasby, Baron of the Court of Exchequer (1804–79). "In the criminal courts he was never quite at home." (Dictionary of National Biography.)

a divorce at present. You know they are not happy together, and when the children are all grown up—if the parents do not agree better, I suppose they will come to some agreement proposed and urged by Marianne, and only acceded to with the greatest reluctance by her husband, to live apart and not meet more than they can help.

From the Queen

I am not feeling right yet. You speak of my life being so very regular and my therefore being easily tired—by anything different—but my life is constantly and perpetually being broken in upon and disturbed by worries and duties of one kind or another which are very wearing.

Beatrice or rather more Baby is a sweet pretty child, but her greatest merit is her amiable, contented disposition and charming, even temper. She is perfect travelling; everything is always right.

From the Queen

I am so glad that you have got on so well with the Empress Queen. Don't you think it is rare that people do understand the necessities, feelings and wants of others? No one suffers more from this than I do— for I suffer from excitement and fatigue and none will (even of my own children) understand my wants! Towards me the Empress Queen has always been most considerate and kind.

From the Crown Princess

You may imagine how disappointed I was to have another little girl,—if it had been a boy I should have hoped with you for it to have been the youngest for evermore, as really what one has to endure is too wretched but it would be wrong of me to complain, and for myself alone a little girl is much nicer, and she will be a companion for Sophie. Though you take no interest in babies I may mention that this one has got an immense lot of dark hair, which I am sorry to think will not remain.

From the Queen

The dear Empress arrived safely on Thursday. I went down to receive her at the South Western station, and as this was the first time she came as Empress I had a Guard of Honour and a Sovereign's Escort. She is all kindness and discretion and has a civil, friendly word for everyone—for my good servants and all—which pleases so much. She spoke most kindly and affectionately of you—I find her aged, which is natural, in appearance but not in energy.

We expect Leopold of Belgium here for luncheon today. On Monday I go up to town and have three tiring days—a Drawing-room, Afternoon Party and part of a concert at the Albert Hall and then I have done for this year and can keep myself very quiet in the heat or else I fear I may be ill again.

And another loss I have had which has pained me much and which you will regret. Good Baker—my trusty and faithful Police Inspector for 18 or 19 years who was about with me everywhere was found dead in his bed yesterday morning. A great loss.

From the Queen

I am most thankful to hear you are going on so satisfactorily. I never thought you cared (having 3 of each) whether it was a son or a daughter; indeed I think many Princes a great misfortune—for they are in one another's and almost everybody's way. I am sure it is the case here—and dear Papa felt this so much that he was always talking of establishing if possible one or two of your brothers and eventual grandchildren (of which I fear there is the prospect of a legion with but little money) in the colonies. I don't dislike babies, though I think very young ones rather disgusting, and I take interest in those of my children when there are two or three—and of people who are dear to me and whom I am fond of—but when they come at the rate of three a year it becomes a cause of mere anxiety for my own children and of no great interest. What name is this fourth daughter to have?

This day I gave the dear Empress (who is so very kind) my Order as I have always wished to do—and with which she was very much pleased and quite touched by it and greatly surprised too. She was very much pleased with the Afternoon Party which I thought very tiring and tiresome—however it pleased and satisfied people and now I have done with everything for this year. This afternoon we are going to the first part of the concert in the Albert Hall where Gounod directs; then we come back here and go back to Windsor at ½ past 6.

From the Queen

WINDSOR CASTLE, MAY 11, 1872

The names of the baby are for once (forgive my saying it) all pretty.[1] Feodore is a dear name which I love to see repeated. I am a little surprised at the Crown Princess of Italy[2] but know Fritz has a great liking for her.

From the Crown Princess

NEUES PALAIS, MAY 11, 1872

How I should have enjoyed hearing Gounod direct a concert. I am a devoted admirer of his genius and think his music so sweet, graceful and heart-stirring. I admire it so much more than Wagner's about which some people here are quite crazy.

Marie Goltz who has been staying here for a fortnight, left yesterday. I shall miss her very much. She was kind enough to read to me an English novel (not a new one) by Wilkie Collins called *The Moonstone* most likely you have often heard spoken of—it keeps one in a great state of suspense until one reaches the end.

From the Queen

WINDSOR CASTLE, MAY 14, 1872

The dear Empress left yesterday early in dreadful weather. She was so very kind and seemed to enjoy everything so much and then she is, excepting Aunt Feodore and Aunt Alexandrine, the only one of my own position who is not of a much younger generation whom I know well. No visit ever went off more pleasantly, and she is so clever. I have heard of but not read *The Moonstone*. Have you read *Squire Arden* and *Hannah*?[3] I think you would like both. The latter is written with a particular object. Leopold is going on quite well, but he must be carried and won't be able to walk. It was his own carelessness again alas! as well as overdoing his standing in London—that evil-doing place which I perceive makes everyone ill, which caused this new misfortune.

---

[1] Margaret Beatrice Feodore.
[2] As godmother.
[3] *Squire Arden* was written by Mrs. Oliphant, and *Hannah* by Mrs. Craik, author of *John Halifax, Gentleman*.

From the Queen

Poor Leopold is really himself to blame for he is so foolish, and over-excites and tires himself in standing and going about so that the weak leg gets tired. But I am always right in my anxiety—in which I am generally opposed by the family so that my anxiety and difficulties are always increased instead of lessened. When your large family grows up you will see and feel (and I think bear less patiently than me) the constant struggles of one's children to oppose what parents do solely for their good. It is a sad thing—and certainly far more in the higher classes where people have not to work bodily or mentally for their bread—to see how ungrateful children are, how they neglect telling their parents what they do and how little they will take good advice. I feel myself that one has constantly to put up with small neglects and want of *égard* especially in one's sons. Often I believe from mere thoughtlessness—but it is these trifles which hurt one as much as the observance of them pleases one.

I am also a very great admirer of Gounod's though I never heard any of his things hardly given in full till his Te Deum which I will send you.

From the Crown Princess

I have not read the two books you mention. There are several new German novels—of which we are reading one—but I do not think that you would like it much though it is very well written and by one of our best authors. German novelists are usually bad,—and their style not pleasant, the exceptions are but a few amongst whom Freytag, Spielhagen, and Hackländer are the best. Shall I send you some in case you might like to look them over?

I think the Emperor looking very well indeed, though he walks quite lame on account of the bandage he is obliged to wear round his knee.—The "great man" is not ill either, he is tired and fussed and bored, and then says he is ill. I think he wishes to save himself up for the future, also as I hope and trust and believe this future is far more distant than he thinks, so he may make a mistake in his calculations. The King[1]

---

[1] Emperor.

is not aged in habits, appearance or health but I believe is much slower over his business than he was and that does not suit the impatience of the "great man".

From the Queen

BALMORAL, MAY 21, 1872

As you can ask Catholics I think it very nice to ask the Emperor and Empress of Brazil. I suppose you don't mean to ask Beatrice to be sponsor? Though I believe the not being confirmed does not make the least difference. I was Godmother to poor Elisa Hohenlohe when I was only 11. So many people in England formerly never were confirmed at all so that naturally they stood sponsors and as you ask Catholics and so many sponsors it would not imply any responsibility.[1] I should be thankful for any very good German novels. I am not very fond of sensational ones. The worst is I don't read German—from want of habit—very quickly and still more because the print is generally so small that I am obliged to read with "specs".

From the Crown Princess

NEUES PALAIS, MAY 22, 1872

What you say about children opposing their parents is but too true, I know, but is it not natural also—and the case all over the world? Are not the cases very rare where the wills, opinions, and characters, of children agree with those of their parents even when the most tender affection exists between them? Is there not also a great difficulty for children to understand that they ought to accept whatever their parents design, and for parents to remember that their authority has a limit, and that if "the strings of the bow are drawn too tight it will snap" as the German proverb goes. Young people chafe at all restraint, and older ones at all opposition; this seems to me to be in the course of nature and it is difficult on both sides to make allowances and give way.

You speak of dear Leopold—and your general remarks applied to him, I think. You of course must know best what is necessary for his health—and a great and heavy responsibility it must be to have charge

---

[1] In the eighteenth and early nineteenth centuries when bishops were more static than they are today confirmation was a difficulty. "Ready and desirous to be confirmed" was often a substitute for the ceremony itself.

The Crown Princess explained in her letter of 25 May that she had written to ask Princess Beatrice to be one of the godparents—only not having done it before because she thought the Queen would not have wished it.

of him. But is not the lonely and secluded life he leads—also a danger? When he is once his own master will he not be tempted to rush into the very extreme of excitement and amusement, and will it not be doubly hurtful to him then? Forgive my saying so. I have no wish or no right to interfere in any way and I do not pretend to know better than more experienced people. I only say that a young man pining for liberty (justly or unjustly) is not likely to make the best use of it once he gets it within his reach. That his brothers and sisters should often pity him for being obliged to forgo all the pleasures that life and the world offer to others his age—is really not out of mere opposition.—Most likely this natural compassion is not always expressed judiciously but I cannot in conscience tax myself with making him dissatisfied with his existence, or long for things he cannot and must not have but I wish with all my heart he were happier. One can not help fearing that his fine disposition may become soured and his views one-sided from not knowing and seeing the outer world as it is.—I hope that you will not be annoyed at what I am saying. I have already a taste of the many difficulties which assail a Mama in her endeavours to do her duty by her children so that I in no way wish to increase yours or make you think me ungrateful.

From the Queen

BALMORAL, MAY 25, 1872

Lenchen is 26 today. She looks much older.

From the Crown Princess

NEUES PALAIS, MAY 25, 1872

The Archduchess Sophia[1] seems dying—which will upset all our arrangements as the Queen Dowager is at Sans Souci. Poor thing I am sorry for her (I mean the Archduchess) but she has done Germany and the good cause of progress and liberty more harm than anyone. Neither Austria nor Prussia have any cause to be grateful to her. Her intrigues and her Jesuits have done a great amount of mischief. Most of all to her own son.

---

[1] 1805–28 May, 1872. Daughter of King Maximilian I of Bavaria, sister of the Queen Dowager and mother of the Emperor Francis Joseph.

The Royal Family at Balmoral. Left to right: Prince Leopold, Queen Victoria, Princess Beatrice, Prince Arthur, Princess Louise, and the Prince of Wales, with members of the Queen's Household. *Reproduced by gracious permission of Her Majesty Queen Elizabeth II*

Thanksgiving Day, February 27, 1872. Triumphal Arch at Oxford Circus. *Illustrated London News*

The Queen at the Show of the Berkshire and Hampshire Agricultural Society in the Home Park, Windsor, June 20, 1872. The judging of the horses. *Illustrated London News*

From the Queen

Beatrice is quite delighted—and good Baby is such a good child that I was pleased she should have this little distinction. Otherwise she will be kept very quiet and at home—which will be much better and happier for her and for me. Everyone says this and many who urged Lenchen— and Louise still more—going out say it was a great mistake to have done so with them.

29th   I could not finish my letter yesterday so I do today and wish especially to correct an evident misapprehension relative to Leopold— and the opposition and ingratitude of children in general. What I meant about Leopold was—not that he pined for liberty or amusement for he does not—nor when he is living with Baby and me alone is he ever discontented or unhappy (but always when large family parties are in the house) but that he would not be careful of himself or save himself or rest himself and was cross and disagreeable to those who warned and reminded him of not tiring himself—not being careful in walking etc. standing etc. And that instead of pitying him and lamenting over him on what he could not do, he should be encouraged and cheered by all around him especially by his own brothers and sisters to look at the numberless advantages which he does enjoy and which others, to whom balls, dinners etc.—which are I suppose considered the only object in life—do not enjoy,—instead of at what fortunately Leopold does not consider such a desideratum. As for his being kept tight etc. it is only what the doctors recommended and what I am sure every young man would be the better for. Leopold—from the healthier life (not "secluded one" for the house is never free from strangers and we are constantly moving) he leads is the only one of the brothers who looks well and healthy. Affie and Arthur both look quite wretched. Leopold can never do what anyone else can and will probably never be his own master in the same way. I cannot now say more about this but time will show what I mean. Besides I think all of you might show the two younger ones that it is a duty as well as a pleasure to devote themselves to their sorely tried Mother who has the heavy burthen of State as well as of a large and much over indulged family on her shoulders unlike any Mother in the world! But gratitude to parents, respect for age and authority are not what they should be in these days! And yet, as good Doctor McLeod said to me the other day, gratitude to parents "never can be strong enough"; for the anxieties and sufferings which parents go through for their children—beginning with what a mother goes

— 45 —

through paying nearly and often with her life, the very existence of her child—can in fact never be repaid by the children. How much beloved Papa felt this and how cruelly he did suffer already for his son's conduct. You say older people can't bear opposition which is not true but what they do really feel acutely is when merely from opposition and often without any real pleasure and enjoyment therefrom—they do precisely the contrary to what they know is right and to what they have been brought up to and accustomed to look up to and respect. I could write volumes on this sad and difficult topic but must end here. I did not mean you had encouraged Leopold in "rebellion" but there are some in the family who are always wanting to interfere and meddle —and cause much trouble.

Odo Russell's brother is (most unexpectedly) become Duke of Bedford, and will be most enormously rich.[1]

From the Crown Princess

NEUES PALAIS, MAY 30, 1872

The Crown Prince and Princess of Italy will pay us a visit today. I am very anxious to see her, as all gentlemen are always in raptures about her and say she is so graceful and charming.

Bertie seems to be amusing himself very much at Paris which I hear is as gay and brilliant as ever—how much misery and sorrow this gay and giddy life may hide one does not know, but the horrors of last year must have left many an awful trace behind them which the *beau monde* ignores and tries to forget. It will always be so there as the world of frivolity and fashion there is comprised of the pleasure-hunters of the whole world and there are but few French comparatively among them. Americans and Russians make up the greater part, I believe.

From the Crown Princess

NEUES PALAIS, JUNE 2, 1872

I agree most entirely in all you say. I think the disinterestedness of a parent's affection is its greatness—the feeling that one gives far more than one can ever receive. Some parents never know how much their children love them; dear Papa I am sure never knew how passionately I adored him—as from half shyness and awkwardness I never could show it, and naughty, disagreeable, troublesome child as I was—I do

---

[1] He succeeded his cousin the 8th Duke, a recluse, who dropped dead in the hall of his house in Belgrave Square.

not think you could guess how much tenderness was at the bottom of my heart, in spite of all my cross temper and opposition.

The Crown Princess of Italy is a very charming, graceful creature, naïve and merry like a child—looks very delicate and reminds me in face of Aunt Clementine and Amalie Coburg—less really pretty but more piquante and attractive. Her husband is greatly civilised and improved, much nicer than he used to be, but he is an original. He rolls his eyes like his extraordinary Papa and his sentences come out in a funny abrupt manner and a hoarse gruff voice; he speaks very little indeed, is not so shy as he was, and seems to be sharp and have plenty of sense.

. . . I saw Hélène Reuter yesterday, and thought her looking well poor thing.[1] Darling Uncle is so odd about some things—perfectly incomprehensible to me. Matters are not comfortable at Coburg and I fear never will be. Dearest Aunt secludes herself more and more and it is so bad for them both.

From the Queen

It gave me much pleasure to receive your dear letter, dated 2nd, as it showed me that you can understand what I meant about the relations of children and parents. The higher the position the more difficult it is. —And for a woman alone to be head of so large a family and at the same time reigning Sovereign is I can assure you almost more than human strength can bear. I assure you I feel so done by the amount of work and interruption all day long that it affects my health and also my spirits very much at times. I feel so disheartened. I should like to retire quietly to a cottage in the hills and rest and see almost no one. As long as my health and strength will bear it—I will go on—but I often fear I shall not be able for many years (if I live). If only our dear Bertie was fit to replace me! Alas! Alas! I feel very anxious for the future, as I see by your observations in your letter of the 30th—for which many thanks also—that you also are. And so is every one.

---

[1] "A certain dreadful person has tried to persuade Uncle Ernest that Hélène Reuter is not his daughter, and that he need not support her. Everyone likes Hélène." The Crown Princess, August 25, 1871.

From the Crown Princess

NEUES PALAIS, JUNE 12, 1872

Writing of Fritz Carl's family the Crown Princess say:

It is sad for those poor girls not to have a more comfortable home—as they are quite old enough to feel that their parents do not live as happily together as they should. It is too strange as neither of them have anything to reproach themselves with. He is harsh, domineering and violent though he loves her and the children. She is gentle and forbearing, but dislikes him and does not seem to care much about her children. Her increasing deafness and ill-health makes her very unhappy. This is a lamentable state of things for which I see no cure—and which promises for them both (and I pity both) a miserable old age. You can imagine how difficult the position is for the poor children and the members of the household.

From the Queen

WINDSOR CASTLE, JUNE 19, 1872

You do, I know, grieve at the irreparable loss we have sustained in our dear, excellent, distinguished friend Dr. Norman McLeod. He was so kind and encouraging to me in the early days and months of my great sorrow, and in all religious matters we agreed so well, and I always felt the better for all he said and preached. His was truly the religion of Love. He wished to impress all with the feeling that God was our loving father and not a hard judge.

From the Crown Princess

NEUES PALAIS, JUNE 19, 1872

The Queen of Bavaria is here, again a round of dinners and parties—one does so wish for a little quiet and real country life. All the potentates of Europe have an unfortunate liking for coming here at all times of the year: the only one whose coming would make us happy, cannot be induced to do so—that is your own dear self! We are to have the Emperor of Austria in September. Poor Prince Otto of Bavaria is in a worse state than poor Charlotte of Mexico even, and quite as incurable. He has to live in a padded room, and barks like a dog all day long. For such a young creature it is too sad. His Mama seems to take it very quietly as she does everything else; it is a dispensation of Providence and therefore she does not trouble about it.

From the Queen

WINDSOR CASTLE, JUNE 22, 1872

You were, as I was sure, greatly grieved and shocked at the death of our dear Dr. McLeod, but I think you hardly know what a loss it is. How wide world [sic] his influence for all that was good and wise and tolerant and large minded—was! His place cannot be replaced. There is no one to replace him. It is one of those "dispensations of Providence" which you seem to think it absurd to take with courage and resignation! It is the feeling that it is God's will and that He sends us these heavy trials for purposes unknown and not understood by us—which enables us to bear the trials which are put upon us. But I fear that with you and Alice I shall find but little sympathy and [illegible] in these great truths which grieves me often deeply for I know the misfortune it is to you both, and which as you live longer and go through more and more sorrows and trials you will feel the want of.

The poor Queen of Bavaria has indeed terrible trials and this mad son is an awful affliction.

Those constant visits are such bores. It's very kind of you to wish me to come too—but it would be utterly impossible dearest child. Mama can bear very little now.

From the Crown Princess

NEUES PALAIS, JUNE 22, 1872

I was sure you would feel excellent Dr. McLeod's death very much. He was so much devoted to you and had your welfare so deeply at heart. Stockmar's book of his father's life has appeared, I wonder what you will say to it; it is sure to interest you as you are the chief person in it. I have only read parts as yet. I suppose he has sent it to you?

From the Crown Princess

NEUES PALAIS, JUNE 25, 1872

Many thanks for your dear letter and copy of a letter about poor dear Dr. McLeod's death. I was well aware how extended the sphere of his usefulness was—and what a loss he will be.

You have quite misapplied my words relating to a dispensation of Providence. I thought you knew how much I admired courage and resignation in suffering and trial. What I do not admire is a habit of using a phrase—when one is too indolent to feel keenly any misfortune that happens to those we love—a sort of indifference which is beyond me, and which is more Mussulman than Christian, and in which I can see no merit. I only spoke of Mariechen of Bavaria who is so passive and inert that the greatest calamity might happen before her eyes without her trying to prevent it and then she would say, if God had not intended it, it would not have happened. At that rate there is an end to all noble incentive for action in this world; it avails not whether we be good or bad—whether we suffer or not, as Providence has arranged it beforehand. This is very like Mohammedan fatalism and for those who have not keen feelings and warm affections, no doubt a very convenient form of faith—but one hardly worthy of an educated and reflecting individual. I think I had however better not discuss such points but carefully avoid them for the future as I am sure to be misunderstood and to shock you, and I ought not to have mentioned poor Marie of Bavaria in my last letter but I was so struck by so pious a person talking as unconcernedly of her son's madness as if she were speaking of the weather. I thought it so unlike a mother's love, and did not wonder that she has no influence on her children and that they behave ill to her, —and yet you know how thoroughly good natured and excellent she is, a negative kind of goodness.

We gave a party yesterday evening out of doors for all the guests who were here for the confirmation of Fritz Carl's girls. The ceremony itself was most touching and I could not help crying all the while, the two girls looked so gentle and modest, like two white lilies, or like two white doves,—it was very solemn and impressive. Mariechen— who is really a pearl of goodness,—looked very sweet, and so quiet and dignified, self possessed and not occupied with herself. She is a charming girl and beloved by all who know her—she is so upright and honest and so sensible. The church was crammed full of people, and covered with flowers. Marianne is going to England soon as I said before, might I kindly solicit your asking her to luncheon at Windsor once, so that she may see the place? Would Lenchen see her once, and would Christian object as she is Fritz Carl's wife?[1] Marianne goes alone with only a lady and a gentleman—and wants to see all England in six weeks incog: how she will manage this I do not know, she has no one about her who has ever been there before or who can speak a word of English.

---

1 Over Prussia's seizure of Holstein—to the royal family of which Prince Christian belonged.

From the Queen

WINDSOR CASTLE, JUNE 26, 1872

I have been this morning (driving round) to the Agricultural Show of the Counties of Hampshire and Berkshire held in the Home Park where the one in '51 was held. It is very prettily arranged and there are some very fine beasts.

I come now to this very important subject of the position of the working classes. You know that I have a very strong feeling on that subject. I think the conduct of the higher classes of the present day very alarming—for it is amusement and frivolity from morning till night—which engenders selfishness, and there is a toleration of every sort of vice with impunity in them. Whereas the poorer and working classes who have far less education and are much more exposed—are abused for the tenth part less evil than their betters commit without the slightest blame. The so called immorality of the lower classes is not to be named on the same day with that of the higher and highest. This is a thing which makes my blood boil, and they will pay for it.

Then as regards education—I quite agree with you that it should be enlightened and that the Protestants may not in Germany at least be as earnest as the R. Catholics. But while no one abhors intolerance or spiritual despotism more than I do—no one also has a greater horror than I have of attempts to teach doubts in God's and our Saviour's love and mercy and power, or in His all pervading influence. Teach them to doubt these—and you at once destroy their respect for and faith in anything and that is one of the causes of Communism, for the respect for God and religion goes hand in hand with the respect for authority and law.

These two points I consider are the great dangers and cause Communism. The Jesuits are a fearful body—and I am doubtful whether any laws can be severe enough against them. But I really do not know the state of the case abroad sufficiently well; still I know dear Papa always thought they should be turned out of any country. The case of the women is one which I have a very strong feeling upon. I think they should be sensibly educated—and employed whenever they can be usefully, but on no account unsexed and made doctors (except in one branch), lawyers, voters etc. Do that, and you take at once away all their claim to protection on the part of the male sex. I have not written this well for I have been sadly interrrupted but I hope to explain myself better when I have more time. Could you let me have it back to get it copied?

From the Queen

I quite agree with you in that dreadful idea that whatever happens you are to do nothing to prevent it etc. That, in my opinion, is going against the laws of an all-wise all-merciful and all-loving God and Father, not to use them as He has ordered and willed—and the sort of strange indolence of Mariechen of Bavaria strikes me as very strange though I know how little one ought to judge by outward appearances. Still one cannot help doing so.

It is most beautiful and enjoyable here and I am sorry I didn't settle to stay here for a week. The trees and the grounds and the country all round is so beautiful and it is so quiet—no eternal bells and drums etc. as at Windsor which are I think so very trying to the nerves. I shall stop at Weybridge on my way back this afternoon to visit the graves of the poor French Royal Family, one more being added since I went in '69—poor dear Lina[1] as I believe they may be moved to France at any time. When do you go to Berchtesgaden and do all the children go?

From the Queen

I received it [the Crown Princess's letter] just after returning from the great memorial to beloved Papa which is entirely finished excepting his statue and that will not be for some time.[2] Therefore there has been no ceremony—which will only take place when the statue is completed. But everything else being now finished and really beautiful I was asked to allow it to be opened to the public—after I had seen it—so I went there on Monday and met all the Commissioners, all who had anything to do with it, all the sculptors etc. etc. and spoke to each and thanked them all. It is very gratifying to see at length such a great work so completely successful and carried out within the amount of money subscribed.

From the Crown Princess

Did you read the account of the Great Concert given by a Mr.

---

1 Difficult to decipher but the Duchesse d'Aumale who died in 1869.
2 The Albert Memorial in Hyde Park.

Gillmore at Boston; it was so absurd that really it was worth reading; it made us laugh so much.[1]

From the Queen

WINDSOR CASTLE (FROGMORE GARDEN), JULY 10, 1872

I now come to what is a painful subject but which I must and will write quite openly to you upon. It is about our beloved old Baron's life. You have asked me twice what I think of it.—I have not had time to read it through yet—but I have looked at parts of it—and others, most interested in it from various causes, like Van de Weyer, Mr. Martin and my own Gentlemen etc. have, and the impression of us all, is one of astonishment and pain at the want of discretion and tact shown in it. I have so great a regard for Ernest Stockmar that it pains me very deeply to have to blame him very much—as I must—for the way in which without (as he was in duty bound to do, from the very intimate and quite exceptional position of confidence in which his father stood towards Papa and me) asking me if he might touch upon some very delicate subjects which I have most carefully kept out of the *Early Years* and which Mr. Martin also will touch with the greatest delicacy, intending only that these should be known in 40 or 50 years hence! I cannot understand how he, who is so clever, could think of speaking of Papa's feelings towards Lord Palmerston—of the Pamphlet—saying (which naturally never has been avowed) that the Pamphlet was instigated by Lord Palmerston—all without feeling what storms of controversy and what painful discussions might thereby be roused, injurious to Papa, to me and to his dear father whose charming, loving, affectionate character is not brought out as it should be. He appears as a sort of hard, political intriguer in this book and this hurts me so much. Then again why rake up that, thank God! long-buried, terrible story of Lady Flora Hastings which his dear father had nothing whatever to do with, and which happened when he (the old Baron) was away? And it is put in such a way that it would appear as though I allowed all these things, young girl as I was, in full knowledge of what they implied which God knows I did not dream of—or it never could or would have taken place. Why rake this up? And then again how could he publish the very unflattering description of my grandmother and uncles etc. written by the old Baron solely for himself—and which he never, with his kindness of heart and personal discretion, would have wished

---

[1] The International Peace Jubilee when the musical entertainment marked the harmony of the principal European nations.

to make public. If only Baron Ernest had consulted me, he would have prevented all what now alarms all who are anxious to prevent scandal and controversy; he sent me one most imprudent part, which shocked Sir Thomas and me greatly and which I asked him at once not to allude to—and I therefore hoped and trusted he would have done so again. I offered him the use of any of the letters not touching on any political or confidential affairs from me to his father wishing that my affection and regard for him should be known—and the publication of which would have explained a good deal and would have shown the soft, loving side of his father's nature, but no—he refused them. If E. Stockmar was not the son of the most intimate friend Papa and I had, I would not be so much astonished and shocked, but as he stands on such a very intimate and confidential footing with you and was so well known through his father to dear Papa, though I think he never lived enough here to understand the affairs of the interior of our house and of the intimate working of things, I must say I am greatly hurt and pained. It will be absolutely necessary for the translator into English to leave out things and for it to be clearly understood that I was no party to what has so injudiciously been published. It grieves me more than I can say to have to say all this, and I hesitated as long as I could but I cannot withhold the truth from you. I have not yet thanked E. Stockmar for the book and feel greatly embarrassed now how to do it. Bunsen's life is such a contrast to this. The most delicate subjects are treated in a way to hurt no one's feelings. I wonder that E. Stockmar's wife has not felt the imprudence of touching on the things I have alluded to. And I had thought him so very prudent and discreet! I have let Morier know what my people and I feel on this unfortunate subject.[1]

---

[1] Ernest Stockmar (1787–1863) "the Old Baron" was originally a doctor in the service of King Leopold. He was subsequently confidential adviser to that King and to Prince Albert and Queen Victoria. "We confided everything to Stockmar and he was adored in this house." *Letters* Vol. 1, page 100.

His son, Ernest (1823–86) "the Young Baron", acted as secretary to the Crown Princess in Berlin. The Young Baron's biography of his father was to cause a breach— though short-lived—between the Queen and her daughter. Some of the Crown Princess's letters for this period have been destroyed but it is clear that she defended the Young Baron against the Queen's attacks.

The English edition was published this year, was reviewed at length and widely read; it carried a judicious foreword by Professor Friedrich Max Müller, a Fellow of All Souls, which made several of the Queen's points, especially "I shall not disguise a certain measure of disappointment at not finding more of the inner life of the man".

The English edition included an allusion to the "antagonism" between the Prince and Palmerston and to the former's disapproval of the latter's "restless and interfering" foreign policy. In the book there is the following reference to the Pamphlet, supposed to have been written after Palmerston's dismissal in 1851, "at Broadlands by a certain Mr. Ph.

From the Crown Princess

VILLA ALPENRUHE, BERCHTESGADEN, JULY 19, 1872
We arrived safely here at 5 in the afternoon, and are busy getting our funny little house in order, and unpacking our things.[1] The villa belongs to Fraulein von Waldenburg, one of the daughters of the late Prince Augustus of Prussia,[2] and the situation is quite lovely. The beautiful mountains surround us, and the little town is just at our feet. I was quite delighted with Munich and only distressed to have been there so short a time as there is so much to see. The whole place seems to me like one vast museum where days would be spent as quickly as hours—and for anyone fond of art there is an immense deal to see and to learn.—We were at a most comfortable hotel. Mariechen [the Queen] was most kind to us; we dined with her both days—and she had the Schloss and everything shown to us. Of the King she knows nothing; she had received neither letter nor telegram for 6 weeks— and no one seemed to know exactly where he was. His oddity must surpass everything that is known if half the stories are true that one hears; people at court seem quite shy even of mentioning his name.

From the Queen

OSBORNE, JULY 20, 1872
I am reading E. Stockmar's book with the greatest interest and have thought it best to read first the parts relating to ourselves and England. It is extremely well put together, but I grieve to say that the extreme imprudence and indiscretion strike me more and more. I quite tremble at it. Aunt Feodore (who knew the dear old Baron so very well) writes to me that she was not pleased with it, "as telling

---

On reflection Palmerston suppressed the Pamphlet". There is also a note in the English edition saying that these rumours were subsequently contradicted by Palmerston in the *Morning Post*. But see *The Greville Memoirs*, 1938 edition, Volume VII, page 8. The author of the Pamphlet was Samuel Phillips—a journalist. It is clear from Greville that Palmerston did inspire the Pamphlet and that a few were still in existence in 1854. The Queen is therefore perfectly correct in what she says.

The Queen's grandmother is described as "small and crooked" with "a true mulatto face", and many of the Queen's family are described in language which, though it is often quoted, is exaggerated and wounding.

Sir Thomas is Sir Thomas Biddulph, Keeper of the Privy Purse, and the passage to which the Queen alludes, no doubt covered Stockmar's reforms in the Royal Household.
[1] "Our little villa here is a would-be Gothic erection in the style of the Rosenau or Reinhardtsbrunn: it stands on a little elevation with a background of dark, pine wood". Crown Princess, July 28, 1872.
[2] With whom Princess Charlotte, George IV's daughter, fell tempestuously in love in 1814.

too much of the private affairs of you [me] and Albert and the family. The father Stockmar would not have allowed it." (That I am as sure of as I stand here.) "And this ought not to have been published without your permission." I must say I feel this very strongly indeed. Mr. Helps is very much shocked and says he "is so thoroughly penetrated with a sense of the indiscretion which he may himself commit in any literary work that he always takes care to show it to two or three severe critics before he ventures to issue it and even then there are sure to be some foolish things which escape criticism". I cannot tell you how grieved I am to say all I have said of a person I respect so much. But it is terrible to see such indiscretion towards anyone but above all towards people in such a high, responsible position as ours—though nothing can be kinder or more flattering than the terms in which he speaks of dear Papa and me. About the former however I think there are opinions of him in his youth which ought not to have been put in.[1]

From the Crown Princess

BERCHTESGADEN, JULY 25, 1872

Fritz returned from Ischl yesterday evening. The Emperor and Empress were most civil and kind, and he spent a charming day with them. He says Crown Prince Rudolph is smaller than Willy, he has 5 gentlemen always with him. The Archduchess Gisela does not look grown up yet, Fritz says—and yet they are going to marry her next April. The Emperor and Empress kindly expressed their wish I should come to Vienna next spring for the Exhibition which I shall certainly do.

From the Queen

OSBORNE, JULY 31, 1872

What an idea that that poor young Archduke Rudolph or Crown Prince—I don't know what they call him—should have 5 gentlemen. That way of bringing up young Princes with loads of people about them, never letting them feel that they are human beings like others— is dreadful. I always feel what a blessing and advantage it was for me to have lived in such very simple and restricted circumstances— almost humbly—and that is why I dislike so living in great Palaces etc. My tastes are simple and humble.

---

[1] "The love of *espiègleries* and of treating men and things from the comical side." *Memoirs of Baron Stockmar*, ii, 6.

From the Crown Princess

BERCHTESGADEN, AUGUST 7, 1872

It pains me much to see how my letter has been misconstrued—
and that you should think its tone wanting in respect or affection
when you must know, dearest Mama, that nothing in this world can
be farther from my intentions. I hope you will forgive any words—
which certainly were not chosen with any other thought than that of
trying to explain what I meant in the best way. As I see I have so
utterly failed, I will not attempt it again nor refer to the subject any
more—though I cannot help feeling much aggrieved at a reproach I
hardly feel to deserve—or it must have been awkwardness on my
part—which of course I blame myself for.[1]

To my horror Henry will get a uniform on his birthday as he is ten
years old. His poor ugly face will look worse than ever,—and he has
grown if possible much plainer still since last year. Willy will have to
wear a Russian uniform when the Emperor comes—to my horror.
I am of course not asked and all these things are arranged without my
having a voice in the matter.

From the Queen

OSBORNE, AUGUST 10, 1872

You know the Russian project is over.—The young lady won't
hear of marrying as she is very happy at home and I believe her
parents don't wish to part with her at all and wish her to marry in
Russia. Affie must and will look about but he will only choose someone he really fancies—and no sister better interfere with advice.

From the Crown Princess

VILLA ALPENRUHE, BERCHTESGADEN, AUGUST 17, 1872

You are looking out at hills also from your window at this moment
as I am from mine. I weary my companions here I am sure with
comparing Scotland and our hills there with these, but it is our constant topic of conversation, and I find myself getting very prosy over
it and beginning again every day; somehow one cannot help it.

Fritz spent a nice day at the Miramar where he saw his Mama and

---

[1] The letters over this period are, in part, missing. The subject was almost certainly
Stockmar's book, or the marriage of Princess Louise to Lord Lorne.

then went on to Stuttgart where he was most enthusiastically received;—"Tis" of Weimar's marriage is off—the young lady could not make up her mind when it came to the last. The Empress and all the Weimar's are very much offended of course, but I think it is only natural.

From the Queen

BALMORAL, AUGUST 17, 1872

I pity you indeed to have to be at Berlin (or will you be staying at Potsdam?) for that week of Emperors.[1] How ever will you manage between the Emperors as to rank? For in fact every Sovereign is alike—and no one yields to the other in rank in spite of the greater size and power of the Kingdoms. I suppose the Empress will be led by both or what will happen? I should really be amused to hear. It has never happened to me but twice I think and that was the Emperor of Russia and late King of Saxony. And on the Rhine in '45 Uncle Leopold and the King of Prussia—when we were there but then the former was the guest of the latter.

From the Queen

BALMORAL, AUGUST 21, 1872

Only think how sad, poor Leopold lost his faithful old dog yesterday by driving over him. He is in the greatest distress for he was like a friend so devoted to him and he had him ever since he was a little boy of nine.

From the Queen

BALMORAL, SEPTEMBER 3, 1872

I was quite surprised at Abbat's engagement of which you never told me a word. The young lady is, I believe, a nice girl. But I fear that this choice and the breaking off of Tis's marriage are great disappointments to the poor Grand-Duke and Grand-Duchess of Weimar and to the Empress who writes much annoyed and hurt that one of the young Weimar Princesses is not chosen and that the young Princess of Oldenburg (whom Alix told me was a charming girl) had taken back her word.[2] You know what the poor young man really is—

---

[1] The visit of the Emperors of Russia and Austria to Berlin at the beginning of September.
[2] Abbat is Prince Albert, nephew of the Emperor; he was engaged to Princess Marie of Saxe-Altenburg. Tis is Charles Augustus of Saxe-Weimar: he was nephew to the

and how plain and unhealthy those three children of the Grand-Duke are; but one cannot say that to the parents whose great misfortune it is—nor to the Empress and I am very sorry indeed for them. But I ventured to tell her that one can't interfere in affairs of the heart and that it was far more honest to speak out before the marriage than when it was too late.

In your dear letter of the 26th you speak of beloved Papa and his irreparable loss and how few if any were like him. But I feel and see that if he had lived he would have suffered cruelly from many inevitable things which have taken place and which he never would have approved. And the opposition to which would have injured him in the eyes of many. The Irish church and changes in the Army would have been excessively (and in my opinion rightly) but vainly opposed by him and he would have been severely attacked for it.—That I know. In the same way the style of life of your elder brothers which he could not have prevented would have shocked and angered him. He foresaw this and often was greatly depressed in speaking of it to me, and it is this which makes me often sad when I see things go on so exactly contrary to what he would have wished and liked—but which cannot be avoided. I often say "thank God! he is spared this"; I rather bear the burthen alone and submit to what I cannot prevent, doing all I can to prevent serious evil. He could not have borne it—after what I saw him suffer!

From the Queen

DUNROBIN, SEPTEMBER 9, 1872

Our journey on the 6th was fatiguing from the crowds at every station—and the presentation of Addresses at Aberdeen, Elgin, Inverness and Dingwall but no Sovereign since poor Queen Mary has been in any of those places except Aberdeen. The loyalty and enthusiasm—so peculiar to Scotland and the Highlands—was great. This is a fine place—but I am much disappointed with it. The exterior is fine (I will send you photos. of it) and so is the position but the scenery is not the twentieth part so grand as about us—nor the house as cheerful or fine as I expected. The rooms are very dark—excepting those quite upstairs and the air is not light and bracing as at dear Balmoral. Affie told me this and that no place in the Highlands and no scenery did he

---

Empress. The Crown Princess had been anxious for Abbat to marry Queen Victoria's daughter, Princess Louise. Hence the Queen's interest. The "plain and unhealthy" daughters of the Grand-Duke of Saxe-Weimar eventually married; Tis married his cousin Princess Pauline of Saxe-Weimar.

admire as much as our dear, beautiful Balmoral nor any people did he like as much as our dear, noble-hearted, honest, clever Aberdeenshire people. There are besides too many trees near the house. This morning I laid that stone to the Memorial which the clansmen and tenantry of the Duke are going to raise to the memory of my dear Duchess[1]—and I made a little speech. She was adored by all here and her name is reverenced and loved by the poorest. I have walked in the mornings and driven in the afternoons. I have this evening seen a Mr. Stanley, who discovered Livingstone, a determined, ugly, little man—with a strong American twang.

From the Crown Princess

NEUES PALAIS, SEPTEMBER 12, 1872

At last this fatiguing time is over and our Imperial guests are gone. I think we may all congratulate ourselves on the visit having gone off as well as possible. The reception was on so huge a scale that of course all the details could not be attended to—and there was much confusion of course, it was more like an immense bivouac than anything else, but that is the style here and our guests did not miss the comfort and order with which a grand reception at Windsor or Buckingham Palace used to be done. I did all I could, but was not present at everything. The Emperor of Austria was most amiable; the Emperor of Russia showered favours and honours and distinctions rather too lavishly, I think, which rather diminishes their value.

The Grand-Duke of Weimar is of course much annoyed about his son's engagement being broken off which is very natural, but I think they are too hard upon the poor young Princess—who tried all she could not to deceive the bridegroom elect as to her sentiments but he did not seem to take the hint and did not release her from her engagement as I think she expected, consequently left her the pain and the blame of taking the initiative. Of course the Weimar family only feel the offence, but all the Russian relatives, who saw the young lady's distress take her part. I myself think the young man was too naïve or obtuse not to perceive that she never liked him.—It is a blow for the proud, ambitious, wordly-minded Grand-Duchess of Weimar who dotes on her son. I think her a cold, heartless woman and have little sympathy with her since I have seen more of her. The girls are such good creatures, but fear they will not easily find husbands as

---

[1] Harriet, Duchess of Sutherland; the Queen's closest friend who had died in 1868.

besides being very ugly they are so unhealthy; they are not very happy at home and would gladly marry.

To return to the letter I wrote from Berchtesgaden I see you misunderstood my meaning. It was simply as a question of historical interest that I wished to know about the precedence of the different reigning families. You know that I consider all these things as totally unimportant myself, and all the fuss which is made about it is very ridiculous—but you are quite mistaken, dear Mama, if you think that my father-in-law's Court is the stiffest and most ceremonial. It is true there is no place where any of us could live a simple, quiet, retired country-life like private individuals. It is true that many obsolete traditions and habits are kept up—which are hurtful and irksome in the extreme—and make it very difficult to educate our children sensibly, but on the other hand there is no court that is so accessible to everybody, that is so liberal and hospitable. We receive everybody who holds an employment under the Government, every artist or man of science—there is no distinction made as to their rank in society. At Vienna, Dresden, Weimar, Strelitz and Schwerin such a thing is unheard of.

You say the Empress does not care about rank. She is the only person here who really does care—and I have so often wondered at it—I can tell you a thousand instances. What you say about Fritz is not untrue, only it does not proceed from pride with him. He does not quite *ménager* the susceptibilities of other Princes I think enough, I am often telling him so,—and appealing to his kindest of hearts and sense of justice. I know quite well from whence his feeling of irritation against what he considers undue "pretensions" comes—and if you lived in Germany and knew all the ins and outs you would also, but I am always for not hurting the personal feelings of others even when they have too great an opinion of their dignity—such as often is the case. All these things are very complicated and it is difficult to explain them in a few words.

From the Queen

BALMORAL, SEPTEMBER 17, 1872

Poor old Prince Albert could you enquire after him in my name and express my sympathy to his children? And offer my best wishes to Abbat for his happiness, which I must ever take an interest in, though I unfortunately could not agree to his wishes. But it must make me take a sincere interest in his welfare.

From the Crown Princess

It gave me even more pain that it can give you, to see my poor children made victims to an absurd and obsolete tradition to which their grandfather so strictly adheres. It does them harm and it makes a very difficult education more difficult still. No one wishes more than I that every compliment possible—every grateful and graceful acknowledgment [be] shown to our splendid, heroic and glorious army, of which no one can be prouder than I, and nothing can give me more pleasure than that my sons should stand in the same ranks and do their duty by the side of many a noble peasant's son and many a scion of an ancient and illustrious family. But I can only regret that this is carried to an extent which is no longer understood in our days. What was natural two hundred or six hundred years ago is now not only absurd but mischievous in more than one respect, and now it is high time such customs were abolished.

From the Queen

BALMORAL, OCTOBER 8, 1872

You never answered my message I told you to give Abbat on the occasion of his marriage. Whether this was accidental or deliberate I don't know but if it was the latter it would not be right. Why be sulky about a thing in which I am far the most aggrieved person— from the way in which you tried to force him upon me on two different occasions? I only told you why it would not do, and I think you would be furious if I in future years tried to force people upon you for Charlotte and Vicky. And yet it would be far more natural that the grandmother should try and interfere than that the child should with her mother. The thing being quite at an end and amicably so and Abbat being about to marry—it is far better to let bygones be bygones, and to be civil and friendly as before.

From the Crown Princess

NEUES PALAIS, OCTOBER 11, 1872

A photographer from Manchester (a Scotsman) a Mr. McLachlan is here doing some photos of Fritz and of Willy, for an extraordinary group of yourself and us all (i.e. your children and children-in-law and 1 grandchild from each family). This group is represented sitting in the green drawing room at Windsor and the picture is for the Town Hall of Manchester I believe.[1]

From the Crown Princess

As you have heard from Fritz by telegram poor Uncle Albrecht is no more. As soon as we heard the news—we hurried to Berlin to see his children whom we found greatly distressed. Countess Hohenau, his poor widow, I did not see—only the eldest of her sons—a charming, handsome, intelligent young man of eighteen, who was dreadfully cut up. The Countess showed Fritz his Uncle's will and the letter in which he takes leave of his family—which is very touching; after thanking the Countess for all the happiness she had given him, he asks her to choose his last resting-place, begging her to arrange so that she can once [one day] be buried by his side. Prince Albrecht thanks his two eldest children for their kindness to his second wife and her sons. She has always behaved as well as possible.

From the Crown Princess

Many most affectionate thanks for the lovely and precious prints of dear Papa's, the one I wanted to give away was for good old Count Usedom who is such a true and devoted admirer of dear Papa's and such a kind and valued friend of ours. He spoke so much of dear Papa's beauty when he saw him at Brühl in '45—and I always think Sir William Ross's miniature renders the regularity of his features so exactly.

You ask, dear Mama, why I did not answer your message in one of your former letters. I thought silence was the best answer I could give, knowing your intention to be a kind one. I am not in the least "sulky" as you suppose. I hope my cousin will be very happy indeed with a nice and good wife as he promises to be, but I can hardly be the bearer of any message from England,—which you would understand I am sure if you knew the effect it would produce. Bygones are bygones, my cousin never alludes to them or names the sisters, and I scrupulously avoid ever mentioning them or England or yourself—out of delicacy. His hopes and wishes (never encouraged by me—as I knew almost for certain he had no chance of success much as I wished he might have) met with a decided refusal from you, and therefore until he is married

---

[1] See Preface page xii.

—and some years have passed by—I cannot revert to the subject. Whoever thought of doubting your having every right and the best reasons of your own for not wishing this alliance? I for my part hope and think it is all for the best, but I would beg you not to forget that the fact of being thus excluded from every chance of presenting oneself, is neither flattering to an individual nor to a family. Dear Aunt Feodore and poor Countess Blücher would say that more strongly than I do here.—I consider the matter completely at rest—and would never have taken it up again did you not mention it again. As for my "forcing" anyone upon you for one of the sisters,—it is no use my discussing as I think the expression a rather unjust one—and I know you will always resent the part you suppose I have taken in the matter —whereas I can not help feeling that I was not justly used in more than one respect. Perhaps in later years when you may like to talk it over you will convince yourself of this—and in the meanwhile dear Mama I know no earthly reason to be or seem sulky; all parties whose well-being I wished are as happy and satisfied as possible. I can only hope they may remain so.

October 19 I could not finish my letter yesterday. Fritz and the nearest relatives (not the Emperor) took the coffin to Charlottenburg where it is temporarily placed in the mausoleum in an empty vault behind the one where the sarcophagi of Frederick William the Third and Queen Louise are placed.—The Emperor was very much affected and when the guns fired he sobbed so much that I gave him my arm to lean upon. He very kindly embraced poor Countess Hohenau who with her two boys was opposite the coffin. I shook hands with them— but could not see her face as she was completely hidden in her crepe veil. I am afraid the Empress will dislike our having taken any notice of her, but it was impossible to do otherwise, it would have been very unfeeling and unkind; the poor thing is in the deepest grief and the boys will only now begin to feel how uncomfortable their position is. They are exceedingly good looking. (I believe the Countess is very ugly.)

From the Queen

BALMORAL, OCTOBER 25, 1872

I wish just to answer what you say about my message to Abbat etc. I quite see your difficulty about it, but you should at once dearest child have said so—and I would at once have understood it. I will later send a civil message through an impartial channel. Let me just say only that it was not out of incivility towards the family or towards himself that I repeatedly refused to entertain the project but from a

conviction that it would not be for the happiness of the people themselves or for the families or countries—which Countess Blücher
herself told me, she was convinced of, though she knew how you
wished it. And what I so bitterly complained of was—that after I had
very firmly though civilly put an end to it in '64 and '65 you began it
again in '68 and even behind my back with Louise. Alice also. That
was what I so deeply resented—knowing as I did how also very much
dear Papa was against it. I have quite forgiven it—only such a pro-
ceeding must never occur again.

As I am once on this topic let me just say a word respecting your two
brothers. It is that you will understand that while I shall ever oppose
any person whose character I could not approve, I must leave (this
applies now only to Affie) them their free choice for it is useless to
attempt to dictate to them, especially to Affie who is 28 and will not
be forced into anything. And you know how often what one would
most wish does not come to pass. I say this in case you should hereafter
think that I had made plans, which others might not like. My course
is simply to say—there are these few unmarried Protestant Princesses—
whom I hear generally well spoken of—choose for yourself amongst
them. As regards the Russian marriage you also did not answer me,
probably because Alice (who has all along been deceived as to the real
feelings of the Russian family) says it can still be—but we know from
the relations as well as from the Minister that, while anxious to be as
civil as possible, the Emperor and Empress do not wish it because the
girl herself does not wish to marry at all for some time, and because
they wish to keep her in Russia. And for Affie to go on pressing the
suit *ad infinitum* would be, as I, Bertie and the Government think,
undignified for my son and bad for his future.

How very affecting the funeral of poor Prince Albert must have
been, and I feel deeply for the poor Emperor. Pray tell him so again;
for to see the youngest go is very trying and sad. I think also that at
such a moment you could not do otherwise but be kind to his widow.
Who was she, and what was the great objection to her?

From the Crown Princess

NEUES PALAIS, OCTOBER 25, 1872

The Emperor is still in very low spirits about his brother's death
also about politics. The Church question seems to disturb and pre-
occupy him, the more so as he and the Empress cannot agree on the
subject.

Did I tell you that Sir Michael Costa is at Berlin for a few days? I was so glad to see him again, and have an opportunity of singing which I am so fond of—though my voice is not and never was anything like yours.

From the Queen

BALMORAL, OCTOBER 29, 1872

I was interrupted by going out—to see a poor dying man and to visit my Girls School (where there are a few little boys) which with a little group of infants would I think have delighted you. They are such pretty picturesque children all of whom I know from their birth almost—amongst others a child of Maggie Gow—whom you remember well I am sure and who is the living image of her mother. Lizzie Stewart who with Mary Spense were such lovely bairns—is my housemaid here, and a very nice, good girl.—How can you doubt my being interested in your dear children? Of course it is the very greatest interest to me to hear how your dear children go on. I only wish I could be of some use to them and as for the boys I hope they in later years will often come to see Grandmama.[1] They should travel and come here to the Highlands for fine air and to see the life and people.

I send you a book which Sir A. Helps has edited (not written) by Mr. Brassey's son which he says it would be very important and useful to be read by the working classes and I therefore think you might like to see it. I have not had time to read it myself.[2]

From the Crown Princess

NEUES PALAIS, POTSDAM, OCTOBER 29, 1872

Many thanks for your dear letter of the 25th. To all you say I can find no reply which in a letter might not convey a wrong impression of what I think. As to Alfred, I only know what you have told me; Alice and I have hardly written to each other at all and she has not mentioned the subject to me. The Emperor of Russia wished to open a conversation on the topic with me, but I cut short whatever he wanted to say when he began *"Nous avons reçu une charmante lettre de votre frère qui nous a beaucoup touché"*. I looked at him with surprise and said *"de quel frère parlez vous?"* Upon which he looked at me with astonishment and said nothing more, therefore I absolutely know

---

[1] In her letter of October 25 the Crown Princess said that the Queen's Prussian grandchildren "will seem like strangers to you".

[2] Thomas Brassey (1805-70) the Railway Contractor. Helps wrote his biography this year, and also edited the book, to which the Queen refers, by the son, afterwards the first Earl.

nothing of the matter. You know I think the young Princess charming, and quite understood that Alfred took a fancy to her, and think they might have been very happy together.

You ask what the objection to Countess Hohenau is, and who she was? She was a Fräulein von Rauch, Lady-in-Waiting to Prince Albert's wife, Princess Marianne of the Netherlands,—and the only objection was that the late King was by way of never having given his consent to Prince Albert's marriage to Mademoiselle von Rauch. This is only upheld by my mother-in-law and Princess Charles, whereas my father-in-law maintains the contrary and has the letter in his possession (as he told me last week) in which the late King consents to the marriage taking place at Meiningen.

From the Crown Princess

NEUES PALAIS, NOVEMBER 2, 1872

I met the Emperor at the railway station today to say goodbye, and I thought him looking tired and preoccupied with the present political complications, which I own seem very absurd to me—but which put the Emperor in no pleasant position, as his all powerful Chancellor continues digging fishponds at Varzin—and no summons or entreaties can persuade him to come to Berlin for business or say when he means to come—which as the Government is in a fix of his making seems to me rather hard on the Emperor.

How vexing and annoying it is that the award in the San Juan question is given against us. I could not help feeling frantic, and yet I suppose nothing else could have been done. I think people at home are wonderfully good tempered not to have been more angry and put out. How those odious Americans will crow over us—they will be more unbearable than ever.[1]

I hear the Empress is terribly excited upon the Church question, I grieve to think of how unhappy she makes herself not without a cause, but to no purpose. From another point of view than hers I come to the very same conclusion as she does—and agree with her entirely as to the dangers incurred by the course our Government has taken only I see no earthly use, and only harm, by trying to oppose the measures which are being carried out.[2] I am happy to say the Empress and I seldom disagree now—she is most kind in all her letters, which is a

---

[1] A dispute over the island of San Juan close to the British possession of Vancouver. The matter was submitted to the arbitration of the German Emperor.
[2] In the summer the Government had placed the Jesuits under police supervision—a step which led to widespread discontent among the German Catholics.

great comfort as what on earth do I wish for more, than to be on the kindest terms and live in perfect peace and harmony?

From the Queen

In my last letter to you I said I would write at more length next time. I will therefore at once begin about the Russian marriage. You know how matters stood when you left. Affie came back and seemed pleased with the young lady—but as you know the Emperor lectured him very severely—in a way hardly quite justifiable if nothing more was to come out of it, and he was told that for a year he could not see or even be named to the young Grand-Duchess! Well Alice would have he was the favoured one; but from what I since hear, from relations of the family, there never was any serious idea of it. Then Affie begged I would write to the Emperor expressing my interest in the affair and that Affie did nothing without my approval. To this came a civil, cold answer from the Emperor saying that for a year nothing could be said to their daughter who then would be left to do what she liked. Meantime Affie had written also to the Empress and sent a present to the Grand-Duchess to which, after a long interlude, he got a scolding letter from the Empress disapproving this and really speaking to him harshly and severely, and accusing him of want of openness! To this he answered properly asking in what she wished him to be more open? No sign of life ever appeared which Affie felt a good deal hurt at and I—not less. For my son to be a humble suitor of a young Russian Grand-Duchess and to be left dangling, till she condescended to say whether she meant to have him or not—was a thing which I am sure your pride would have arisen against as much as mine. We waited and waited,—inquiring on several occasions through Brunow whether he had heard nothing. At length at the beginning of May there was some communication and I send you what passed. After this it was advised Affie should write to the Empress (she never answered his letter written in October!!) and he asked me to write one for him; I send you here the draft which was translated into German. To this came the answer also enclosed which evidently was a civil ending to the matter; and Affie wrote the rejoinder of which I also enclose the copy. We heard since through Brunow—and through other near Russian relations—that it would not be well taken if Affie tried to force on his suit; that the girl (whom though you thought her charming is said to be quite wonderfully spoilt) did not wish at all to marry and the parents wished her to remain in Russia. So matters stand. I wish you to let Fritz see these letters and for you to be able to answer if questions should be asked exactly what happened. You will see that (while not thinking it would have been a match likely to suit here or in our family) I did all I could to help Affie and promote it, which he knows—only now he must not expose himself to a rejection which he has not received. Keep the letters till you see Fritz and then send them back again.—As eldest sister I wish you to know the truth.

As regards the different interests and paths of the members of the family it no doubt does not tend to unity which is a great grief to me as it would have been to beloved Papa; though he could have helped me in many ways—still in others his difficulties with his sons would even have been greater. But still I think there might be a unity of affection and feeling even if the interests are different which is the one great difficulty and drawback in Royal Families, and I think it ought to be a rule as well as a principle for them not to talk at and about one another—which I'm grieved to say has been (with some) a great practice; not with you,—and therefore as the eldest of the family I do ask you always to help in preaching this, for *l'union fait la force*. If I saw you I could tell you more. One remarkable exception is in the Danish Royal Family; they are wonderfully united—and never breathe a word one against the other and the daughters remain as unspoilt and as completely children of the house as when they were unmarried. I do admire this.

This award is very unfortunate but we have no right to complain— only I think that the people here are again irritated against Germany which is my great distress always. There is always something unto- ward happening to provoke or rekindle this. I must end this very long letter. Please just telegraph that you have received it.

From the Queen

BALMORAL, NOVEMBER 16, 1872

These lines are to offer you my warmest and heartiest good wishes for every possible earthly and spiritual blessing on the occasion of your dear birthday! May you see many many and happy returns of it and may God bless you and yours here and hereafter when "the wicked cease from troubling and the weary are at rest".

From the Queen

WINDSOR CASTLE, NOVEMBER 27, 1872

As regards the report of A.'s engagement, it is not true; but you
— 69 —

know I cannot make A. marry exactly whom I might choose and he has seen the H. girls[1] as well as F. Charles's daughters and may see more. He is 28 and you know neither I or anyone ought to take the responsibility of such a step. I can only forbid what is really bad. Thyra's engagement is totally without foundation. Augusta Stanley is here since Tuesday and has told me much of what I wish to hear.[2] The Dean has also been here for two nights. The friendship of A. for the Metternichs[3] I have warned and shall warn against and it annoys me much.

Towards the end of November the Crown Princess had gone to Bex in Switzerland where she was to be joined by the Crown Prince who was shooting with his father. Unfortunately the Crown Prince fell ill at Carlsruhe, and the Crown Princess had to abandon all her plans and join him there in the house of the Grand Duke and Duchess of Baden. The Crown Prince was suffering from a small inflammation in part of the bowel. The Crown Princess wrote that "the air, and the country here as well as the mode of life does not at all agree with me and I think the place as melancholy as a grave".

From the Queen

WINDSOR CASTLE, DECEMBER I, 1872

Pray thank Wegner for his letter. Sir William Jenner to whom I have shown all the telegrams etc. says that dear Fritz must not make any exertion for some time and any return to dinners, parties, etc., too soon, might be very serious.

Lenchen's baby looks strong, healthy and good humoured and sits up like a much older child, but is excessively plain and quite unlike the others.[4]

From the Queen

WINDSOR CASTLE, DECEMBER 5, 1872

I have just received the Japanese Ambassadors in hideous modern uniforms. Such a pity.[5]

---

[1] Probably Hanover.
[2] About the death of the Queen's half-sister, Princess Hohenlohe. Lady Augusta had represented the Queen at the funeral.
[3] Prince Richard, son of the Chancellor. He was Austrian Ambassador in Paris during the Second Empire. Princess Pauline, his wife, said of herself "I may look like a monkey but at least I am a fashionable one".
[4] Princess Marie Louise 1872–1956.
[5] Sionii Twakuri and suite. They had landed at Liverpool, and one who met them noticed how modern reforms had changed their oriental customs. "They speak pure English, dress as we do, and in perfect taste."

Affie is here. I am so distressed at his not going to see you—and feel sure that he is sorry too—but Alice I blame for not sending him off at once.[1] He did see your three eldest children I am glad to hear at Berlin and thought the Emperor quite wonderful, so fresh and young and in such high spirits.

From the Queen

WINDSOR CASTLE, DECEMBER 9, 1872

The weather is very unwholesome. Such a frightful south west gale last night, that eight trees were blown down in the Home Park, in those avenues not far from the river—and the water is out in every direction.

I cannot tell you what I felt and feel about Affie's conduct and can only hope you will forgive him as I have had to do so often, but I am very unhappy about him altogether and I fear he will never be really happy.

From the Crown Princess

CARLSRUHE, DECEMBER 11, 1872

Of course I do not resent dear Affie's strange proceedings, I love him much too much for that, and would never think of owing any one of the dear brothers and sisters a grudge. I only felt hurt because it proved so clearly to me how little he cared for his old sister who is so fond of him. He could afford to give Princess Metternich and other amusing ladies plenty of his time, and had none left for me. But I know I must be a great bore to young men who like fashionable society, and our life has nothing to attract or amuse young people and no doubt appears very dull to them, so that I make every allowance for Affie not being in a hurry—especially now when he has been told Heaven knows what about our wishing to interfere with his affairs.

---

[1] "We do feel a little hurt at Alfred's not having thought it worth while to see us." He was shooting with the Duke of Saxe-Coburg in Alsace.

From the Queen

WINDSOR CASTLE, DECEMBER 14, 1872
Writing on the anniversary of the Prince's death the Queen alludes to his tender love which remains and goes on:

I would, too, willingly help you far more than I do if I could feel that you two sisters cared the least for your mother's loving and may be sometimes warning voice.

As regards Affie I must just say a word for him. In the first place as regards his going to Berlin he is not to blame; before leaving England at the end of September he had intended to go there, and after his other visits in Austria I insisted that he should pay his respects to the Emperor. Nothing against you has been instilled into him; and it was merely I suspect slyness, and fear of being asked questions, which was very foolish, for you would not have done so, and if anyone had, he need not answer them unless he liked. I think he misses gay society less than Bertie.

From the Queen

WINDSOR CASTLE, DECEMBER 21, 1872
Everyone grieves for poor Mr. Disraeli's great loss, for their marriage was so touching an example of mutual devotion and affection and it is an example which is refreshing and wholesome in these days of dissipation and disbelief in chivalry and disinterested attachment.

From the Queen

OSBORNE, DECEMBER 27, 1872
I could not, to my regret, write sooner having been so occupied with Christmas, and arranging for the two trees and presents for the servants—which comes to between two and three hundred people and which is given on New Year's day.

1873

From the Crown Princess

WIESBADEN, JANUARY I, 1873

It was such a pleasure to receive your dear, kind letter early this morning and the lovely New Year's cards to Fritz and the children and myself. The children were all assembled when your letter arrived, each was delighted with his or her card and Waldy asked "which has Grandmama sent to me?" When I told him Grandmama most likely thought him too little for a New Year's card he laid himself on the floor and hid his face in the carpet in the greatest distress.

From the Queen

OSBORNE, JANUARY 4, 1873

I send here a New Year's card for poor little Waldy who is not too little to get a New Year's card; the fact was I had such quantities of grandchildren (their name is legion) to send to—as well as my own and other relations and friends—that I got confused and bewildered about the ages, and omitted to send it which I do now. I suppose he is still rather wilful as he used to be—dear little fellow.

From the Crown Princess

WIESBADEN, JANUARY 6, 1873

Our three eldest left this morning at six—they were so dreadfully distressed last night and nearly cried their eyes out (I did mine too)— but this morning the delight of a railway journey seemed to have comforted them, lunching in the railway carriage is the greatest of pleasures. We shall miss the dear children so much. Willy is loud and rough, Charlotte is very troublesome and Henry most provoking at times—but really they are very dear and nice—and I am very proud of them. I can see them improving so rapidly and they are so affectionate and happy to be with us and give me great pleasure.

From the Queen

Here the very sudden death of the poor Emperor[1] after such cruel suffering (which I think accounts for a great deal at the time of the war) fills everybody's mind and much sympathy is felt and shown here—where he was much liked personally and because he certainly was a faithful ally of England and at times, when if he had not been, he might have done us great harm. It is too horrible to be tortured as he has been, only to die! The disgusting and horrible publicity of his illness which went on every day after the operations—and the details of the post-mortem today (though I dare say they had to have it) make me furious and I would like to punish those surgeons who always seem little better than butchers to me!

From the Queen

I have just heard by telegraph that Bertie, Affie and Christian have been (by my desire) to Chislehurst to pay a last mark of personal respect to him who was excessively kind to them always and who lay in state today! Tomorrow at half past ten is the funeral and as immense crowds will come, though it is by way of being private, it was thought better, for fear of political demonstrations, that the brothers should not attend, but we all send gentlemen (Lord Sydney a personal old friend and who lives close by and Lord Bridport—from me).

From the Queen

I hope the weaning will go off well for both parties. It should be done gradually I believe; dear old Sir James (who I think was the best and wisest doctor—as well as one of the kindest men—I ever knew) was so very strong upon that always.

Let me now say one word in great confidence which I beg you not to mention to Alice as having heard from me—viz—the Russian match has cropped up again!! The Emperor sent a direct message through Count Schouvaloff saying they never intended it to be broken off!! And as Affie still seems to wish it so much—I can't, of course,

---

[1] Napoleon III died at Chislehurst on January 9.

after what has passed, entirely refuse these (to me somewhat suspicious) *avances*. I could not leave you in ignorance after what I told you, dearest. Have you heard anything indirectly for I should be grateful to know? But don't let Affie or anyone suspect I told you anything. Would you let me have those letters back.

From the Queen

I wish to make you a proposal—which I hope might perhaps be acceptable and possible. It is that you should come to see me at the very beginning of May and stay with me till I go to Scotland in the middle of May—and then spend ten days or a fortnight at B. Palace where you would be able to see the brothers and sisters and all you wished—without being oppressed with the great heat, and when I also could see you comfortably. I mention this to you as I think it far better you should know when I could comfortably receive you. You could bring two or three children but I would ask not more. I am really not up to large family parties. I should be at Windsor from the 1st of May and leave for Scotland D.V. about the 16th and shall be in London for two days during that time. I have not mentioned this to anyone.

From the Queen

That clock of the poor Emperor's is what she has sent me as a recollection; was his travelling clock and was with him everywhere and will be a most interesting relic hereafter. I shall leave it as an heirloom; it stands in my room.

The German Press is very savage against us again and seems to try to set us against the Russians and vice versa. I don't see exactly why?

From the Queen

Poor Alice's little Fritz seems to be sadly delicate.[1] I think it is a good deal accounted for by the state of anxiety and distress she was in before and after he was born. This peculiarity of poor little Fritz, like

---

[1] He is believed to have suffered from haemophilia.

Leopold's which is such a rare thing and not in the family, is most extraordinary. It is a sad anxiety for nothing can be done—beyond general strengthening and fresh air.

From the Queen

OSBORNE, FEBRUARY 8, 1873
I have been so annoyed and vexed at that business about Dr. Hessel, which you must have seen in *The Times*, that I told Mr. Sahl to write all about it to M. de Normann. It is so very humiliating for us.[1]

From the Queen

OSBORNE, FEBRUARY 12, 1873
Alice's little Fritz is better but I am afraid he has the same constitution as Leopold. Only where does it all come from?

From the Crown Princess

WIESBADEN, FEBRUARY 12, 1873
I am so glad the English Government have been so generous to Doctor Hessel, though it is no more than right, because it was a most unfortunate business; and I was so provoked that he should have been a German—as of course it only adds fuel to the flames which are not needed.

It is in all our German papers that Affie is engaged to the Emperor of Russia's daughter.

How very kind of you it was to send a sum to the poor creatures who have lost everything by the inundations on our north-east coasts, a great deal of money is being collected for the sufferers, we belong to a society who are occupied in raising sums, and the help will be very effectual I am sure.

There is court mourning again—the poor old Empress Caroline whom I saw at Vienna; our Queen Dowager feels her sister's death

---

1 Harriet Boswell or Clara Burton was found murdered on December 23 in lodgings in Great Coram Street. The police arrested Dr. Hessel who was a German clergyman. He was subsequently acquitted at Bow Street. £1,200 was collected for him in England, and to this the Queen contributed £30 as a token of individual regret. On his release Dr. Hessel was entertained in London by the German Gymnastic Society—a social and athletic centre for Germans living in London.

very much as she was much attached to her in spite of their seeing each other so rarely and there being such a great difference in their ages.

From the Queen

I am sorry Alice and Louis mean to take W. Ruland *à trois* with them to Italy.[1] He is not the man to be treated with familiarity, that I know to my cost and before Alice married Louis took great exception to him, and considering his conduct to me about what you know, they ought not to take him. Can't you still advise against it? Believe me it is a bad thing. I wonder how Alice can wish to do it.

From the Queen

What I meant about the poor Emperor's photograph taken after death was—that it should not be put into an album but you would be sure not to do that.[2] You will I think like to hear about my visit to Chislehurst. We left this at $10\frac{1}{4}$—(Baby, Jane Churchill and I—Colonel Maude acting as equerry) went by rail over London[3]—which was wrapped in a thick yellow fog to the station at Chislehurst which we reached in about an hour and from thence we drove to the little Catholic Church, a pretty rural little place, quite like a village church; smaller a good deal inside than half of Whippingham Church. To the right of the altar or rather below it—and nearly opposite as you enter, behind a railing—in the smallest space possible—rests the earthly remains of the poor Emperor, covered with a black velvet pall embroidered with golden beads and covered with wreaths of Immortelles flowers—a number of which also are lying in a heap outside, to which Beatrice and I each added one. Father Goddard the youngish priest, a quiet sort of man, showed us about—and also showed us the plan of the small separate chapel which is to be added on. The Sydneys (who live quite nearby) had met us there. Thence we drove to Camden House where at the door instead of the poor father who received us so kindly always—was the poor Prince Imperial looking very pale and sad—and a few steps further, in the deepest black, looking very ill,

---

They were also accompanied by the Princess's English lady-in-waiting—Emily Hardinge.
[2] Sending the photograph the Queen had begged the Crown Princess not to put it in an album or show it to people "who had no feeling for him".
[3] The Queen almost certainly used the West London Extension Railway by which it was possible to travel from the Great Western to Clapham Junction above the chimney pots.

very handsome and a picture of sorrow—the poor Empress—who would come down to receive me. Silently we embraced each other, and she took my arm in hers—could not speak for tears and led me upstairs to her little boudoir—very small, full of the few souvenirs she could save of all she formerly had! She cried a good deal but quietly, gently and that sweet face, always a sad one, looked so inexpressably sad—as you can easily imagine. She described the poor Emperor's death—how terribly sudden it was; she was just going to Woolwich to tell the Boy, who wanted to come, but who they thought would fidget his father by going continually in and out of his room, as he loved him so much, and that the Emperor had had a better night, when they told her—better not go—"*l'Empereur a une petite crise*" and she took off her bonnet and went towards the room which is close by —and as she came closer to the door—she met Dr. Corvisart calling out "Father Goddard, Father Goddard" and at once saw there was danger.

When she came in—and kissed his hand, they said to him "*voilà l'Imperatrice*" and no longer able to see her—he still moved his lips to kiss her. And five or ten minutes afterwards all was over! He had suffered fearfully and going in the carriage was agony already in September when they were at Cowes! The dreadful preparations, the hammering and knocking in that small house were dreadful she said. Prince Napoleon behaved abominably—wanting to take the boy from her "*tout ce que j'ai*" she said—and not to leave him here but she was firm and she is by the Emperor's will his guardian. He likes being at Woolwich which is only half an hour's ride or drive from Chislehurst. She showed me the poor Emperor's two humble little rooms— left just as he left them—all his things on the tables! So sad to see, as I know but too well.

She was dressed in the deep widows' dress worn here—with crape almost up to her waist but no white whatever; on her head—a black crape cap quite flat coming very forward, with a sort of point and a short black veil something like the back of my white cap of an evening.

One of her nieces is with her,—and old Princess Murat, a nice old lady were there. It was a very sad visit—and I see her sad face constantly before me.

From the Crown Princess

WIESBADEN, MARCH 2, 1873

The people at Berlin are going to give Fritz a brilliant reception which is very kindly meant and touches us very much, but it also makes us rather shy and nervous, and we hear the Emperor does not half like it[1] which makes us more uncomfortable still.

From the Queen

I am vexed I could not write to you on Saturday but I was so flurried and hurried and tired in London I could not—and yesterday the result was a violent neuralgic attack in my face which I have not had for a long time—but I have been overworked and worried and overdone for the last three weeks and it was brought to a climax in London the other day. I am free from pain today but very tired.

The good old Duchess of Inverness is really improving. Poor Bernstorff is very, very ill. The cupping operation which took place on Thursday has temporarily relieved him but the general state is very serious. I went to see her poor thing on Friday and found her looking very ill, a shadow of herself from sitting up every night and from great anxiety—but she bears up wonderfully. She said she was dreadfully tired.

I had before been to Victor and Lolo and to the studio of the former where I saw his model for the monument of beloved Aunt at Baden which will I think be very fine.

From the Queen

I wonder Alice is not frightened to go so far away from little Fritzie with that sad propensity to bleeding. Since '62 I have never been any distance from Leopold. At least no place which could not be reached within 24 hours and that only once! Tennyson (whose fine Epilogue no doubt you have seen) is coming here today to see me and I am going to show the Mausoleum to him.

The Prince Imperial came to luncheon here on Tuesday. He is a very dear, nice boy—with such charming manners—reminding me much of his father and yet he is like her too. The tears come to his eyes whenever he speaks of the Emperor. His nose is getting like the Emperor's and the shape of his head as well as the colour of his eyes—

---

[1] Meaning—only half likes it.

but the shape of his eyelids, and eyebrows and his smile—a very sweet one—are the Empress's. His hair is very dark.

The Irish University Bill[1] suddenly threatens a crisis.

From the Queen

BUCKINGHAM PALACE, MARCH 13, 1873

I am in the midst of a Ministerial crisis and could therefore not write yesterday or in time for the post today. You will have seen how very great the opposition to and dislike of this Irish University Bill had become. The adverse vote on Tuesday night or rather more yesterday morning led to Mr. Gladstone's resignation today. I saw him twice yesterday—and again today when he told me two courses were open—either to advise me to dissolve or to resign as they could not submit to such a vote, and that they thought the latter course the best. I then sent for Mr. Disraeli, who says he can't undertake a Government in this Parliament and did not ask me to dissolve, but hoped Mr. Gladstone would resume office. Here we are and no farther, for I have sent to tell Mr. G. this and I don't know yet what the result will be. But all is quiet and I hope tomorrow we shall see our way. Good Mr. G. is not judicious and this "mission" to redeem Ireland— which has signally failed—has been the cause of his defeat. It gives me of course a good deal of trouble. Please tell the Empress from me as I can't write to her.

The good old Duchess of Inverness is really better! I went to see her this morning and she was so pleased to see me and said "you are a darling". There is something so touching in an old and very sick person who blesses you and is so kind to you. She always blesses me and all my children.

From the Crown Princess

BERLIN, MARCH 13, 1873

I had not time to write since our arrival, which you must kindly excuse. You have no idea what a rush we fell in to the moment we arrived, people to see and receive, visits to pay all day long. The opening of the Reichstag, the church service, a large dinner at court, last night a soirée which lasted till 1 at the Empress's, and I with a

---

[1] Two years earlier Oxford and Cambridge, formerly restricted to members of the Church of England, were thrown open to men of all creeds. The Irish University Bill arrived to create a new university where Roman Catholics would attend but which would not offend the susceptibilities of a Protestant Parliament.

violent sick headache! Fritz is very tired, and I feel quite done up, then tomorrow again a party besides which all the things in the house to settle and arrange which is almost too much for me. We were very kindly received, and everybody who sees Fritz again expresses their pleasure in the kindest way but a regular reception there was not, much to our relief.

From the Queen

What I told you of already—on Friday has ended in Mr. Gladstone having to go on. I think all this might have been avoided but he has no tact. He has been very tiresome and obstinate in this business and I think has done himself no good. I shall see him today, and tomorrow the explanations will take place. The excitement, anxiety and hard work have made me feel ill and upset today as it always does when a crisis of any kind is over. I am sorry to hear you have so much to tire you on your return, but that was, I fear, unavoidable. You ask about Affie. Do you think it possible that such a thing could be true, and you know nothing? Matters are as they were, and time will show if it is to be—or not.

Yesterday being Louise's birthday I had some music in the afternoon and Joachim played very beautifully as well as a Mr. Ap Thomas whom you have heard—and a young Italian called Rendano on the piano.[1] He has a beautiful touch.

From the Queen

Your dear anxious letter of the 17th reached me quite safely and I hasten to tell you first of all how pleased I am that you should open your heart to me as you did to beloved Papa and as I hope and trust you will always do upon any subject, if you are in any doubts or in any trouble. Secondly I will try to relieve your anxiety. The crisis is over and the Government has not changed. But if it had I don't think you need have feared a *rapprochement* with the French. People are too disgusted with them now to wish that. The Commercial Treaty (about which the French behaved very ill) is merely a question of trade which would be seriously affected by any war—and if the Conservative Party came in at present with a Protestant cry it would certainly prefer

---

[1] Ap Thomas (1829–1913). A distinguished harpist. Alfonso Rendano (1853–1931).

supporting Protestant Germany to Roman Catholic France—the more so as Bismarck's policy is entirely anti-Catholic. As for a war of aggression, France is in such a state that it is simply impossible for her to attempt anything and I think it is very unwise to appear to think so in Germany. You will no doubt have read the Ministerial explanations in yesterday's papers.

You ask about Count Münster. He would certainly be very *présentable*, and popular in society though the Cambridges would I think take exception to him, but that does not signify.

From the Queen

WINDSOR CASTLE, MARCH 26, 1873

You asked if I am not "rather shocked" at that horrid George of Meiningen's marriage. I think it disgraceful and an outrage to the memory of the dear wife he so shamefully neglected for this very woman! The poor children! What poor Ada and brothers will feel! Thank God! beloved Aunt is spared this. I hope you will mark your sense of his conduct if ever he shows himself.[1]

From the Crown Princess

BERLIN, MARCH 24, 1873

The last few days have been so horribly fatiguing, and the exposure to suffocating heat in the rooms and violent draughts on going in and out of the houses has been such that I am very unwell. The blood goes so frightfully to my head from the fatigue, heat, noise, bustle etc.— and having a cold besides gives me a dreadful rheumatic headache so that I can hardly move my head—a swelled face, sore throat and pain in my limbs! Poor Fritz looks so tired, so worn, so different to what he did a fortnight ago that I shall send for some other doctor and have their opinion as to whether he is fit for this knocking about! Pray do not say anything to the Empress as she takes it very ill if he asks to take care of himself. She is too odd about it! Two months ago she was in a dreadful fuss and fright about him, and now she will not hear of his taking the least care—or absenting himself from any dinner or party. His parents are both of them most marvellously constituted; the more of this kind of thing is going on the better they seem to feel and look—it is quite astonishing.

---

[1] He had married Princess Hohenlohe's daughter, and subsequently made a morganatic marriage with Hélène Baronne de Heldeburg.

From the Queen

Poor Count Bernstorff ended his sad suffering on Wednesday rather suddenly. People keep asking me who is to replace poor Bernstorff; I said I did not know, some thought Arnim others Perponcher. I asked Lord Granville what he thought of Count Münster and he said he would do very well. So you can make use of that if you require it.

From the Queen

I asked Lady Caledon to write you an account of my visit to the Victoria or People's Park today—which is beyond Bethnal Green and we had to drive through the poorest and worst parts of London— but nothing could go off better or the enthusiasm be greater. We had no escort and I am sure there were as many people out as on the Thanksgiving Day! The population really is fearful. Baby—Lady Caledon and Jane Churchill were with me, and the three other ladies and the Lord-in-Waiting in the second carriage. It was a splendid day. In few countries could such a sight have been seen.

From the Crown Princess

We gave a large dinner the day before yesterday at which Prince Bismarck and Lord Odo sat next to me. I did not like to say anything to the former about Count Münster but I think all chances are not lost, though nothing is decided. Most people of judgment here think Count M. would be the best as he would get on so well in London. Without being a very clever or remarkable man, he is such a gentleman, and an easy, good-natured, good-tempered person with whom it is really difficult to pick a quarrel.

William passes an examination today before some masters from one of our gymnasiums to see whether he is as far advanced as other boys who are in the upper third class. He is only examined in Latin, Greek and Mathematics. We have not decided whether we shall take him to Vienna or not; there would be so much to be seen which would be both instructive and interesting but I am afraid it will make real work very distasteful for him afterwards. How kind and civil people have been in England to poor Countess Bernstorff; it is really very touching; but in no country in the world so much sympathy is shown to people in sorrow and misfortune.

From the Queen

WINDSOR CASTLE, APRIL 5, 1873

Lenchen's baby is wonderfully improved in looks and is a splendid child as big as one a year old, almost too fat—but it is quite firm. She has been entirely brought up by hand and I certainly never saw a finer specimen.

This is what poor Victor wrote to me about that horrid George of M.'s marriage "I hardly know how to express my utter disgust of George's heartless and insulting conduct. Even putting us relations out of the question, how can a man of honour insult the memory of his wife, not dead much more than one year, in this disgraceful way and knowingly lower himself in the eyes of his own children and the world? What will become of those two poor boys of our darling Feo?" I quite agree, but there is not much honour nowadays and actresses and singers are made so much of, that it leads to these lamentable results. What will the children do? Surely the poor daughter can no longer live in the house?

I send you a little poem Dean Stanley wrote on the poor Emperor Napoleon's clock being given to me.

From the Crown Princess

BERLIN, APRIL 6, 1873

It was utterly impossible for me to write yesterday as I was quite in bed—and next to insensible with the frantic violence of neuralgia in my eye. I cannot describe what I have suffered these last three days. I have been nearly mad. I took arsenic without any effect, tried hydrate of chlorate in order to make me sleep—I did not sleep and was only very sick—I tried smelling carbolic acid, and rubbing acoustic salve over my head but all to no purpose. Today I am able to stand on my legs.

I was so glad to hear of your successful visit to Victoria Park. No! indeed in no other country could such a thing be seen; there is a something in the expression of British loyalty which nothing else is like, the spontaneous, warm, touching way in which it comes out. John Bull has more heart than anyone alive, that I know and feel and see every day of my life!

From the Crown Princess

Master Willy is going to Vienna with us and now that Doctor H. is away—he is leading quite a dissipated life for him, going with us to see pictures etc. and enjoys himself immensely; he is growing such a big boy and has changed his voice which has now become very like his Papa's.

From the Queen

I am rather sorry you take dear Willy[1] as I fear it will make him old before his years and bring him too forward. Where has Dr. Hintzpeter gone to? You ask about Affie. I thought I said to you (I am sure I did) he was going to pay a visit at Sorrento and that the result was in God's hands! I will however tell you exactly how matters stand as I can entirely rely on your discretion. You know about Count Schouvaloff, well a long time elapsed and there were even unpleasant reports about the girl which made me very anxious but which have been removed. But finally only a fortnight about ago—the Empress wrote to say she would be glad to see Affie at Sorrento about the middle of April; so A. wrote to say he would be there on the 21st and hoped his presence would be agreeable to the Grand-Duchess. Two things I have made a *sine qua non*—viz that there must be mutual attachment and if there is—then they must be married within this year or else it must finally be put an end to.

From the Crown Princess

I am so glad it is settled now about Count Münster: the Emperor seems to like the appointment, most people here think it is a good one. He is devoted to England as you know, and has been particularly civil and kind to me at all times. I hope you can persuade Bertie and Alix to like him as of course the Cambridges (not Uncle George) will do their best the other way. I heard from Bismarck's own lips that he is most anxious to please you—and said your wishes in the matter would be his guide. I did not use your name nor mention Count Münster's— though I know Fritz did the latter.

---

[1] On an official visit to Vienna.

B. is too dangerous a customer to deal with so I never say a word to him, even when he is in the best of humours, which he can make any use of against me, and particularly not in connection with England —as that would always be the point on which he would attack me if it suited any purpose of his to be spiteful, which it does not at present, so he is as civil as possible.

From the Queen

OSBORNE, APRIL 16, 1873

My beloved Baby—who is really the apple of my eye—and who is very much with me—though not of an evening as I keep her as young and child-like as I can—and who I pray God may remain with me as long as I live for she is the last I have and I could not live without her— was very happy.[1]

From the Queen

OSBORNE, APRIL 18, 1873

You will I hope not allow dear Willy to stay up late at night or only once or twice as you and Bertie did when you went with us to Paris. Willy is older by a few months than Bertie was when he went with us then.

Affie is at Rome, and leaves for Naples and Sorrento on the 21st— so the next week will be a very anxious one. As sweet and gentle a creature as dear Alix or as loving and dutiful a daughter and as good a sister to you all, it will be very difficult to find. I don't think you need fear Bertie's not being very amiable to Count Münster; quite the reverse, and I think Alix too and Uncle George. Both spoke in a very friendly way of him when I mentioned him as a candidate. But Aunt Cambridge and her daughters will at first I suppose be angry and (but this I beg you to keep quite to yourself) Christian and Lenchen are inclined to look on him with disfavour as they say "he behaved very ill to the King of Hanover". Now I certainly am not one who approves of faithlessness and disloyalty to your Sovereign especially when in misfortune, but I never heard that Count Münster had been guilty of personal faithlessness to his King. I think if you, without alluding to what I have said as to their feelings, were to write to Lenchen about

---

[1] Her 16th birthday.

Count Münster recommending him and (if you can) disproving any of these accusations it would be a very good thing.

As for me, for the very recollection of his parents and sisters, whom I knew so well when I was a child, I would be sure to be friendly—though I can't quite forget the cradle of my family being swallowed up.

The ceremony on Thursday of the Presentation of the Colours[1] was very pretty and very successful. It is a splendid and very gallant Regiment and they have presented me with their old colours—which I shall greatly value. They were through the Indian Mutiny and had sent for their former Chaplain a fine, tall-looking Presbyterian Minister who had been 14 years with them and had the Indian Mutiny Medal, to bless their new colours which he did in a very pretty prayer. You will see my little speech, which I had learnt by heart, in the papers.

From the Crown Princess

BERLIN, APRIL 20, 1873

Merely a word to say the wedding has gone off quite well.[2] The bride looked very pretty in the handsome dress which is anything except that of a bride. I think the whole most trying—and not in keeping with our ideas of what is nice—however I do not say so.

From the Crown Princess

BERLIN, APRIL 22, 1873

What you tell me about the reception Count Münster is likely to meet with, interests me very much. Of your kindness I felt assured also dear Bertie's now that you tell me he is not against Count M. The ladies of the Cambridge family—no one doubts will not be agreeable, Christian's and Lenchen's prejudice I know of. It is most unfair. The facts are so well known to me that I can hazard saying that Count M. behaved loyally and conscientiously towards his unhappy Sovereign—who requited his services and received all his advice as ill as possible. Had the King followed Count M.'s advice he would still be King of Hanover. The whole Augustenburg family (Fritz excepted) have a violent prejudice against Count M. Their accusations (which I know of old) are totally unjust. Poor Count M.'s position *vis à vis* of King

---

[1] The 79th Regiment—Cameron Highlanders.
[2] Abbat with Princess Marie of Saxe-Altenburg.

George is very trying and painful, and I think he is as tactful as possible —and behaves just as he ought. Today is my sweet little Mossie's birthday. She is such a little love—so forward, so pretty and so good, I think she would find favour in your eyes in spite of her being my pet.

I must end here dearest Mama but first let me say Willy is quite incog: at Vienna, does not appear at dinners or parties but goes to bed quite early as he does here. We do not wish to bring him forward in any way; he is only to have the treat of seeing the Exhibition.

From the Queen

OSBORNE, APRIL 23, 1873

It was very dear and kind of you to write to me twice in the midst of those festivities. I own I think that a good part of them belongs to those times which are now gone by. I thought of you and of what you had wished and was sorry you should feel disappointment.—But let me for the last time say that you may believe me, when I say it is better so, for you and for all parties.—I sincerely hope that they may be happy and your new cousin prove a pleasant and amiable companion and friend to you. What did you think of the *fackeltanz*? Is it not very odd? And what dress did you wear—and what was the bride's dress at the marriage? My Grandmother, Queen Charlotte, wore the same sort of dress, and robes![1] But I refused to wear anything but a bride's dress. My Aunts wore all white, silver, etc., but no robes.

You will find dear Bertie much improved and most kind, affectionate, and reasonable. It is his own particular wish to go to Berlin after Vienna. But think how unfortunate, the Grand-Duchess Marie is ill—has got a fever but I think and hope it is only malaria, though that is very bad; and there is unfortunate Affie, who was to have gone there on the 21st, obliged to wait till she's well enough to receive him!!! I heard it first through a cyphered message from Affie on the 20th— and then through Alice saying that poor Prince Charles had the same! It is very awkward. I am very glad you liked the locket for little Margaret. It is indeed like a sort of Order for my very numerous grand-daughters. 13 I have. And I hope that number won't increase—nor the grandsons—whom I like less—for some years! The family becomes too enormous.

---

[1] "An endless mantle of violet-coloured velvet, lined with ermine dragged itself, and almost the rest of her clothes, half-way down her waist." Horace Walpole.

From the Crown Princess

Fritz particularly wishes me to say how much Lord Odo is appreciated here—and how excellent in every respect the position is which he and Emily have made for themselves. They are as much respected as they are popular, and consequently are treated by all as your representatives should! There is but one opinion in all classes here on that subject, from the Emperor and Bismarck down to the youngest lieutenant. Of course we are delighted and only hope you may be able to give a good account some day of Count Münster who is at present in a state of beatitude.

You wish to know what I wore for the wedding festivities—a red velvet gown, and my pearls, a coiffure of black feathers and diamonds. For the wedding a lilac satin gown and train with silver, for the gala dinner a blue velvet gown and train with gold, for the gala opera a yellow tulle dress with bunches of grapes. It is the dressing and undressing which fatigues me and which I hate most of all! I dread Vienna so much, the Exhibition interests me immensely but I am so sick of ceremonies, etiquette, dress, show, fatigue and waste of time that I would give anything to get out of it, and we shall have it all over again for the Shah of Persia. How charming and touching the ceremony of your receiving the old colours must have been. I suppose you will keep them at Balmoral in the Kirk or in your room?

From the Crown Princess

Prague I thought most interesting, but the hotel in which we were was so horribly dirty, cold and wretched, and the journey so miserably cold that I am thankful it is over. Willy is a good bit taller and twice as broad as the little Crown Prince Rudolph, who is a slight graceful boy with very nice manners. I fear Willy seems rather a bear or a schoolboy beside him. I heard in a roundabout way from a diplomatist here, a friend of Count Schouvaloff, that at St. Petersburg they seem to consider A.'s marriage to the G. Dchss M. as quite a settled thing and I thought I should tell you.

From the Crown Princess

The ceremony was grand and imposing but my thoughts were far
— 89 —

away and recalled the brilliant and touching scene 23 years ago—which the sun lit up so magnificently.[1] I saw you standing on the Hautpas, and darling Papa looking so beautiful and reading that never-to-be forgotten speech! I saw it all before me the glass fountain, the crystal dome, etc., and the reality before me seemed gloomy and matter of fact compared with that. Others who cannot share those precious recollections no doubt were much impressed with the immense size of the building and the crowds (mostly seemed in morning dress) which filled it. It was wretchedly cold, and it rained and blew. I was much put out to walk first with the Emperor before the Empress, but he was most kind, civil and amiable. The Exhibition was only one third part ready and not near so striking as the Paris one but it is almost too soon to judge. This is a very pretty little rococo schloss with a nice garden and very comfortable. The whole Imperial family are very civil and kind but you can imagine what visiting—audiences, etc., this quantity of people entails. I was so glad to see dear Uncle Alphonse who looks much altered grown old, grey and bent! I made his wife's acquaintance who seems very nice. Aunt Clémentine was quite gracious and kind to me after she had got over the first few minutes, her three children are so nice (the little one I have not seen, and Clotilde is away so I can only speak of the others). Philippe and Marie Flanders are here and endless other distinguished visitors and the going about is exhausting. We are half an hour's distance from town which makes our movements and arrangements rather complicated. We have to drive through the very ugly and dirty and wretchedly poor and neglected-looking suburbs of Vienna before reaching this pretty spot which is close to the fine park of Schönbrunn.

From the Crown Princess

VIENNA, MAY 8, 1873

Nothing can be kinder than the Emperor and Empress are to their guests and to us in particular. The Empress's beauty seems more marvellous to me each time I see her; it is not the regularity of her face but the most picturesque and striking ensemble which I do not think one can see again, the complexion and colouring, the figure, and the extraordinary hair which is arranged without much taste. I saw her on horse-back yesterday for the first time but did not find her riding up to my expectation as one hears so much about it.

.

---

[1] The opening of the Great Exhibition.

We find the young Countess of Girgenti very nice also. Poor thing she is the Queen of Spain's daughter, not pretty, but I think pleasing and agreeable. You know her husband shot himself after he had gone mad![1] She always lives with the Archduchess Rainer who has much to say in her praise. Her brother Don Alphonso is here at school in the Thérèsianium and gets on very well I hear.

From the Queen

WINDSOR CASTLE, MAY 12, 1873

I am glad you understand why I can do nothing in my Household for good MacKay.[2] Of course you can't do all as you like as I can, but I regret you can't make a good and faithful servant comfortable, and thus retain him about you. But British servants—especially men—are, as a rule, not fond of being abroad.

From the Crown Princess

VIENNA, MAY 18, 1873

Bertie seems to have been of great use to the English Committee, and certainly the English department has come out best, has been the best arranged, the first to be ready, and has almost the finest show of things. Mr. Owen seems to be a most excellent organiser and has done wonders.

From the Crown Princess

HOTEL DE VILLE, MILAN, MAY 24, 1873

As my ladies were obliged to stay behind,[3] I have a charming young lady with me—Countess Dohnhoff *née* Camporeale—the daughter of Madame Minghetti whom you may have heard of, as being a very charming and clever woman. This daughter of hers is beautiful, very small but a real Italian type, she is very clever and nice and a delightful companion.[4]

---

[1] He was the son of Francis II of the Two Sicilies.
[2] The Crown Princess's page who does not "feel comfortable in Germany as I am quite unable to make him so".
[3] The Crown Prince and Princess, after leaving Vienna, went to Venice and Northern Italy. The Crown Princess's Prussian ladies stayed behind in Vienna.
[4] Princess Camporeale was stepdaughter to Marco Minghetti, the Italian Prime Minister. Her marriage was declared null by the Holy See in 1884, and she then married Prince Bulow, the German Chancellor. She was an accomplished pianist and the pupil of Liszt.

From the Queen

BALMORAL, MAY 25, 1873

Indeed you are right in saying how many trials I have gone through since '61 !! I have lived a whole, sad life, losing friends and becoming more and more isolated and worried and tried in a very exceptional way. I feel certainly worn and tried and tired by it all. But though I have lost so many and beloved Aunt is one of the heaviest (and I missed her dear letter so much yesterday) I have many blessings left—loving children, many kind and devoted friends sent as a help and as a comfort, and the loyal affection of a whole nation.

One great worry is Affie's affair. You have seen all the letters which I sent Bertie and I must say I think it is very uncertain and very un-satisfactory and all that you say in your letter is just what I feel and think about the way in which he is being treated by the cool, not to say insolent, conduct of the Russians.[1] This A. does not feel as he ought. He has no pride, no right pride or dignity though he has plenty of false pride when it ought not to be there.

It gives me so much pleasure to hear you speak so lovingly of dear Bertie for he deserves it. He is such a kind, good brother a very loving son and a very true friend, and so kind to all below him for which he is universally beloved; poor A. is not at all, either by high or low.

I am also very glad to see how much you like the Emperor and Empress of Austria—and Willy the young Archduke Rudolph. It will be of such use.

From the Queen

BALMORAL, JUNE 2, 1873

And now comes this dreadful calamity at Darmstadt which will so deeply move you.[2] How awful! How dreadful! Only God was very merciful in taking the little darling so painlessly and peacefully. But oh! the dreadful shock and recollection of it! I think it is merciful that no unhappy nurse or other person was to blame as that would have added to the misery. But I think little children, unless you are doing nothing and can be constantly watching them, should never be left without a person to watch them. I know how alarmed I always was about win-dows and fire. And I have always lived in dread of something happen-

---

[1] "It is so strange to give him a chance, and yet not seriously intend to accept him." The Crown Princess, May 8.
[2] Princess Alice's second son, reputed to be a haemophilic child, fell from a window and was killed.

ing to Alix's children as she used to have and has all five together in the room—even when the youngest could hardly walk—without any nurse—writing herself—and not hearing! It is so dangerous.

I send you here the copy of a letter I wrote giving the account of my visit to the Royal Vault at Windsor which I know will interest you and where perhaps I may take you some day.[1]

From the Crown Princess

The Shah of Persia leaves this morning. He is a strange guest, and of course the manners and customs are very extraordinary but he seems to know a great deal about all the countries he is going to visit, his questions are intelligent, and one gets to understand his snatches of French. He talks most of England and of you, was kind to the children particularly to Waldemar to whom he took a fancy. His unpunctuality is something dreadful—to keep everyone waiting three quarters of an hour is nothing at all out of the way. Some of his suite are very intelligent. He is a curious and not uninteresting person, but certainly not easy to manage. The Shah of Persia dislikes Russia and I fancy was not so civilly treated as he wished, at any rate he preferred being here.

From the Crown Princess

The day before yesterday was Princess Leignitz's funeral.[2] We were not a large company only the Royal family and their suites, the poor

---

[1] "Walked with Beatrice to the Deanery and went, with the Dean through the Wolsey Chapel, into St. George's Chapel and down to the family Vault, there being quite a good staircase. A small passage leads to the Vault, which is shut off by iron gates. It is wonderfully roomy and airy with an arched roof like a Chapel. In the centre, quite close to the entrance, on a sort of long stone platform stood my poor dear Father's coffin. It was indeed solemn and moving in the extreme for me, his only child, who had never known him to be standing near his earthly remains. The Dean translated the inscription on the coffin. Next came poor Princess Charlotte's and that of her little infant son, then William IV's, dear Queen Adelaide and George IV. At the end, facing the entrance are the coffins of George III, Queen Charlotte, Princess Amelia and the little Princes Octavius and Alfred, and on the shelves to the left, as one comes in, those of the Duke of York, Aunt Augusta, dear Aunt Adelaide's poor little child, a little child of the late King of Hanover's and the old Duchess of Brunswick (sister to George III and mother to Queen Caroline). All the coffins, excepting those of the Kings are covered with crimson velvet, and the former with purple. It was a very impressive and not painful sight. As we ascended the organ was being played in the Chapel, and the fine voices of the choir added to the solemnity of the whole. It was in making the passage to the Vault, that the long missing coffin of poor King Charles I was discovered." (From Queen Victoria's Journal, 15 May 1873.)

[2] She was married morganatically to Frederick William III—the Emperor's father.

Princess's family that is, her brother Count Harrach, his wife, their three sons and daughter-in-law (the Countess Pourtales's daughter). The day was splendid and the quiet walk through the garden of Charlottenburg to the mausoleum was very beautiful. At the side entrance stood the whole household of the Princess—all her servants etc. The little vault was all draped with black and lit with massive silver candlesticks, and the coffin, also black and silver, was covered with flowers; the sunlight poured in through the leaves and boughs and the little windows lighting up poor Uncle Albrecht's coffin which stood close by; the birds sang so loud that they almost drowned the clergyman's voice. The service was short and simple. We all walked back to the Schloss with a soothing and pleasant impression in our minds. A marble slab with the Princess's name will be let into the floor between the lying statues of Frederick William III and Queen Louise just above the spot where the Princess's coffin stands. Yesterday the ceremony was of a very different kind in the Doma[1] with all the pomp and solemnity of a military funeral. The North German flag covered the coffin. The effect of the firing of soldiers outside the church, and the cannon, the organ pealing loud and the bells ringing while the blessing is being pronounced is so moving that there was not a dry eye in the church.

I said that the Shah of Persia was extraordinary. It is not easy to understand his French, though I got on well with him, and found him very intelligent. He is brusque and rough. He gives himself the greatest trouble to eat like other people at dinner, but cannot manage the knife and fork—perhaps that will have improved before he reaches England. The poor man kept cutting his fork—but never managed to get a piece of what was on his plate safe into his mouth. I suggested cutting everything beforehand but no one must appear to notice it, or it offends him very much. He has a perfect adoration for England and everything English. He has not an idea of time, and no one dare tell him of it; he kept the troops, the Emperor and Empress and us all the railway train and everything else waiting three quarters of an hour every day. I hope all the sickening stories of his awful cruelty are not true: they are almost too horrible to relate but I fear they are not totally without foundation. He gave the Empress and me his order, which I cannot say is very pretty—but I thought it very civil as I did not in the least expect it. I fancy the Persians cannot be rich, there is none of the splendour about them that the Indians display and they seem much less civilised—and have less good manners, but I do not think they are so indolent.

[1] The cathedral at Berlin.

The Shah of Persia always has a lamb roasted in his room which he pulls to pieces with his fingers distributing it to all his Ministers and attendants all sitting on the floor. The Shah drinks water out of the spout of a golden teapot, before everybody, after dinner or at a parade; he also throws his pocket handkerchief across the room at his Prime Minister when he has used it, upon which this dignitary makes a profound bow and puts the handkerchief in his pocket.

From the Queen

Your account of the Shah is most amusing and interesting and has somewhat relieved me—as such exaggerated accounts of his eating etc. reach me. But I think if these Eastern potentates wish to travel they ought not to carry their uncivilised notions and habits with them! He arrives at five this evening at Buckingham Palace. Affie is gone down to Dover to meet him; Arthur is there. The Césarewitch and Césarewna arrived on Monday. It is rather unfortunate they should all come together.

From the Queen

I was so grieved to see by your dear letter of the 17th received on the 19th that you had caught so bad a cold in that dreadful Vault, the description of which is indeed horrid and a great contrast to mine of the Vault here. But surely could not the Emperor be told to have it looked after?

The Shah's visit yesterday went off admirably and he certainly is very intelligent but I thought him very dignified. There was nothing to shock one at all in his eating or in anything else. The whole reception was the same as when I received the Sultan. He is delighted with England and with everything here and contrasts it favourably with all he has seen abroad especially in Russia where he was not pleased. I gave him the Garter and he gave me two Orders. After luncheon I took leave of him and he rested for half an hour and then drove round Virginia Water and went straight back to Town. On Tuesday there is a Review here to which he and everyone is coming and about which the good people here are gone slightly mad, as they do upon occasions by over-exciting themselves upon a subject till it reaches a pitch of half craziness. It was much the same when the Sultan came, but the

Shah has produced almost a fever and Mr. Gladstone says he can hardly get the House of Commons to sit!![1]

The Césarewitch and Minnie came to luncheon today. He is very good natured and kind and Minnie very simple and unaffected but she is not (excepting her eyes) pretty and she has not the distinguished face and appearance of dear Alix, though in manner they are much alike. It is unfortunate they should be here now when the Shah is here as he dislikes Russia.

From the Crown Princess

It seems so strange to me when I consider that it will not be many years before Willy is confirmed and almost grown up! For that occasion I trust you will come! For once in your whole life and in my whole life be my guest! How much I wish it I cannot say. For many a long year I had hoped that such a day might come—perhaps it will then! At any rate I may hope it and enjoy the hope of it be it ever so faint.

From the Queen

The review yesterday was a tremendous affair but succeeded extremely well—all excepting the railway arrangements. The Shah (who has never kept anyone waiting here though he is dreadfully tired) left B. Palace at three and reached Windsor Castle at five on account of the dreadful blocking on the line;[2] Bertie, Alix, the Grand-Duke and

---

[1] The Shah has left an account of his visit to England which supplements the Queen's account. "Friday 20th. June. We have to go to Windsor Castle, the residence of Her Most Exalted Majesty Victoria, Sovereign of England. . . . At the foot of the steps of the Castle we alighted. Her Most Exalted Majesty the Sovereign advanced to meet us at the foot of the staircase. We got down, took her hand, gave our arm, went up stairs, passed through pretty rooms and corridors hung with beautiful portraits, and entering a private apartment took our seat. The Lord Chamberlain, who is the Minister of the Court of the Sovereign, brought for us the insignia of the Order of the Garter set in diamonds; i.e. the Knee-tie which is one of the most esteemed English orders. The Sovereign rose, and with her own hand decorated us with the Order, and cast the ribbon upon us, presenting us at the same time with a long stocking-tie. . . . I received the Order with the utmost respect and sat down. I too presented to the English Sovereign the Order of the Sun, set in diamonds with its ribbon, and also the Order of my own Portrait, which she received with all honour and put them on herself. . . . The age of the Sovereign is fifty, but she looks no more than forty. She is very cheerful and pleasant of countenance." J. W. Redhouse, *Diary of the Shah of Persia* 1874.

[2] Not an accident, but the concourse of trains taking people to the Review.

Minnie, Augusta Strelitz—Mary etc. having come with them, and all having been expected here at ½ p. 3—the Review to begin at four! You will see the account in *The Times*. I can only say that the Shah behaves admirably—with great dignity and does most kindly whatever he is asked to do. He is immensely pleased with everything here to the intense disgust of the Russians who cannot disguise their annoyance (excepting dear, gentle, sweet Minnie whose unassumingness and simplicity are very striking)—and it is very unfortunate and *gênant* that they should be here at the same time for no one takes any notice of them hardly. He (the Césarewitch) seems to be just what you say. I think him so like the Grand-Duke of Hesse. The husband of Eugenie Leuchtenberg was also there; plain but gentleman-like and pleasing. We only got back at half past seven when everyone got a little refreshment and left at eight for London! Lord Granville's dinner had to be given up and they only went to the party at the Foreign Office a little before twelve. The poor Shah was most kind to me; I received him at the entrance and took him down again. He took my hand in both his and then put his on each of my shoulders in taking leave, like a sort of benediction. Today he goes to Greenwich. Tonight is a State Ball at B. Palace.

From the Crown Princess

NEUES PALAIS, JUNE 28, 1873

I am so glad the Review went off so well, and that the Shah was so much pleased and produced such a good impression. Here where people do not care a straw for royalty of any kind and are only disposed to laugh at anything that is outlandish they did not like him at all and were annoyed at what they thought the unnecessary fuss that was made with him, particularly the Empress who thought doing him the honours a great bore. I think Fritz and I were the only ones who liked him and were interested in him! I did not think him undignified but the Empress did! Berlin and our newspapers were full of disparaging anecdotes, some very funny and mostly all untrue. I think that the visit in England must do him good and give him the right notions. It would be of such immense importance if his Country could be opened to our civilisation which is the only one that does good! The French cannot civilise—and the Russians are half savage themselves! If it were only possible to induce the Persians to give up their barbarous cruelty they so often practise. I suppose you have heard a great deal about it!

From the Queen

The Shah continues to meet with the most enthusiastic reception wherever he goes and to impress everyone with his intelligence and cleverness. His visits to Liverpool and Manchester have been great demonstrations. The Russians are not judicious enough to conceal their anger and jealousy. The fact is the Shah seems at his ease and pleased with everything here—which he was not at St. Petersburg. The Empress disliked the Sultan also which I cannot understand and the Shah—though less handsome—is infinitely cleverer and more intelligent than the Sultan was. Today I am going (a great effort and fatigue) to Bertie's Garden Party at Chiswick where I have not been since you were there two years ago. The Shah will be there. On Wednesday the Shah comes in the afternoon to wish me goodbye as he leaves on Thursday and I shall take him through the rooms; and Leopold will take him to see the kennels, dairy, gardens and mausoleum besides stopping for a moment to see Lenchen. I hope you will tell the Emperor that we all like him so much.

You say dearest child you wish me to visit you when Willy is confirmed. It is kind and dear you should wish it, but it would be wrong if I let you indulge a hope which cannot be realised. I cannot go abroad except in the completest quiet and incognito; to go to a capital I must go in state—especially to Berlin or Potsdam, and that I cannot possibly do. Dear Papa deprecated such a thing even in his time for many, many reasons—but for me now, at my age, very easily exhausted and fatigued, very nervous and alone it is simply impossible. Even here, anything like State is extremely difficult and trying and years only increase this. This is the same with any large Court and Country, and you must not be disappointed by what I say—though I fear you will, dearest child, which grieves me.

From the Crown Princess

What you say about never coming here is alas what I expected but very sad! Of course I know that all state and ceremony is very trying and fatiguing to you and that you would never take it up again! I never thought you would visit Berlin! But I thought a short visit here for such an occasion as your eldest grandchild's confirmation would be an effort you might be inclined to make for that child's sake as well as his parents —for instance on your way to Switzerland—say three days here—and all being arranged not for pomp and ceremony—but for your comfort and convenience; I am sure we could devise a method which would not be unpleasant to you and not partake of the *gêne* and stiffness of an official visit. Many a circumstance may change in the next two years which would make all that simpler and easier so that you yourself will see many a difficulty and objection removed! You know that the happiness you bestow would be far greater than the trouble, fatigue or inconvenience it would be to you (if I may be allowed to say so) and which it would be our study to seek to lessen or avoid!

You do not know how sad it is to think that you have never seen our *intérieur*, never been our guest, and never shared our life under our own roof for one day in fifteen years!—I am not urging or pressing. For the present I know there is no hope and I do not indulge in one, but when the time comes, who knows? My dear Mama may feel stronger or in better spirits or may think it more important and less impossible. This at least I may think! Then perhaps Lord Odo Russell, Count Münster, Kamme and myself can put our heads together and see whether you cannot, having given your permission, be transported from Windsor here without ever finding it out! At any rate building air castles of this kind is a very pleasant and very harmless occupation!

From the Queen

WINDSOR CASTLE, JULY 3, 1873

I am very tired. For you know everything comes to me—questions of every kind and sort which I cannot allow to be settled and decided without my knowledge or else the stupidest mistakes occur; and even down to the Court Circular; then come letters—correspondence and all, independent of the public affairs, despatches—signing, etc. In short if you knew all that weighs me down—you would not be surprised at my inability to do more. I am much touched at all you say in your letter of the 1st but believe me it is not for want of love and interest in you and yours or even for want of spirits—but without declaring long beforehand, about what I cannot and will not do, which, as you say, circumstances may change—I must not deceive you with false hopes. One thing I may say and that is that I cannot travel again in summer and that it is not likely that I shall ever go again to Switzerland then. If I do such a thing then it must be independent of other visits. And as for Lord Odo and Count Münster being able to help—I fear they would be the very reverse. Even Kamme (though he knows better now) hardly knows how easily I am knocked up and tired with the life abroad—where moreover the air never suits me.

The breakfast at Chiswick was very pretty but very hot and very full and I was very tired. On Monday afternoon Minnie and her husband with Bertie and Alix came here. The two sisters drove with me. I had (for me) a large dinner and yesterday morning Bertie and Alix showed them all about and then left. At half past three arrived the Shah in the same state and I received him in the same way—at the door—I wore the Koh-i-noor as a brooch and the two orders the Shah had given me. I then took him through the rooms—the North Corridor where all the swords and guns and curiosities are, which he examined most carefully, and took him through all the State Rooms and the Library where he was much pleased, as well as his old Uncles, to see some very fine Persian Manuscripts, which we have there. I was surprised to see his knowledge of history and of Nelson, Wellington, in short it is quite astonishing for a person living in such a far off and uncivilised country. We took some refreshments in the White Room (only fruit—ice and tea) during which he spoke most kindly of his visit—his earnest wish that the closest alliance should be maintained between the two countries and from this time a new era should commence; that he hoped I would keep him and his Country in my remembrance and not forget it, which I replied was very reciprocal on my part. I gave him a nosegay and my photograph which he kissed (I hear) as he was leaving the station! I took him again down and he kissed my hand! Leopold then drove with him down to Frogmore—where he visited Lenchen for a few minutes and then went to see the Mausoleum where he placed flowers and then planted a tree near the aviary.

From the Queen

WINDSOR CASTLE, JULY 5, 1873

Count Münster dined here on Thursday. He is sensible but rather heavy and his position, in consequence of his father and the King of Hanover—not so easy; these causes are in fact a disadvantage to him.[1] —The swallowing up of Hanover (not the taking away of many Sovereign rights, for a Head, Germany required) I can never certainly forget or excuse, and feel always.

---

[1] His father, who died in 1839, was greatly in the confidence of King George III and his sons—a loyal friend to the Kingdom of Hanover.

Above: The Queen receiving the Shah of Persia at the Sovereign's Entrance, Windsor Castle, June 20, 1873. Prince Arthur and Prince Leopold are on the Queen's right. *Illustrated London News*
Left: Princess Beatrice dressed in the clothes she wore for the Thanksgiving Day ceremonies, February 1872. *Reproduced by gracious permission of Her Majesty Queen Elizabeth II*

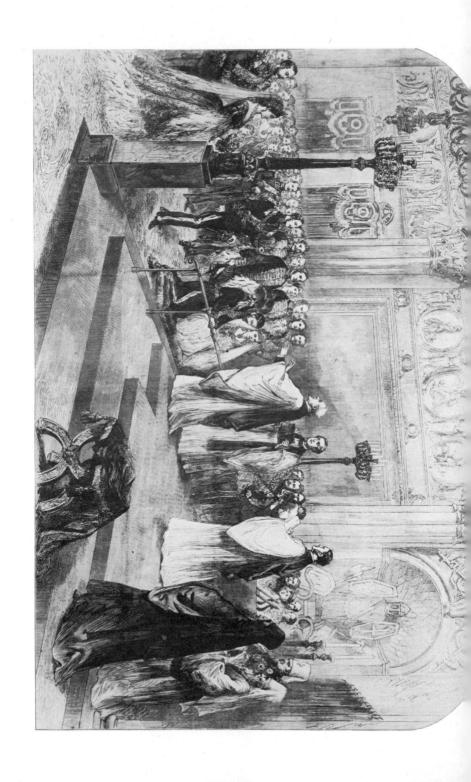

Left: Sketch by N. Chevalier of the Russian Marriage Ceremony of Alfred, Duke of Edinburgh, and Grand-Duchess Marie Alexandrovna of Russia, in St. Petersburg, January 23, 1874. *Reproduced by gracious permission of Her Majesty Queen Elizabeth II*

Below: The English Marriage Ceremony in the Alexander Hall of the Winter Palace. *Illustrated London News*

Above: Crown Prince Frederick of Prussia with his sons Prince William and Prince Henry, June 1874
Below: The Princess of Wales with her sons Prince Albert Victor and Prince George, August 1874.
Reproduced by gracious permission of Her Majesty Queen Elizabeth II

From the Crown Princess

I hope the Shah may be induced to make great changes for the better; he is not wanting in intelligence and, as you say, I too observed how much he knew about all the countries he was about to visit. If only he could be led to abhor and forbid cruelty—I think the treaty with the Sultan of Zanzibar is such a triumph for the British government, that is what I call *"marcher à la tête de la civilisation"* which the French fancied they did, and certainly have not done. England is the only country at present which devotes all its energies to the cause of "culture" and real civilisation. How much is being done in India since your Reign and how much more might still be done; it is always my dream that England should release the whole of the East from the yoke of barbarity, by exerting its wise humanising influence, not through missionaries and by trying to convert people to Christianity against their will and without the great principle of loving one another being understood by them, but through giving them by degrees as many of the advantages of our ways and customs as possible. I am sure you think and feel as I do. There are such grand resources in the East. Neither France nor Germany could ever do what England can in this direction.

From the Queen

One thing however I wish to say today viz:—that it is not true that the Shah is so cruel, quite the reverse, for I asked the English doctor, or rather more Scotch, Dr. (now Sir Joseph) Dickson who has been for twenty five years in Persia and has saved the poor Shah's life when two years ago, he was very dangerously ill—and he said that these stories were quite untrue, that he was very kind to all about him and very amiable; and when I took an opportunity through Lord Granville and Sir H. Rawlinson to recommend to the Shah the gradual adoption of milder punishments like with us, making due allowances for their customs and nationality, it turned out that there had hardly been any capital punishments in the later years of his reign.

From the Queen

The murder is out! I say nothing but that I pray God to bless both and grant that it may be the cause of harmony and peace in the family!

It is, you know, not what I wished or like—religion—politics—views of Court—and nation, are all contrary to ours and I own I foresee many difficulties, but I shall receive Marie with all love and affection and if she can alter his hard, selfish, uncertain character she will be a blessing to us all, and I shall be the first to acknowledge it—but I personally cannot rejoice yet; as you perhaps can understand though you will hardly feel the religious part so much as I do. What I'fear is the moral impropriety and the coarseness which exists in Russia. Her brother Alexis has got into a scrape with a maid of honour which if it happened here I think would upset the Throne and I fear this—it is got over very easily—though the young man himself can't return to Russia at present. Then Vladimir is very bad and so is Sanny's son; and the young Leuchtenberg is dreadful, and his Mama not exemplary. So what do you say to that? All this is not what I like or can like. However I must make the best of it now—and the parents-in-law seem pleased. They were so afraid I think of the other possible marriage that they wished this.

How terrible is dear old Winterhalter's death, quite irreparable. His work will in time rank with Van Dyke.

From the Queen

OSBORNE, JULY 16, 1873

Affie and Marie seem very happy and I pray she may continue so, for she really seems a very sweet girl, who marries him entirely for his sake (!!)—I wonder—but never mind that. She has written me such a pretty letter in English of which I will send you a copy another day. Difficulties there will be and delays and troubles but if she is so amiable and dear, much will be got over.

From the Queen

OSBORNE, JULY 19, 1873

I send you here two letters from Affie and Marie which will please you. I must try and see her before the marriage, as really when I think that the princesses who marry Russian grand-dukes are sent to Russia, often some months before, alone, and have to change their religion besides—I think they are bound to bring her over to me before. I had wished the marriage to be at the end of October or beginning of November but the Empress won't hear of the winter, as she calls that, as it is unlucky and wished for the spring but the Emperor overruled that and they propose it should be in January which surely is still more in the winter. They have only Clarence House in England and more I cannot tell you. I fear there will be many difficulties and that Affie will be ready to yield to everything. The parents have not written to me which I think they ought. However I am ready to write if they wish it. I fear Affie will be ready to be quite a humble servant of Russia, and Alice is also quite on their side. So that it will be better at once to put all negotiations into the hands of Ministers. All this worries me and gives me so much to do.

The day before yesterday Affie's marriage was declared in Council. The vote in Parliament will soon be brought forward and I fear something rude or vulgar may be said.[1] What I feel painfully in the religion is that it is the first departure since 200 years nearly from the practice of our family since the Revolution of '88! We must be very firm—or else we may pack up—and call back the descendants of the Stuarts.

From the Crown Princess

NEUES PALAIS, JULY 22, 1873

I remember so well when we were little children thinking it very grand to abuse Catholics; and I recollect your saying you could not bear that and thought it very wrong, and that you had seen so much vulgar prejudice and foolish violence against the Catholics in former days that you had felt shocked and hurt by it. It struck me then; I remember it now as showing how just and tolerant you were—and how much above the nonsense the ignorant talk about a thing they hate. These are times when the spirit of Christian charity and tolerance towards others and respect for the belief of others is recognised as a duty, and I think there is none more ennobling and softening! But to return to the subject I must say I don't see any great inconvenience arising from a Greek. She will have her chapel and her service and priest but I am sure go to the Protestant church whenever she is asked as Maroussy does and never dream of making converts or being bigoted. The Greek religion is singularly foolish in its rites I think—and not quite so preposterous in its doctrines. At any rate the Greeks are very much more harmless than Catholics and more tolerant and in some places the Russian grand-duchesses have answered very well—as in Weimar and formerly Wiesbaden. I am afraid that they will not be able to bring Marie to England before the marriage as their plans are all fixed and the time is not very long—but I think it too bad of the Emperor and

---

[1] He was granted £10,000 a year. This made his total grant £25,000 and the Duchess was to have £6,000 a year if she survived him. Mr. Gladstone described the grant as avoiding parsimony and excess. Eighteen members, including a Conservative, voted against it.

Empress not to have written to you first, and I hope you will not be the first to write. You are so much longer on the throne than the Emperor and you are a lady so he ought to have double respect. But the Russians do not know what that is. Their ideas about their own rank are in the style of the Shah of Persia.

From the Queen

I cannot entirely agree with your religious ideas as I feel much more strongly and deeply than you do. As regards prejudice, I cannot understand how you can say that one's dislike to one's child marrying a Greek is "a prejudice". Does not every true Protestant feel the errors of a superstitious religion—full of strange observances repugnant to all the simplicity of our Saviour's teaching? Do you really think that the exclusion of Roman Catholics from the possibility of marrying any of our family merely a political necessity? If you love your children and then they marry, is it not a terrible bar to be unable to talk to them on religious subjects except with totally different feelings and to have no sympathy with them? If you don't feel this, I fear you cannot feel really deeply and earnestly on these subjects. Then you say one ought to be very tolerant; certainly I would never persecute others for their religion and would always respect it, but we Protestants are not aggressive and when I was a child, our Church was not in danger of the alarming innovations which its unfortunately too Catholic nature and forms have exposed it to and which are most alarming. In Germany you can afford not to dread these terrible High Church and ritualistic attempts and movements—which are mere aping of Catholic forms and an undermining of Protestantism, because your Church is really Protestant and all Catholic forms are expunged from it. But here flowers, crosses, vestments, all mean something most dangerous! Thank God the Scotch Church is a stronghold of Protestantism, most precious in these realms.

You will probably have heard, or perhaps not—that the Empress of Russia in the coolest way telegraphed on Wednesday night to me to meet her at Cologne tomorrow!!! I think it almost an impertinence. Knowing that I cannot travel in the heat, and even if I could how could I a sovereign and lady be ready in three days to run after her? I own I am very indignant and not a little shocked to see how Alice takes the part of the Russians (ever since she saw first them in '64) as if she was a Russian and not a British Princess. I know your judgment is not warped in that way. My people were greatly shocked.

I think I ought seriously to condole with you at there being no baby coming. What a misfortune when you have only seven children—and only three boys!! Is Mama very naughty?

From the Queen

OSBORNE, AUGUST 2, 1873

Affie seems very well satisfied so far—but I find no improvement in him as yet—otherwise. There is the same ungracious, reserved manner which makes him so little liked.

I am going North on the 14th straight from here to Balmoral and have only to leave two hours sooner than from Windsor.

Affie's annuity has passed fairly enough though not however without some rude remarks,—and the religion has been observed upon several times. And I think we shall hear more of it.

From the Crown Princess

WYCK—ISLE OF FOHR, AUGUST 2, 1873

About the telegram asking you to come to Cologne, nothing was said and I only knew from your letter. If she had known you and your habits, etc., I am sure she would not have proposed it, but travelling is to them such a common occurrence on short notice that I suppose they never thought of the inconvenience it would be, and of its not appearing civil. As to the religion I see that I must have explained myself very badly and quite have failed making my meaning clear so I think it is better not to begin again. I only wish to say that living on the continent has nothing to do with what I think on the subject.

From the Queen

OSBORNE, AUGUST 6, 1873

At length after more than a week I received your letter from Wyck, which gives me an account of your meeting of the Empress and Marie. I trust that when Marie lives always with Affie she will still be as wrapped up in him—which I own I cannot exactly understand. He is 29 today!

From the Queen

OSBORNE, AUGUST 13, 1873

Sacha and Minnie leave today (tonight) and I tomorrow night; that is we start from here at 5.30—and from Gosport by train at $\frac{1}{4}$ to 7—arriving D.V. at the usual hour at dear Balmoral on Friday. You will be surprised to see in the papers the changes of Government. I can't see how they can last. But there have been disgraceful squabbles and proceedings in the Government (without positive dishonesty) and I don't know how Mr. Lowe will ever do at the Home Office or Mr. Gladstone be able, worn out as he is, to bear additional work! But if this had not been done they must have broken up![1]

From the Crown Princess

WYCK, AUGUST 23, 1873

I think it was a good thing that Fritz should have an opportunity of paying a little visit to the Danes, perhaps it may create a little more friendly feeling—though it is hardly likely. There is a cousin of Christian's here, a very good looking Count Danneskiold and his wife and children but they cut us completely—and do not even return a bow! It is funny considering I know the eldest brother quite well and have seen him since the war. It is so rude to demonstrate with one's political feelings I think, and I should have much liked to have been civil to a relation of Christian's.[2]

From the Queen

BALMORAL, AUGUST 28, 1873

Many thanks for your loving words on the dear 26th—ever dear, and the loss of Him great and irreparable; but he could not have borne many of the things which have taken place at home and abroad; with his strong conscientious convictions about them. I really don't know how he would have borne them! And if, as he most likely would as he was so fearless—he had taken a strong line against them, it might have done him harm. I feel more and more he has been spared much which he could not have prevented.

From the Queen

BALMORAL, SEPTEMBER 3, 1873

It is strange that you should dream so often of beloved Papa, while I do so seldom—and so much oftener of dear Grandmama, and as if I lived with her. You see, your life has not changed, whereas mine has

---

[1] Nearly a million pounds of public money had been improperly used for the extension of the Telegraph Service. Lowe, as Chancellor of the Exchequer and therefore responsible, was transferred to the Home Office.
[2] Prince Christian told the Queen that Count Danneskiold never "looks at them even".

entirely. Married life has totally ceased and I suppose that is why I feel as though I were again living with her.[1]

I am going on the 9th with Baby for a week's excursion to the West —Lord Abinger having lent me a small place of his near Fort William called Inverlochy. We shall have a very long day, which is rather tiresome, but it is rather an awkward place to get at. We go by rail to Kingussie and have then to post fifty miles to Inverlochy.

From the Crown Princess

NEUES PALAIS, SEPTEMBER 4, 1873

You will receive a parcel from me if you have not already done so, containing a snuff box in bloodstone—a relic—as it belonged to Queen Caroline Matilda of Denmark (unfortunate woman). It passed through different hands as an heirloom and was at last the property of a Countess Brockdorff who was married to an old Professor Michelson well known to Christian and all the Augustenburgs (a very talkative funny old man but an authority in science). This good lady his wife heard that you had expressed yourself convinced of the innocence of that much injured Queen and your sympathy for her terrible fate. She (Mrs. Michelson) full of loyalty and devotion for the memory of Queen Caroline Matilda, was so delighted at hearing of your feelings that she wished to present this box to you which was so precious to her, but feared appearing intrusive so she left it to you in her will. She died some months ago and when I saw the husband a few weeks ago he gave me the box begging me to send it to you. I know how strict the rules are for not accepting presents, still I thought I can hardly refuse to send this object and that you would make the Professor happy by accepting it. Will you tell me what I am to answer him?

From the Queen

BALMORAL, SEPTEMBER 8, 1873

I am touched and pleased at the old lady appreciating my deep feeling for my poor and most cruelly treated Great Aunt, and shall greatly value this relic of hers. Pray thank the old gentleman in my name. I have asked Christian to send him a print of me as he knows him so well.

I am looking out for ladies for her [Marie], unmarried not too

---

[1] "Is it not strange that I continue dreaming about him, fancying I am holding long conversations with him?" Crown Princess, August 26.

young ones (three she is to have as Grandmama had) but besides, one married lady for London, and I am happy to say I have secured Fanny Baillie which is most agreeable and which Affie himself wished. This is a great security.

From the Queen

INVERLOCHY CASTLE, SEPTEMBER 14, 1873

This is a nice little house, with some very pretty rooms, neat, good servants' rooms, and beautiful views from my sitting room. Ben Nevis is just before you—quite clear and to see it all pink yesterday evening was beautiful. Today has been fair but not bright but anything without rain or mist is very acceptable. We walked (Baby and I) just a little about here this morning. And this afternoon we drove up Glen Nevis which, after Glencoe is the finest, grandest and wildest thing I have seen here. A beautiful green valley just under Ben Nevis finely wooded at the bottom with alders and ash with the greenest grass up to the very top of the very high hills, not a single habitation but one farm with an avenue of ash trees to it, but this is not half way up the Glen. On Tuesday 16th we return to Balmoral by the Caledonian Canal and Inverness.[1]

I hope the cold at St. Petersburg will not be too much for you. I shall feel not being present for the first time at the marriage of one of our children, but at the same time I dislike now witnessing marriages very much, and think them sad and painful, especially a daughter's marriage.

From the Queen

BALMORAL, SEPTEMBER 19, 1873

Certainly the Highlands are the most beautiful, wild, romantic country with an amount of solitude and historic interest—which you quite miss in Switzerland.—Independent of my love for the Highlands I do admire it, with its purple heather and "swelling blue" more than Switzerland, glorious as that is.

I really cannot imagine who could invent that idea of my going to Homburg! There never has been the slightest idea of my going abroad this year, nor do I think I shall next year. D.V. when I go again it will be in the spring to Baden to visit my darling sister's grave and to go for a few days to Coburg.—But that even I doubt of doing next year.

---

[1] In *More Leaves from the Journal of a Life in the Highlands* the Queen described the journey along the Canal as "very tedious".

Homburg would be far too relaxing for me, though I feel very grateful for the kind offers, and then a great schloss is a thing which I have enough of at Windsor and am always thankful to escape from.

Pray offer my respects to the King of Italy who you must be well on your guard with—on account of what he says.

From the Crown Princess

NEUES PALAIS, SEPTEMBER 20, 1873

We had an English officer the other day to dinner, a Captain Clayton who has just returned from Persia, and it was very interesting to listen to all he had to say. The poor Grand Vizier is sent away as a prisoner—to the place where the last Grand Vizier, husband of the Shah's sister and a very good useful man, was put to death by the Shah's order without any great reason. Perhaps this poor man will share his fate.

From the Queen

BALMORAL, SEPTEMBER 23, 1873

This is a sad sad anniversary on which my beloved and precious only sister was taken from me. It is sad and painful to me that none of her children will go to her last earthly resting place on this first anniversary. Were it a Catholic family they would go from any distance. No doubt there our treasure is not, but it is all we can do to show our love and respect! Unfortunately it is a time when they are all away and separated, and so far off. The dear kind Empress, whose goodness last year I can never, never forget will be there and place a wreath for me. I have sent some from England.

You are misinformed, I must think, about my poor friend the Shah; in the first place as you will see in the papers, which is quite borne out by what Sir H. Elliot told me, that it was an intrigue of those horrid old Uncles and I believe the favourite wife, to upset the Grand Vizier and that the Shah, who I know likes him, resisted with all his might but was overpowered. But it is thought that he will be reinstated. Then as regards the late Grand Vizier there must also be a mistake. The Shah has only one sister who is married to Zahzah Khan (with a great scar in his face) who is the brother to the present Grand Vizier and is all powerful with the Shah and very clever and agreeable and is with him now—just the same.

As regards this report about Thyra I should be grateful if you would tell me all you hear. I told you exactly how matters stand—viz. that

Arthur saw her—and liked her, but could come to no decision till he saw her again. Both are quite free still. This was understood beforehand, but strange to say they seem to have expected him to propose—which after a first acquaintance would not have been right. Plain she certainly must be, and I think Arthur ought to see other Princesses before he goes again but pray keep this quite to yourself. That young Princess of Mecklenburg is said to be charming and will have some money.

From the Crown Princess

NEUES PALAIS, SEPTEMBER 25, 1873

The visit[1] is passing off very well indeed. He spoke of dear Papa and your terrible bereavement with so much feeling that I was quite touched. I am always on hot coals—for fear of not having the drive of the conversation quite in my own hands and of his saying anything awful; but not a word has escaped which was improper except one phrase which was so very funny that I could not help laughing! Rolling his eyes—he began *"Cette nuit, m'est venue une idée, je m'en vais écrire une lettre au Shah de Perse, pour lui dire de ne pas couper la tête au Grand Vizier, et pour lui demander des nouvelles de son sérail."* If you had heard the way in which it was said you would have gone into a fit. I fear he does not much fancy the poor Shah as he said *"C'est un animal—il a éplumé des poulets dans mon Scalar, et il a tué des chèvres dans la chambre de ma mère!!!"* The King told me that out hunting at Rome *"je suis tombé dans un buisson d'épines, je ne pouvais plus en sortir et j'y ai laissé ma barbe."* Anything so funny as he looks now you never saw, he is about four times the size he was then[2] and dyes his hair and moustaches pitch black. He told me you had been so kind as to give him a cream horse, and that he was keeping a person travelling for three months to find some Sardinian ponies which would be good enough for you. In spite of his extraordinary ugliness the King has a great deal of dignity—and makes a good impression on the Germans.

From the Queen

BALMORAL CASTLE, SEPTEMBER 30, 1873

I am glad the King of Italy's visit went off so well. He has a warm heart and some noble qualities but bad education and society ruined

---

[1] Of the King of Italy.
[2] When he came to England in 1855.

him. To me he has never been the same, since he undermined his own Uncle's Kingdom and took that, as well as other peoples, near relations, of his own; and it used to be my pride and dear Papa's to be able to say that your excellent father-in-law would never let himself become a tool of Bismarck's ambition as the King of Italy had been of Cavour's. Alas! I can say that no longer, and '66 destroyed that bright difference. This does not mean that the unity of Germany was not right, or not wished for by me and dear Papa. We both earnestly wished for that— for one head, one army and diplomacy; but not for dethroning other Princes and taking their private property and palaces. No, that was and is a grave mistake. And I never could live in their palaces if I were the Emperor or you. Today is the dear Empress Queen's birthday. May that true and kind friend of mine be long spared to us all.

From the Queen

BALMORAL, OCTOBER 4, 1873

I overlooked answering your question or rather more observation respecting the French Pilgrimage. I think it too ridiculous and also disgraceful that English people could go! Really in the nineteenth century it is monstrous![1]

How grieved you will be for our dear old Sir Edwin Landseer. For him it was a release as he was in a very sad state. But one can't realise his also being gone! Such a loss! He and Winterhalter—our old friends —and two such unrivalled artists both gone within three months of each other.

From the Queen

BALMORAL, OCTOBER 7, 1873

I understand your view of the question but as regards India I am bound to say that no one feels more strongly than I do about India or how much I opposed our taking those countries and I think no more will be taken, for it is very wrong and no advantage to us. You know also how I dislike wearing the Koh-i-noor.

I give a ghillies' ball tonight for Bertie and Alix. The accounts of Uncle Ernest's conduct are too distressing!

---

1 "What do you say to all the absurd nonsense of Paray-le-Monial? It is so like Lady Herbert to go there—how people can make themselves so ridiculous." Crown Princess, September 20. Five hundred English Roman Catholics left Victoria Station on 2 September for the Pilgrimage to the shrine of Marguerite Alacoque 1647-90, foundress of the cult of Sacred Heart. The Annual Register gives us an entertaining account of the expedition.

From the Queen

I am sorry you again change your maid! Time was I remember when Schmalz was everything. It is a pity to change so often for there can be no mutual attachment between mistress and maid—without which I think there can be no good or pleasant servants. But I think you don't care much for the inestimable comfort and value of a truly devoted and attached and trustworthy servant.

What you say about Uncle E. alas! alas! is what I have heard from but too many and is most painful and humiliating. Really one cannot go to Coburg when Uncle is there. You will have seen in the papers the account of dear old Sir Edwin Landseer's funeral and the great feeling shown at it by all classes and especially by the people.

The Empress of Russia wants to keep Marie now till near the end of February which considering that she is to be married on the 21st January is not right, or respectful towards me who have never even seen her. Do you remember what a fight we had to keep you only for a week after your marriage and with no expectation of seeing you soon again,—on account of the reception at Berlin? And Alice also just the same. But the Russians expect to have everything their own way.

From the Queen

You asked me some time ago if Beatrice was going to be confirmed this year, and I said no,—which was true. But I do intend she should be confirmed early in January '74, so as not to clash with the excitement of Affie's and Marie's arrival. This will however prevent your being here at that time unfortunately. But it can't be helped as I know your good wishes will attend her all the same. It will however make no other difference, as she will be only 17 in April (alas that she should already be so nearly grown up!). As to her appearing at state parties;—as she is my constant companion and I hope and trust will never leave me while I live, I do not intend she should ever go out as her sisters did (which was a mistake) but let her see (except of course occasionally going to theatres) as much as she can with me. I may truly and honestly say I never saw so amiable, gentle, and thoroughly contented a child as she is. She has the sweetest temper imaginable and is very useful and handy and is unselfish and kind to everyone. *Unberufen* she has very good health. Thank God too she is not touchy and offended like several of her brothers and sisters are. That has increased with poor Lenchen (partly from health and partly from Christian's inordinate spoiling and the absence of all actual troubles and duties) to a degree that it makes it very difficult to live with her. But pray keep this to yourself and say nothing to anyone about it—but it grieves me to see it and to see what poor health she has. She won't either do anything to get better and says she don't care if she is ill or well!!—which is a great mistake.

From the Crown Princess

NEUES PALAIS, OCTOBER 24, 1873

You can imagine that I should feel disappointed and distressed at dear Beatrice's confirmation taking place without my being there— even being thought of! I have never been at the confirmation of any of my brothers and sisters—and this is the last—and I am Beatrice's Godmama! I know I shall not be missed—therefore I must try and console myself but it is hard to become quite reconciled to the fact that one is an utter stranger in the home of one's happy and blessed childhood and to one's own sister.

An incident happened here two days ago which has caused a deal of excitement among the children. The dog of a gentleman living in the Palace went mad—and bit our dogs—so it was proposed to shoot all our poor pets the same evening! You can fancy my horror—my dear little dog who is always in my room, the handsome collie of the children's—and Fritz's two charming greyhounds. I resisted so firmly that the dogs have only been sent to Berlin to the veterinary school. But fancy our poor pets so spoiled and made so much of shut up for 13 weeks in iron cages. Is it not distressing?

From the Queen

BALMORAL, OCTOBER 25, 1873

I am so glad that the Emperor bears his visit so well but I fear he is again doing too much.[1] I quite agree with Fritz in the great security for the peace of Europe which is ensured by the very satisfactory good feeling which exists between Germany, Austria and Italy and also Russia. It must prevent France making any attempt to disturb the peace of the world.

---

[1] To Vienna.

From the Queen

BALMORAL, OCTOBER 24, 1873

In my letter of Tuesday I omitted to say with what interest I had read the correspondence with the Pope and how much I and everyone admired the Emperor's answer. Pray thank Fritz for his kind, long and interesting letter. I also feel sure that the conduct of the R.C. Bishops in Ireland is one and the same thing; all over Europe there is an attempt made to resist authority and to defy it, by the Priesthood; and the ritualists in England are a stepping stone to this—wherefore we should all try and unite the Protestant Churches as much as possible together in order to make a strong front and protest against sacerdotal tyranny —as well as against unbelief.

From the Queen

BALMORAL, OCTOBER 27, 1873

I had such a dreadful sick headache that I could not write as I wished to thank you for your dear letter of the 25th which however distressed me as you have taken up dear Baby's confirmation in the wrong light.

From the Crown Princess

NEUES PALAIS, OCTOBER 28, 1873

We see the Emperor's letter is much approved in England, the same as it is here. The only feeling I have in the contest between Catholics and Protestants is one of regret. I do not think it belongs to our age.[1]

From the Queen

BALMORAL, NOVEMBER 4, 1873

I will send for the book you mention without telling anyone who named it.[2]

---

[1] The Pope wrote protesting against "the destruction of Catholicism" by the German Government adding that he had heard that "Your Majesty does not approve the harshness of the measures". The Emperor in reply explained that he could not disapprove the measures since the laws in Prussia required "my consent as Sovereign. I shall maintain order and law in my states against all attacks as long as God gives me the power; I am in duty bound to do it as a Christian monarch, even when to my sorrow I have to fulfil this royal duty against servants of a church which I suppose acknowledges that the commandment of obedience to secular authority is an emanation of the revealed will of God."

[2] "There is a book which I think is most interesting to read, it is called *Die Petersburger Gesellschaft* an account of all the principal persons about Court. Fritz and all those well

From the Queen

What you say about the proceedings against the Roman Catholics I quite understand;—but as I said before, while I detest intolerance as much as you, I do not think they can be treated as people of other religions. They will not be conciliated and wish to persecute and, by foul means or fair, to obtain the upper hand. The real thing to meet them with is a complete and strong union of all Protestant Churches as one—to oppose them, and the Rationalists, against whom naturally they have a great hold.

I am quite unhappy and indignant about the shameful and tyrannical treatment of your poor dogs! It is extremely cruel; as for being ridiculous to mind it—I should be shocked if you did not mind it, and deeply feel it. A faithful dog is a valuable and true friend. Besides to shut them up in that way is very foolish and might make them go mad. They should at least be taken out walking muzzled.

What extraordinary events in France! But I think that it is a good thing that the restoration and fusion did not take place.[1]

From the Queen

BALMORAL, NOVEMBER 11, 1873

I like my new Lady, Lady Erroll very much. She has a great deal of pleasant conversation, is very cheerful, is wonderfully unselfish and devoted and very useful and practical. She reminds me of my dear Lady Ely in that respect who I am thankful to say will join me at Windsor after having been very ill.

From the Crown Princess

NEUES PALAIS, NOVEMBER 11, 1873

We have been rather uneasy about my father-in-law—not that he is seriously ill or that the doctor was the least alarmed but he feels so very wretched. He is not in bed nor on the sofa nor even in an

---

acquainted with Petersburg say it is quite excellent and very true; of course it is not what the Court would approve of—as there are some dreadful truths in it, and if you read it, which I strongly recommend, pray do not tell dear Affie that you had it from me, because it might shock the Russians." Crown Princess, November 1.

[1] Marshal MacMahon continued as President when the two branches of the Bourbons failed to come to terms.

armchair—only sitting about the room with a cap on his head, looking very depressed and uncomfortable though his face is not pale and drawn as I have often seen it after his influenzas in the winter time, and he is able to talk of business and of serious subjects with all his usual interest and clearness—but his voice is weak and he keeps his eyes closed! I do feel so sorry for him! He cannot endure to be pitied or nursed in any way—and I dare not interfere or try to make him a little more comfortable—I should like to do so so much, and would do anything in the world for him, read and talk to him, keep him warm, amuse him, make his tea and invent little delicacies to make him eat—but he will not hear of it—and those about him will not allow it! Pray do not mention to the Empress what I saw or how I find him, I can tell you whenever we meet why, let me entreat of you![1]

From the Queen

BALMORAL, NOVEMBER 14, 1873

I am distressed at the accounts of the Emperor. As I told you, in my last letter I felt rather alarmed at his own answer to my telegram and the Empress's anxiety too by what she wrote me. But why do you always think that I repeat everything again? At 54, at the head of a large Empire for 36 years—and of late years with an enormous and very indiscreet family (by which I do not mean you for you do not repeat) I am well accustomed not to retail and repeat tittle tattles! Some of your brothers and sisters are famous for indiscretion and mischief-making (most likely unintentionally) I grieve to say.

Marie Alexandrina continues to write me charming letters and I feel almost to know the dear child, whom I shall be most anxious to be a real mother to.

Our poor Leopold is just the same, and as he dares not be moved till some days after the bleeding has entirely ceased we may be kept here longer than next week. We were to have left on the 21st D.V. It is a terrible anxiety for me and for all who take care of him; but this severe warning will show himself and all that quiet and prudence are the only things to keep him well and able to enjoy air, exercise and occupation. You only speak of him and not of my constant anxiety and the terrible difficulties I have to contend with from foolish, ill-judged people suggesting things which bring on illnesses. No one knows the constant fear I am in about him.

---

[1] Probably because his indisposition was made worse by quarrels with the Empress over Church questions.

From the Queen

I am thankful to hear that the Emperor is better. I can well understand that you would have wished to nurse him but few men like it. Dear Papa could not bear it.

From the Queen

I give the good people and my servants here a dinner in the servants' hall tonight[1] as I did last week for Bertie's birthday. I am sure I told you dearest child that Leopold's bleeding was from the kidneys, and you will therefore understand how it showed itself. It has however entirely stopped since Tuesday and he has been twice out—and walked a little from room to room.

I did not mean that what you said was disrespectful respecting the Emperor and my writing to the Empress. I was only grieved that you should think I should repeat what I do know well—it would never do. I have seen and heard enough to know that the Emperor and Empress are better apart when ill, and long before you could know I saw how little harmoniously (though respecting and trusting each other mutually very much) they got on together—dear Papa knew it well for the Empress spoke openly to him about it and he grieved over it. You may be sure I never would say anything which could add to these or any difficulties. But she wrote to me she had been very anxious but that the Emperor would not be nursed and had absolutely forbidden her coming.

From the Crown Princess

I am quite ashamed of disliking living in town so much during so many months! But this place does spoil one so—the space and the charming rooms—the liberty of roaming out of doors riding and walking—one does miss that so much!

---

[1] The Crown Princess's birthday.

From the Queen

The Ball in the servants' hall on your birthday was one of the gayest
I ever saw. Brown had said to me two days before—having had a Ball
on Bertie's birthday, "Your Majesty should have a Ball for the Princess
Royal,"—my first born—and so we did and much enjoyed it was.
Baby danced everything almost.

From the Queen

Poor Alice looks very ill—and is so weak, unable to stand or walk
hardly and already so large. I am very anxious about her, poor dear
child. She is grown so gentle, and patient, and so resigned to all God
sends! It is very touching to see her! But I try and cheer and divert
her as much as I can and she is quite cheerful. I am going to give her
an Aberdeenshire granite sarcophagus just like dear Grandmama's for
her poor dear little darling's earthly remains.

From the Crown Princess

The Emperor gains his strength slowly but of course he cannot do
much business of a serious nature which is very awkward just now—
in the midst of this perplexity caused by the Church laws and the
opposition of the Roman Catholics. The Ministers are in despair at
not being able to get the Emperor's signature and consent to different
and very important proposals. But they must have patience, one cannot
force on a recovery—time alone can restore the Emperor to his former
strength; with his excellent constitution I should think he would be
quite himself again a month hence.

From the Crown Princess

The Grand-Duchess Marie was here yesterday and questioned me
in an alarmed tone—what I thought Marie's position would be in
England, whether it would be easy—whether she would be well received! I said I did not know but I did not doubt it for a minute! In
England people were so cordial so kind in their welcome to strangers
and so pleased to display their loyalty to you! (I did not say that society

and the public at large were more generous to foreign princesses and less back-biting and criticising than they are here but that is the truth!) How very much easier it is for dear Alix to get on and please in London than it is for me here, and I fancy I take double the pains! People make such much greater demands to princesses in Germany than in any other country; what is expected of them is almost impossible to give, if one wishes to have a house and occupation and time of one's own! The Grand-Duchess wishes to know whether Marie was likely to hear many disagreeable things said about Russia. I said that I thought nobody would be unkind enough to say anything to her to give her pain! Then whether she would be tormented about her religion—I said I thought that depended on her own tact and good judgment. Then she asked whether Affie was really fond of her and I said I thought from what I had heard excessively.

From the Queen

WINDSOR CASTLE, DECEMBER 15, 1873

I am so deeply grieved at the kind, good Queen Dowager's death. It is a sad event, and will cast a gloom over everything at Berlin. To me she was always very kind—and I shall never forget her last meeting at Lucerne. The Empress writes very sadly at the prospect (which she still hoped was not near) of her death—as with her so much goes to the grave! Oh! life is a very hard struggle! One by one you see friends and helps drop off and you have to stand more and more alone. I will answer your dear letter of the 13th fully on Wednesday. The questions put to you were not easy but were very well answered. Alas! I wish I felt easy there!

From the Crown Princess

BERLIN, DECEMBER 16 1873

We have spent two sad days! The loss of our dear Aunt[1] is a great grief to us as she was so kind of late years—and one could not help feeling attached to one who commanded such respect and in many ways admiration! She was so modest, hated pomp and show, had been the model of a wife—and was so generous and charitable! During the whole of '66 (the war was of course a more cruel blow to her almost than to anyone) she showed so much tact—and discretion and so much

---

[1] Frederick William IV's widow; a Bavarian princess and aunt to the Emperor of Austria.

dignity. You know how fond she was of her own family, and yet how she rejoiced at the success of the country which she had adopted as her own! I often admired her in this! Those who lose most are Fritz Carl's children to whom she was quite a mother, Abbat and Addy whom she loved as if they had been her children and her two poor ladies-in-waiting—one has been for 30 years and one for 20 with her! As for me I shall miss her much, as of late years I used to see so much of her in summer; Sans Souci is so near the Neues Palais that she used to like one's dropping in occasionally with the children. I was not the sort of person made to captivate her or for her to approve, as all my ideas and ways were too different from what she was brought up to think right, but she had grown fond of me and felt that I loved her and liked showing her any little kindness and attention which was in my power.

From the Queen

OSBORNE, DECEMBER 20, 1873

The Augustus Loftus's dined on Wednesday and he never ceased talking and is in a dreadful fuss about Affie's marriage. I fear their handsome daughter has made a very poor marriage.[1]

From the Crown Princess

BERLIN, DECEMBER 20, 1873

We have just returned from Potsdam after the sad ceremony! It was a blessing the Emperor was prevented from being there as I feel sure it would have upset him dreadfully. All went off well, the weather was mild and rainy—but it did not pour. It lasted all in all two hours. Willy, Henry, Charlotte and Vicky were with me at the funeral!

From the Queen

OSBORNE, DECEMBER 24, 1873—CHRISTMAS EVE

I am glad you took the four children to the funeral. It is right early to accustom them to such sights.

Affie comes here today and will stay here till Friday for the last time as a single man. Oh! may he really enter on this most eventful moment in his life with true earnestness and with the firm resolution to make

---

[1] She married Lord Cowley's youngest son. The marriage was dissolved within ten years

that sweet young creature, who all praise and who really is so attached to him, happy! I feel so much for her and will be so ready and anxious to be a mother to her if only she shows me confidence.

From the Queen

OSBORNE, DECEMBER 27, 1873

Affie left me yesterday morning and was a good deal upset in taking leave and is, I think, very nervous about the whole thing—I mean the fearful ordeal he will have to go through! I wrote to him that I hoped and prayed he felt the very solemn and serious step he was going to take, how I prayed he would make the dear, amiable, young girl—who is leaving all for him—happy and that she alone must have his heart and love—and all old habits must be given up. But he has said nothing in return! Oh if he only does break with old habits! It would be awful if he did not.

Young Richmond who used to paint charming portraits a little while ago—has taken to paint flat, bad imitations of Holbein and I don't know whom, with green flesh and blue lips and Chinese sorts of leaves as a background!! And has done an awful picture of Alix (who will never be really well painted) for me which I can't look at—much less hang up! Is it not dreadful?

From the Crown Princess

BERLIN, DECEMBER 27, 1873

Many thanks for your dear and kind letter by messenger with the pretty Xmas card, they are so pretty and one does not have them here. In a few days dear Affie will be here, what a pleasure for me, I have not seen him for more than two years and a half—and yet last year he was at Darmstadt within two hours of me when I was at Carlsruhe and this autumn at Dresden he was only three hours distance, but both times it was not worth his while to give me just an hour's visit which I was so sorry for, and felt so disappointed at. I would go and travel anywhere to catch a glimpse of my brothers—but he has not the same feeling about it.

Many affectionate thanks for the splendid cold meat for Xmas. The Emperor who has very little appetite as yet enjoyed the cold beef very much. We have now settled to leave for St. Petersburg on the 18th of January after the tiresome *Ordensfest*[1]—which will be in the morning of that day! That will bring us to Petersburg on the 20th.—I shall of

---

[1] Investiture.

course take off my mourning for the whole time there as they are so superstitious. We know very little about my Aunt's will! She has left her houses, furniture, pictures, plate etc. to the Emperor, her money to her sister the Duchess Max of Bavaria and I hear numberless legacies to relations friends servants etc. but of which we have as yet heard nothing.

From the Queen

OSBORNE, DECEMBER 30, 1873

Affie will be with you tomorrow. I hope and pray he thinks as he ought about this very solemn time! I do think much and especially of poor dear Marie and her parents as I know too well from sad experience how very trying these last weeks and days are, and how the poor mother's heart sinks within her when the many visitors and relations of the bridegroom who—one feels quite to dislike—arrive! You, who are so passionately wrapped up in your young girls, will feel this terribly some day.

From the Crown Princess

BERLIN, DECEMBER 30, 1873

All you say about dear Affie is so true, indeed I hope and trust he will undertake his new duties and responsibilities in an earnest spirit— for the young creature who is so fond of him is worthy of being made as happy as possible. She is so good and so nice, it would be too cruel if her life were marred by being neglected or Alfred returning to the old, bad habits which have alas! given him so bad a name, and have done him so much harm. Let us hope for the best, and trust that Marie's influence will draw out what is good in him and keep him from danger. The steady influence of a happy home and a loving wife may do wonders for him and he can be so nice and dear sometimes! I do not envy his being the Empress's son-in-law—because, good and excellent as she is, she is the Empress of Russia which means knowing no other rule except her own will. Still it has an advantage for Affie to feel her authority sometimes. I am sure you will not have the slightest difficulty in getting on with Marie, and that you will find her charming to live with—and she will be so kind to the brothers and sisters and being much accustomed to society will not be shy at all, and please people very much by speaking pleasantly to everyone who is presented to her.

1874

From the Crown Princess

We are so delighted with the beautiful book and do not know how to thank you enough![1] I admire Holland House very much—and the lovely photographs after Sir Joshua Reynolds also. It is so kind of you to have thought of giving us this pleasure!

It is such a pleasure having dear Affie but my pleasure here is marred by the illness of my poor little ones, who have got the most violent feverish colds! Affie has hardly seen them. He seems so happy and I thought full of the best intentions! We cannot make his stay very agreeable for him first on account of the mourning and then because of the formalities at Court on New Year's Day. You were kind enough to mention the desire to see us again, we cannot make any decisive plans now on account of the Emperor, but whatever we do we should mind not to be in your way.

I must answer your questions in your letter. I could not send you a photo of our pictures as they have not arrived from Vienna yet. You asked me whether I think G. von Angeli would paint a group well—for the dining room. I am sure he would do it quite beautifully as he really is the first portrait painter alive now—and universally admitted as such in Germany. He is a far greater artist than Richter. He refuses so many orders—as he is rich and does not care for money and is of opinion that it completely spoils a painting to have to hurry through a picture and undertake more than he can do well! Von Angeli never parts with a picture until he considers it perfect—and as much finished as possible—therefore each one is a chef d'oeuvre—and he will not undertake too many! He has raised all his prices in order not to be overwhelmed with orders.

From the Queen

All you say about Affie and Marie is most true. If only he has principle and shows heart. He can be so hard—and so sharp and unkind in speaking of and to others when he disagrees and he always knows best.

---

[1] *Holland House* by Princess Marie Lichtenstein which was published in 1873.

This makes him not a pleasant inmate in a house and I am always on thorns and *gêne* when he is at dinner. Alix feels just as I do.

I am sorry it [the wedding] is on the 23rd for that is the anniversary of my poor father's death.

I think I did tell you that I have lost my good faithful old Sprague; he was 33 years with Papa and me and used formerly always to attend on the dear old Baron as "Gilbert". He was very unwell in Scotland, so weak and breathless and coughed dreadfully—(he had a heart complaint) but he would not go away—till at last we were obliged to send him back a week before us. He got better and had been to church, and been very cheerful last Sunday at supper. When—in the night—his wife thought he breathed hard; she got up to get a light and he was gone. A peaceful, happy end for him but a dreadful shock for her. He was 62—and had been 10 years in Uncle Leopold's service before coming to me. He was so fond of painting and really copied wonderfully, especially Landseer's things.

From the Queen

OSBORNE, JANUARY 10, 1874

Lady Car has written you an account of the confirmation of darling Baby—and therefore I have not much to add but—it was very touching and simple and impressive and I never saw anyone look more simple, pure, innocent and sweet than this dear good child did. She looked so very young—and her very plain white silk dress—beautiful complexion and very fine fair hair which she wears quite simply and plainly (and wishes to continue to do) was very suitable. The Archbishop delivered an admirable charge which you shall have. The church was very prettily decorated with flowers—and very full but of course the Chancel was only kept for us. Bertie and I stood in the Chancel on one side, the other brothers and sisters on the other. Our pew was filled by all our ladies and gentlemen and the opposite one (which was just behind me) with all the servants. Thurston was there. Unfortunately it was a rainy dull day. When we came back the presents were given. From me she got the usual diamonds, the V. and A. order, dear Grandmama's pearls (which I had worn till now) and the Indian shawl. Tomorrow she takes the Sacrament early in the morning.

From the Crown Princess

BERLIN, JANUARY 14, 1874

Bertie, Alix and Arthur were very dear and kind and took the very bad accommodation we were able to give them most goodnaturedly!

Each time I see dearest Alix again I am struck with her great beauty. She puts everyone else in the shade! She is so dear and kind and the children got so fond of her in a few hours, they would hardly let go her hand. Bertie and Arthur went out shooting yesterday—and on Monday we had a little skating which they seemed to enjoy. It rained all day yesterday so I took dear Alix and Lady Suffield to a picture gallery.

About G. von Angeli painting a picture for you, may I not first enquire more particularly? He is coming here most likely at the end of February—and then I can find out the price which I fear would be much higher than what you might be disposed to give; then I do not think he has ever painted a group, and I don't know whether he would undertake it. Then he always says he cannot paint a portrait unless the person gives him sittings enough and sits really well; I feel with him that it is impossible to do anything satisfactorily without that! Another thing is that he thinks low gowns very pretty in nature but only in very rare cases fit for a picture—however in a group I think he would like it better than in a single figure! Shall I not find out all these details before you give a real order? It is far easier to speak than to write. We gave a dinner last night to all the English—which was very nice. What a great pleasure it was having the Dean and Augusta here. The Dean read a service and gave us a most excellent sermon on Sunday. Augusta looks quite unaltered.

From the Crown Princess

BERLIN, JANUARY 17, 1874

Is it not rather a risk that Bertie, Alix and Arthur go so far and to such a climate without a doctor! I was so glad to see Lord Sydney and Sir John Cowell as so many English faces are a delight which I have not had for a very long time.

I will write to you as often as I can but you know how the time is to be filled up! How I shall stand all those late parties I do not know! Toilettes one has to take are also a great business. Uncle Ernest arrived last night and we leave tomorrow in the middle of the day.

We are very busy packing and getting everything in order. Our pictures I believe are to arrive from Vienna today! Mine is done in an old Italian costume—with a black feather fan in my hand. I wonder whether you will like it. I gave the painter quite *carte blanche* as I know they paint with greater pleasure when they can do as much as possible what they like.

From the Queen

Pray be photographed by Bergamasco[1] who has done all those lovely photos of Marie. Pray ask Alix to be done too. I think Alix does not dress her hair to advantage just now. Too high and pointed and close at the sides for her small head. The present fashion with a frizzle and fringe in front is frightful.

From the Crown Princess

I meant to have written yesterday evening but I really was so knocked up and my head ached so with the dreadful shaking of the railway train that I was unable to collect my thoughts sufficiently. The dear brothers are looking very flourishing; the Emperor and Empress were most kind to me! Dear Alix and Minnie flit about like two little fairies, but I have seen them very little as yet! I spent the evening yesterday—alone with Alfred's Marie which was very nice. She looks very happy and as yet not agitated. She took Fritz, me and Uncle Ernest to see her trousseau today, which is very magnificent of course but I do not think finer than mine was. Her jewellery I have not yet seen. The Empress had not been well but she is always delicate. I have been paying innumerable visits and went out with Fritz in a sledge. It is not very cold happily at present—but there seems promise of it soon becoming so. I also saw the Dean and Lady Augusta today for a short while. We all live very far off from each other and the distances in this building are so immense that going to and fro takes a deal of time. Affie and Marie seem so happy together.

The marriage took place in the Imperial Chapel of the Winter Palace at St. Petersburg on January 23. All the Metropolitans were present including Innocent of Moscow, who was blind. The male guests were in full uniform and the ladies wore Russian national dress. There were no bridesmaids. There were four groomsmen—the bride's elder brothers and Prince Arthur. Immediately after the handing of rings and the crowning of bride and bridegroom, the Duke of Edinburgh and the Grand-Duchess processed round the altar carrying lighted candles and supported by their groomsmen. After this service all proceeded to the Salle d'Alexander where the Dean of Westminster (Arthur Stanley) carried out the marriage service of the Church of England. The bride carried a

---

[1] The celebrated St. Petersburg photographer. The successful picture of the Princess of Wales with her sister, by Bergamasco, was doubtless taken at this time.

bouquet of white myrtle sent by the Queen from Osborne. As the bride and bridegroom processed up the Hall Psalm XXI—"The King shall rejoice in Thy Strength"—was sung but no instrumental music was played at either service in accordance with the rule of the Greek Church. Prince Arthur was the best man. The Dean used the same book—though this was possibly not a tactful choice—which had been used for the marriages of George IV, William IV, Princess Charlotte, the Duke of Kent and the Prince of Wales. Immediately after the service the Duke and Duchess signed a leaf from the Register of the Chapel Royal.

A few days afterwards the Duke and Duchess and the Royal and Imperial families went to Moscow where a Te Deum was sung in the old Cathedral Church of the Kremlin and the Imperial family moved in procession kissing the sacred pictures.

From the Crown Princess

HERMITAGE, ST. PETERSBURG, FEBRUARY 2, 1874

We are just going to Lord A. Loftus's ball and from there to the train which starts in the night for Moscow! Our stay here has been made very pleasant by the Emperor and Empress's great kindness and hospitality. We took leave of the Empress and her younger sons this evening, and she had a long talk with us about her daughter and Affie and about the separation from her—which will indeed be hard for both mother and daughter. Dear Affie looks so radiant and beaming and really another creature—his satisfaction makes him so amiable to everybody!

I cut a sorry figure at balls as my eyes invariably close with fatigue —and I have to make such faces to keep them open! I fear I am more sleepy of an evening than even dear Papa was—it is quite a misfortune as it makes me so unamiable—and is such misery to oneself. I have seen as much as I could of Petersburg—and particularly of the beautiful collections here.

From the Queen

OSBORNE, FEBRUARY 7, 1874

The Government here will be out almost immediately. I thought they would lose—but not to the immense amount they have done! They have already lost 44 seats! It will be a new bother but Mr. Gladstone has not managed well—you know we often talked over all this.

The Emperor and Empress of R. have recommended their dear child to me in such a way that it makes me almost nervous, but I shall do all I can for her and Affie; and he is, I think, not suspicious of me.

From the Queen

We have a large Conservative majority and the change of ministry will take place very shortly!! Mr. Gladstone has contrived to alienate and frighten the country. Since '46, under the great, good and wise Sir Robert Peel—there has not been a Conservative majority!! It shows a healthy state of the country.

From the Crown Princess

BERLIN, FEBRUARY 10, 1874

We arrived last night very cold and very tired! Bertie says it is an affectation of mine but I cannot stand much railway travelling, it upsets me completely, and the life of going about to balls and parties makes me ill, to his infinite contempt! I have felt wretched all the time but there are no reasons of any kind such as you suppose—there is nothing whatever on the road. My three maids, Uncle Ernest's valet and Fritz's valet were left behind by mistake—the train left Dirschau without them so upon arriving here I had to shift for myself for getting up. Also as the unfortunate creatures were snowed up in their train outside Berlin for two hours! A nice beginning of yesterday!

There is so much I would like to say about Russia, but I do not like writing it all down!—Anything to be compared with Moscow as a sight—and as a picture I never saw, so imposing, so quaint, so fine! I was quite in raptures. The streets and houses are like a village—small and ugly but the grandeur of those 300 churches with their gold and green and blue domes, the mighty fortress walls with the beautiful little towers with glazed, green-tiled roofs and strange columns some Byzantine, some Norman and some Romanesque all this with the beautiful glittering snow and the black crows circling round their forest of proud towers and steeples was too magnificent. I could have looked at it for ever—and made a new sketch at every step—for the variety of buildings is quite extraordinary. The Kremlin is unfortunately so modernised that it only contains few rooms of historical and artistic interest but the collections—the riches piled up there are a perfect marvel. I have seen so much that is beautiful that it would take me a long time to describe it all. I am very very glad to have seen it all. And I am only sorry I could not spend a month in Moscow—its beauties seem inexhaustible and what subjects for pictures!!! I admire the peasants, and the sledges and the horses, snow-covered houses, streets and plains with sunlight or in moonlight. Altogether I am very glad I went to Russia, though profoundly thankful I am not a Russian and need not spend my days there—for there is much much that is very sad—and over the whole of Russia there seems to me to hang a dull, heavy, silent melancholy very depressing to the spirits! I do not talk of Petersburg as those who like to live in a whirl of excitement and frivolity can do so just the same as at Paris or Vienna, and have no time to observe anything beyond it or to reflect of the world beyond the brilliant salons, and the *luxe écrasant* of the Palaces and frantic extravagance of so great a Court. Please do not say so to dear Bertie, for he would not understand what I mean, and I would not for the world requite the great kindness and hospitality shown to me with one unkind or ungrateful remark. The Emperor is so amiable and kind and the Empress was so too. I feel myself drawn towards dear Dagmar who has remained so good—gentle, unspoilt, simple, and ladylike that it is a pleasure to see her. The Queen of Denmark is a happy woman; there is not one of her children who is not universally liked and respected. People in society were exceedingly civil to me and I tried to be so to them. The Russians are most hospitable! I got on so well with the Grand-Duchesses. Sanny wishes to be remembered kindly to you— she is as handsome as ever!

From the Queen

OSBORNE, FEBRUARY 14, 1874

Did you ever see such a universal and overwhelming result of a Dissolution against a Minister as there is against Mr. Gladstone? It shows how little he is trusted and how unpopular he is! What you used often to say to me about him and his talented colleagues is most true.[1]

From the Queen

WINDSOR CASTLE, FEBRUARY 21, 1874

As regards the Government you will see that instead of being a Government of dukes as you imagined it will only contain one, and he, a very sensible, honest and highly respected one.[2] The others are all distinguished and able men—not at any rate retrograde, but still not bent on changing everything which was most alarming and had

---

[1] That they were enlightened but not practical.
[2] Duke of Richmond.

alarmed the country. Mr. G. and Mr. Cardwell both have done great harm. I wrote so far—before I had the Council for the outgoing Ministers. Mr. Gladstone I took leave of yesterday and he talks of retiring altogether and letting the Liberal Party feel, as he says, the results of their conduct. He says that they have so far less cohesion than the Conservative Party.

From the Crown Princess

BERLIN, FEBRUARY 23, 1874

I am glad your new Government gives you so much satisfaction! Retrograde men are happily not to be feared in England. A Tory there would be considered an advanced Liberal here by many.

From the Queen

WINDSOR CASTLE, FEBRUARY 24, 1874

There is no fear of the new Government being otherwise than friendly to Germany. I shall see Lord Derby on Friday morning and will talk to him on that subject. You speak of the Liberals being more in accordance with the views of the times;—but many real Liberals would tell you that they all looked with fear and trembling upon "what next?" Everything was being altered and in many cases ruined— and Lord Palmerston was quite right when he said to me "Mr. Gladstone is a very dangerous man." And so very arrogant, tyrannical and obstinate, with no knowledge of the world or human nature. Papa felt this very strongly. Then he is a fanatic in religion. All this and much want of *égard* towards my feelings (though since I was so ill that was better) led to make him a very dangerous and unsatisfactory Premier. He was a bad leader in the House of Commons—too. The Duke of Abercorn after declining it, is going to Ireland again which I am glad of.

From the Queen

WINDSOR CASTLE, FEBRUARY 28, 1874

I went to see Landseer's pictures yesterday morning at the Royal Academy. I went early to avoid being known. That succeeded but it was so overheated that it made me quite sick and headachy.

From the Crown Princess

Fritz sends you the letters back which you wrote at different times to the poor Queen Dowager and also one of beloved Papa's. Lately I have been thinking a great deal about the keeping of letters, and it is painful to see how the wishes and orders of the dead are set aside—not out of curiosity but because it is considered, by some, politically useful. To me the expression of a wish by a person who is no more is sacred! Such and such letters are not to be read, are to be burnt, should be carried out to the letter! But in our position it is over-ruled by the consideration "these papers may be very useful, they may contribute remarkable facts and details to history and they had better be saved— and not burnt or returned." I want your authorisation to burn all I have except dear Papa's letters! Every scrap that you have ever written—I have hoarded up, but the idea is dreadful to me that anyone else should read them or meddle with them in the event of my death. Will you not burn all mine? I should feel so much relieved. It is hard to part with what is so precious, and such a record of our life—so much love and time and labour is spent upon the letters—and yet I am sure that keeping much is a bad plan. I have seen it too often. What will you say to this? Your letters are one of the greatest treasures I possess—but I consider them mine, and would have no other eyes see them and no other hand touch them.

From the Queen

I can not write as long as I could have wished today but shall do so, if I can, tomorrow in an answer to the important question of your dear letter of the 28th for which many thanks. I will give you then my opinion against destruction of letters, and the means of securing them.

I hope I shall keep well when the dear young couple arrive. How my thoughts are taken up with this you can well believe. The excitement here is great! Only two days and then D.V. and they will be here.

From the Queen

The arrival and reception of Affie and Marie, as I telegraphed and Lady Ely wrote to you, was very brilliant and satisfactory. A lovely, bright, warm day—the town beautifully decorated—the streets lined with troops—great crowds and enthusiasm. And now about Marie. She is dear, and most pleasingly natural, unaffected and civil; very sensible and frank and unaffected not pretty (excepting *fraîcheur*) and not at all graceful. At first in her white bonnet I thought her prettier than I expected, but without it—and since—I think her less pretty even than I expected. The chin is so short and runs into the throat and the neck and waist are too long for the dear little child's face though the bust is very pretty and then she holds herself badly and walks badly. She is however quite at her ease with me and we get on very well—and she is very sensible. I hope to see more of her alone and then get to know her still better. It was just the anniversary of dear good Alix's arrival. Tonight there is a great banquet in St. George's Hall which I am dreading, for since '60 I have not done such a thing and I am not very strong. But I shall only remain a few minutes after dinner and then retire. Marie is very civil which is a great thing. She is not a bit afraid of Affie and I hope will have the very best influence upon him.

From the Queen

WINDSOR CASTLE, MARCH 14, 1874

People do not think Marie pretty, but frank and pleasant. Her little short, abrupt way gives a little appearance of haughtiness—but I don't think it is really that. Only the Russian family do look upon themselves as greatly above others, and therefore they have a little that manner. Still she speaks very kindly to all high or low if one names people to her. She is very anxious to devote herself to some charitable and other establishments and fond of serious books.

From the Queen

WINDSOR CASTLE, MARCH 1874 (no day of the month)

First about Princess Wiasemsky. I think her charming and so does everyone. I find her so sensible and calm and serious and right-minded. I have had a good deal of conversation with her about the dear Marie, and I found her and my views so entirely agreed. She is a great friend of the poor Empress's—who is delicate. She and the two gentlemen leave on Friday or Saturday. About Marie's jewels I think the sapphires magnificent and the rubies and the pearls also.

Now about the letters which you wrote to me about the other day. I am not for burning them except any of a nature which affect any of the family painfully and which were of no real importance, and they should be destroyed at once. But all the papers and letters I have, are secured even as to my successor (excepting political ones). No letters can be published or kept if directed to be burned. Your letters are quite safe and would be returned to you in case of my death. If (which is very unlikely) I survived you mine to you must be returned to me—and yours to me and Papa would be equally tied up securely. I would however destroy any of a nature to cause mischief. Do that also with mine—and give directions (as I have done) to Fritz and your son or sons —who are devoted to you—to see that your wishes are carried out and then surely no one could touch them. I am much against destroying important letters, and I everyday see the necessity of reference.

You will see what a strong feeling in favour of the Prince Imperial was shown on the 16th at Chislehurst.[1]

Already 14 years that beloved Grandmama was taken and yet all, all seems so present to me still! What a sweet, tender loving nature that blessed mother's was. And to think that darling Aunt is gone too! That thought—that blank is sometimes very sickening.

It is dear Louise's 26th birthday today. It is a pleasure to see her so happy and so satisfactory, so good and sensible in every respect! She is adored in her husband's home.

From the Crown Princess

BERLIN, MARCH 21, 1874

I will do as you like about the letters but I am not convinced that it is the right thing for this country at least. I have seen people's last will and testament completely overthrown and correspondence read because it contains matters of interest. If they are destroyed nobody can read them who should not.

Marie is really a darling, and I am sure England will be very useful to her as that habit of the Russian family of thinking themselves the first in the world can only be a little counteracted by life elsewhere. I think you will like her dear little face better the oftener you see it.

I am so glad to hear you say dear Louise is so happy—and gets on so well in her husband's family.

From the Queen

WINDSOR CASTLE, MARCH 27, 1874

First let me thank you for your two letters of the 21st and 24th and say how vexed and provoked I am not to have telegraphed as I had

---

[1] His coming of age. Special trains brought thousands of French men and women to a demonstration in front of Camden House.

fully intended to do about the bazaar but my poor head gets really quite bewildered—for public affairs—family affairs (the most trying of all) and Household ones and arrangements all rest on me! Our young people are here. Marie is certainly most amiable and easy to live with, and with an imperturbable, even, cheerful temper and not the least touchy. I think she will require these qualities in her life. You will understand me. Really pretty I cannot think her, but she has beautiful, deep-set, clever eyes—which look so straight and honestly at you, and the forehead and upper lip are pretty and it is a nice little nose; but the underlip is not and the chin is too short.

I cannot understand how you would not trust your own husband and your own sons to carry out your wishes respecting letters! Destroy any which you think could be injurious to anyone.

Poor Adolphus whom I saw yesterday looks very unwell. I am afraid he is not strong. Mary's boys are splendid, but the little girl is very plain.

From the Queen

OSBORNE, APRIL 1, 1874

I think more of the other dreadful case of poor Lord Rossmore from its being so near, and my hearing so often through the day and calling three times myself and seeing the poor mother and friends and doctors![1] Both have increased my horror and disgust for hunting and steeple-chasing.

The review[2] and also making the acquaintance of all the distinguished officers in the evening was very interesting but it was a great pity that the men did not come in their fighting dress. It would have been so very interesting. There was the same long *attente* and general confusion of trains which occurred on the occasion of the review for the Shah, and we were all waiting and waiting for more than an hour and had to have some luncheon (I and the five Princesses) of sandwiches, broth, wine and biscuits, etc., in my sitting room and only sat down to a real luncheon at half past three! I had besides a dreadful headache all day—and had to have that large dinner of officers which reminded me of the Aldershot dinners—and to speak to all (fifteen dined with me) and after dinner the same number were again presented having dined with the Household. As soon as I got to my room the sickness returned.

---

[1] A friend of the Empress, M. de Knause, had been killed in the hunting-field, just before Lord Rossmore (1851–74) had a fatal injury in the Guards Cup race at the Windsor steeplechases. The Queen is believed to have seen the accident when out driving.
[2] Of the troops returning from the Ashantee War.

I am quite overdone, and shall require quiet and rest and bracing air after the Empress of Russia's visit which rather alarms me—though I am to have only two days of it. But without dear Papa, and tired as I get and not equal to *faire les honneurs* as I would wish and like to do—it is very very trying and makes me terribly nervous.

I have almost forgotten to mention that all the sketches in oil, chalks and pen and ink (of which there are an immense number and such beauties) by Landseer are to be sold by auction at Christie's in this or next month and that I wish to know if you and Fritz and the Emperor or anyone of the family would like to acquire any, for they are most valuable. If so I would willingly execute any commissions for that effect.

From the Queen

What you say about Marie and the education in Russia is very true.[1] Certainly she is wonderfully little proud and spoilt—considering—and I think will soon learn English (good not fast) ways! But it is an immense advantage not to have "been born under the Purple" which was my case and dear Alix's and dear Papa's. We strove to counteract it in every way with all of you—but still it is an enormous disadvantage never to feel the difficulties and disadvantages of life, and that you depend much on your own exertions—especially for princes.

From the Queen

Yesterday evening Captain Glover and Captain Sartorius also just returned from the Gold Coast dined here. They were very interesting to see and hear—both so wonderfully dark and sunburnt.

From the Crown Princess

I am so glad that Affie and Marie are with you. I am sure she must like the country and can well understand her thinking the London atmosphere dull and heavy but I flattered myself she would be struck by the stupendous size of the first city in the world, its extraordinary life

---

[1] This letter written on April 4 appears to be missing.

and its vast intellectual resources, its historical recollections, and its extraordinary wealth—compared with St. Petersburg. Compared to it, Paris always appears to me a lovely, charming place of amusement, and Vienna a pretty, provincial town. I am sure in time she will think of all this! I did not when we were children and only thought it a bore to be there. But now—oh how often I would give I don't know what to spend a month there now and then, imbibe fresh ideas, see the progress civilisation has made in a thousand branches which continues so rapidly that each year something new can be learnt. What London is one can only understand when one has lived for years in a German town—and is old enough to reflect on all one sees (and it seems to me that I have only begun to think these last two or three years). I am afraid though of wearying you with this one subject which may be a very tiresome one. I have become very German in one respect that is very "doctrinaire" I am afraid—in the eyes of most English people it is a disadvantage I suppose.

From the Crown Princess

BERLIN, APRIL 25, 1874

Many thanks for the lovely primroses, also for kindly sending the lithographs of yourself and dear Papa. I am very grateful for them. Many thanks for your letter by messenger,—and for one of three days ago. I did not answer it, I felt the unkindness and injustice of the remarks made—and their being so uncalled for—so keenly that I was afraid of answering in a way that might be unpleasant and painful to both you and me so I thought I had better not write at all.[1]

From the Queen

WINDSOR, APRIL 29, 1874

I shall indeed be truly delighted to see you for two or three days at Osborne while you are staying at Sandringham and am only rather surprised at the tone in which you speak of my wishing to see you, and of my being "too fatigued to see you". You know how I wished you to come last year and this year in May and I hope some other year you

---

[1] It is most likely that the disagreeableness arose through an unguarded remark of the Crown Princess on Princess Beatrice's birthday—"may she be as good a daughter as I trust some day a wife and mother". (April 15.) The idea that Princess Beatrice should marry was anathema to the Queen, and that the Crown Princess might promote a marriage for her infuriated the Queen. (See the Queen's letter of April 29.) The Queen's letters and those of the Crown Princess for this period have evidently been destroyed. For a week or two the Queen begins her letters "Dearest" and not "Darling Child".

will be able to come in the spring—part of March or part of April and May—as I could then see you comfortably and you could see London which you yourself delight in—now, but which is a thing I certainly do not.

I am going to see Jacob Wainwright, poor Livingstone's black servant who so faithfully nursed him and carried back his remains at the risk of his life.

I do not wish to continue the painful correspondence which commenced with your letter of the 15th—but this much I must say—viz: that my letter to you, could not have pained you more than yours to me—the remarks in which were "so uncalled for"—did me and they recalled circumstances which had gone before some years ago in a manner which I could but feel painfully and feel bound to guard against.

From the Crown Princess

NEUES PALAIS, MAY 10, 1874

The Grand-Duke Constantine's eldest son has got into such a frantic scrape that they have been obliged to declare him mad—and shut him up![1] But it is all hushed up—and not to be mentioned. Even his own mother does not know what has happened, but the Emperor and the Grand-Duke Constantine are in a great state of distress about it.

From the Queen

WINDSOR CASTLE, MAY 13, 1874

Those dreadful reports about the Grand-Duke Constantine's son have appeared in the English papers just yesterday and today—and in one even, I heard it was said that he had stolen his mother's jewels! What has really happened?

We are all living *en attente* of the Empress's coming and it causes much uncertainty. The sea certainly makes everything very uncertain.

From the Crown Princess

NEUES PALAIS, MAY 16, 1874

The business with the Grand-Duke Constantine's son is awful! I never mentioned it, but since you named it I could say what I know.

---

[1] Grand-Duke Nicholas Constantine 1850–1918; some years later he married the daughter of a police inspector.

He stole the jewels out of his mother's saints' images in her chapel, and carried them to the pawnbrokers—he wanted the money to pay the debts he contracted with an American woman of bad character. He and the other young Grand-Dukes—or at least many of them—lead highly irregular lives and this is what such company and such habits lead weak young men to! The Grand-Duchess had not a notion where her jewels were—and sent to the police who found it out and told the father and the Emperor.

From the Crown Princess

I had thought of going to Darmstadt to see how dear Alice is.[1] I wish she had an English doctor; after my experience of German doctors at the moment, I would not have one if I could possibly help it for anything in the world! I think it a branch in which they are very backward here. They are first-rate surgeons, very good professors— very clever oculists—but I don't think them clever physicians as a rule for they think little of treatment, and for a confinement I really have no confidence in them, but please do not say so.

From the Crown Princess

Charlotte has greatly improved in every way these four weeks. She is gentle and amiable and willing to do all she is told, and much nicer towards the brothers and sisters. I have her now a great deal with me and cannot complain of her in any way. Clever she is not—and never will be; she has few or no interests—no taste for learning or reading, for art or for natural history, so it is no use to expect these things of her— one cannot force them into existence if there is no natural turn for them; if she only grows up a nice and good girl—and in time becomes trustworthy and conscientious that is all I can expect. Her temper is very even and good now! Unfortunately her nose has remained exactly in the same state as it was when we were at Osborne—like a violent cold in the head! It is too tiresome, we now try Ems water, and baths of salt water and Kreuznach mixed! Langenbeck advises dropping Laudanum into her nose! Sometimes she can hardly breathe. Ever since April '71 Wegner has shrugged his shoulders about it and says (as

---

[1] Her youngest daughter was born four days later.

also Langenbeck does) that she is perfectly well and strong in every respect. She grows so little that you would think she was nine or ten, has not an atom of figure, or waist, and shows no signs of her health beginning to change. It is so funny—Beatrice was only a little older when we were at Osborne than Charlotte is now, yet she was quite formed—so were Alice—Lenchen—Louise and I. And Charlotte is in everything—health, looks and understanding like a child of ten! I suppose it belongs to the family here! and Willy is so forward in every way, has changed his voice and become quite a young man! Henry is awfully backward in everything, and does not grow—is hopelessly lazy—dull and idle about his lessons—but such a good-natured boy—everybody likes him though he is dreadfully provoking to teach from being so desperately slow! Willy, Waldy and Vicky have monopolised the brains of the family, and I think that the three little ones will be very sharp and I do not think any of them are downright stupid, and on the whole I must say they are very good. They are rarely without colds which drives me wild; it is our abominable North German climate which is as detestable as the Russian almost and really most disadvantageous for little children.

From the Crown Princess

NEUES PALAIS, MAY 27, 1874

Today I am to make the acquaintance of Addy's mother—she dines with her and we are invited.[1] There is no reason now why we should not just see her! Uncle A. is dead and the dreadful man with whom she existed for so many years is also dead since 2 years—so now in her old age we may hope she will become comparatively respectable, poor thing. She is come to see her grandchildren who are much attached to her.

From the Crown Princess

NEUES PALAIS, MAY 30, 1874

Angeli is doing most marvellous portraits just now at Berlin, I never saw anything to compare to the Emperor's and to Marianne's! How I wish he could do you, Bertie and Alix, Alfred and Marie and Beatrice, you would indeed not repent it! He could not go when it was arranged because the Emperor of Austria sent for him to paint two

---

[1] Princess Marianne of the Netherlands; she married Prince Albert of Prussia in 1830, and they were divorced in 1840. She always dressed in white to proclaim her innocence.

fresh portraits of him—and now the Emperor of Russia has ordered him off to Livadia in the autumn.

It interested me much to see poor old Princess M. of the Netherlands. She looks like an old Dutch picture—with a close white cap round her face—and a little snow white hair at the temples and behind the ears. Her face is so covered with wrinkles and her eyes are so sunk in her head that she looks like a study of Rembrandt, and might be 80! She has associated with us for the first time since she left here—not having met the family at Potsdam or Berlin again. She made a most melancholy impression upon me—to see an old lady—high placed— who has so entirely forfeited all respect—and yet I felt the profoundest pity for the poor thing mixed with all those feelings. To think that one could fall so low as to associate with a footman!! For nearly 30 years she lived with him (not married for 30 years) almost. This low wretch was often tipsy and of late years he used to beat her in the street when they walked or drove!! She stooped to his sphere so completely that she ceased to be a lady at all! Now he is dead, and the family see her again—so perhaps she will have a peaceful and respectable old age. It is so terribly sad to think of a life so mis-spent, and of the sorrow and suffering she has brought on children and grandchildren. Perhaps a little kindness and wise advice in her youth might have saved her, but her husband was neither wise nor good then, and many mischievous people contributed to her fall. She asked much after you—and talks very good English.

From the Queen

BALMORAL, JUNE 2, 1874

I find I have not thanked you for your dear letter of the 27th. That old Princess Marianne should wish to see her children I think quite natural. But I can't understand her not having more pride than to wish to return to be condescendingly received by the family to which the husband belonged who used her so ill and who in fact forced her— unprincipled as she was, into a most immoral life! The lowest born can have the noblest, highest feelings—and vice versa—as indeed one sees daily; but a low immoral life is a thing not to be got over excepting by the affection of her children. Her return to Berlin I think very unbecoming, though I think you were quite right not to refuse to meet her.

Bertie's dear little boys left yesterday;—they are dear, intelligent and most thoroughly unpretending children, who never are allowed to be "great Princes" than which there is no greater mistake. It is already so difficult to prevent little Princes from becoming spoiled as everybody does what they wish.[1]

From the Queen

I am very glad you like poor Marie of Meiningen. Her fate is certainly very sad,—but with her health (she had at one time 28 open sores from scrofula!!) it is hardly to be desired either for herself or for the person she married—that she should do so.[2] She might die if she had children and they might all be full of disease—and that is an awful thought!

Most certainly Bertie gave me a most lovely picture of Venice, which he bought at Berlin as he said by your advice. It is indeed very fine—so "luminous" as dear old W. Leitch used to say.

From the Crown Princess

I am so glad dear Bertie's children are so nice and well brought up,— he is indeed happy to live in a country where there are no absurd and injurious rules and customs about the education of the Princes of the Royal Family—not only laid down, but rigorously enforced! He can bring up his children as he thinks fit and proper and if you did interfere it would not be to the disadvantage of your grandchildren. Here, not only the Emperor has full and despotic power over us and can do with us what he can with none of his other subjects but abuses this power, and is backed up in this by the whole official world—civil and military! Ours is no pleasant position and we have a hard fight to have our own way with our sons—even in trifles. It embitters our existence very much. We are not children any longer—Fritz is over 40 I over 30 and have more experience in education than the Emperor ever had, but he sticks to his traditions with extraordinary stiffness. I often think laughing to myself—if Bertie and Alix were once to change places with us—for a month!!! what would they say. We have not more liberty or independence than babies—compared to them. Neither of my parents-in-law can understand this and the remonstrances are either useless or lead to quarrels, which are best avoided. I really adore the Emperor as he is so charming, kind and amiable when one has no business to transact with

---

[1] The Crown Princess had this passage from her mother's letter copied.
[2] Have children.

him—everyone loves him, and I know how well and kindly the poor Empress means it from her heart, and pity her so much for feeling so unhappy and dissatisfied. Still the "relations" between Fritz's parents and us do not become easier as both parties become older. I am only thankful they are as good as they are, as here fathers and sons in the family have always been at sixes and sevens!

From the Crown Princess

NEUES PALAIS, JUNE 10, 1874

Many thanks for your two telegrams. I answered directly about the accident, which luckily was none but might have been one. The carriage in which Fritz and the 3 boys were, was crossing the rails when the arms (which they have here instead of the gates we use at the places for crossing the line in England) came down and would have fallen straight on the carriage if it had not been stopped in time, the carriage then drove on across the rails, but could not get on to the high road as the other barrier was closed on the other side, the carriage had to stop, and the train rushed by just behind it, so that there was a space of about 6 feet between the train and the back of the carriage! But I do not think they were even frightened, the children told me quite complacently what happened some time after.

From the Queen

BALMORAL, JUNE 16, 1874

I send you today a letter from Mr. Martin which speaks for itself. He is writing the whole admirably and everything which could hurt people is excluded. I mean to wait till you come to show you the first chapters. He has written the whole—and really in a masterly style—for no one writes better. The very chapters he mentions, which were very difficult on account of politics, he has treated with great impartiality.

In your letter of last week you speak of the great difficulties you had with your father-in-law about the children's education. I am very sorry for it, and think it injudicious and inconsiderate; still I think as regards young people (this don't apply to you) the parents should have more power—than they have or at least than the young people think they have. The idea that a young man at 21 knows all that is best and should never consult older people and only come to them when he has ruined himself and them, broken their hearts and yet expects them to help him out of trouble is unnatural as well as wrong in every way. Good parents have only the good of their children at heart and the children ought to be taught to have the greatest respect for them and their advice, which alas! with these new ideas is the very reverse. You will feel this yourself later. I would often wish to get Bertie and Alix to do things which are neglected, but she is rather obstinate about it. One great thing however she does insist on—and that is great simplicity and an absence of all pride—and in that respect she has my fullest support.

I am grieved to hear that you get on less well as time goes on with the Emperor and Empress. You should however both of you never forget what Fritz owes to his mother. Without her watchful care in the midst of a very immoral family, he might have turned out very different to what he is; in which case you could never have married him. And she is so true a friend. To Papa and me, I never saw anything like it.

From the Queen

WINDSOR CASTLE, JUNE 24, 1874

You need not be at all anxious and uneasy about what Mr. Martin writes. He is most careful, and so refined, honourable and discreet that he would hurt no one's feelings if possible, and the extract which I have had copied (as I prefer waiting with all that was yet printed till I can give it to you here together) will I am sure strike you as beautiful and as most useful. I do not think that as so many memoirs of statesmen and people of the same time have been published that it is too soon to publish a discreet life of beloved Papa; indeed much that appeared without permission, or I must think, reflection, in the dear old Baron's life rendered it necessary not to delay in putting things before the world with all the sides to them which did not appear in the other. It will be of such use to posterity and to princes, to see what an unselfish, self-sacrificing and in many ways, hard and unenviable life beloved Papa's was. But I wish to explain that Mr. Martin is in fact engaged on three. The first is the shortest one which is to be published now; secondly the unpublished one carried on with the same detail as *The Early Years* which were not originally intended to be published; and thirdly what is to be published with reference to Public Affairs in 50 to 60 years time.[1]

---

[1] Martin's biography of the Prince Consort was published in five volumes between 1874 and 1880. With increasing confidence in Martin, the Queen evidently agreed that the second of his tasks should be made public, and absorb the first.

From the Queen

Poor Lady Amberley died on Sunday last of diphtheria and yesterday morning the poor only little girl died of the same—and has left
poor Lord Amberley in a state of the most terrible distress which is an
immense grief to poor old Lord and to Lady Russell.

At the beginning of July the Crown Prince and Princess came to England, and
were staying in the Isle of Wight.

From the Crown Princess

WRITTEN ON BOARD THE ALBERTA, JULY 20, 1874

We shall await your orders dearest Mama, when you may wish to
see us. Wd. Sunday suit you? May the *Alberta* fetch us from Ryde if the
weather is fair? We have spent a most interesting and delightful time
in London—though the fatigue of having to crush everything into 10
days is immense! Bertie and Alix have been so very kind that we do
not know how to thank them sufficiently! No host can be so amiable,
and no guests were happier than we were!
Dear old Lord Russell and Lady Russell wish to be placed at your
feet. I was at Richmond yesterday and lunched with them.

From the Queen

OSBORNE, JULY 20, 1874

Our letters crossed. Sunday would not do. The *Alberta* is never used
on Sunday and I should not like to send a carriage to Ryde on Sunday.
But any other day will do.

From the Crown Princess

SANDOWN, JULY 27, 1874

Sophie's remarks about you I must tell you though they are not so
respectful as I could wish! "My dear Grandmama is very tiny—a very,
very, pretty little girl—and wears a veil like a bride."

From the Queen

The Empress[1] insisted on coming over to see me today. We are all disappointed. A great beauty I cannot call her. She has a beautiful complexion, a splendid figure, and pretty, small eyes and not a very pretty nose. I dare say that in *grande tenue* with her fine hair seen to advantage she looks much better. I think Alix much prettier than the Empress.

From the Crown Princess

The Empress of Austria was here yesterday also—she would not take any refreshment we offered, but afterwards we heard that she went to the hotel here at Sandown and dined, which we thought rather funny. She was not looking her best and I think her much gone off since last year but still lovely! She was not dressed to advantage either—because she is really dazzling of an evening. Alix's features and expression are far prettier—but the Empress is more "piquante" than any lady I have ever seen. The lovely Empress is a very funny person with her arrangements. She sleeps a great part of the forenoon on her sofa—dines at 4 and rides the whole evening quite alone—and never for a shorter time than 3 hours and becomes frantic if anything else is proposed. She does not wish to see a soul—or show herself anywhere. All the same I like her very much and she is very kind to me.

From the Queen

I wrote at once to Sir William to settle to be here with Sir J. Paget at 3 to give you good time to talk all over with them, but these great surgeons and doctors do make great mistakes very often and Sir J. Paget has done so on several occasions within my own knowledge. They are so fond of cutting.[2]

---

[1] Empress Elizabeth of Austria.
[2] Princess Charlotte had a perpetual snuffle, and the Crown Princess was dissatisfied with the treatment of the German doctors (see p. 138).

From the Crown Princess

Let me send one more line of tender farewell. You cannot think dearest Mama how a day such as yesterday upsets me! Indeed I think you hardly know how passionate and how tender is my love and devotion to you. I have not the gift of showing it, and a sort of funny shyness, I think also of respect and reverence make me as stiff as a stick and all my repressed feelings only find their vent in tears when I am alone! Parting from you is always the same pain, only I think it is more keenly felt as one grows older and one's experience of life grows deeper and larger—and with it the heart's affections and the sense of what a mother is and how no other tie on earth can compensate for that one sacred one. To see your dear face looking so fresh and radiant so beaming and young with the same dear smile as in former happy years —was the greatest comfort I can take away with me, but also makes me long to stay with you all the more! You must excuse my stupid tears which blot this paper. Osborne was looking so lovely—so green, the sweet flowers are so bright and the sea so blue and calm! It was such a wrench to me as we stepped from the pier into the boat and left the dear spot of which every inch is haunted by sweet and blessed recollections which even the sound of the clock striking in the tower conjure up so vividly before me! At any rate one thing never changes whether one be apart or together—and no separation be it ever so long can alter it— that is the love and devotion, the grateful and dutiful affection of your most loving and obedient daughter Victoria.

From the Queen

I am sitting out near the river the soft, murmuring sound of which is delightful to hear.

It gave me pleasure but also pain to see you waving your handkerchief and then sending a farewell signal from the *Fire Queen.*

You did not tell me if you were pleased with what you saw of Mr. Martin's life as it seems to me so admirably written and so delicately done. He does it all himself and I only suggest, correct and suppress, if I think anything better be omitted or added and then he sometimes points out his reasons for leaving in or out things.

I do perceive that a sort of shyness and stiffness comes over you which you described in your dear, sweet letter—but less towards me than towards others, which sometimes distresses me (let me say openly) as it is unlike your former self and is sometimes misunderstood. You always were a little absent and I think are so still—which when one thinks of and does so many things as you do is very often the case. Still it is a thing to be watchful of.

I know indeed too well what the tie of mother and child is. It is one never to be replaced when gone! though children often do not feel it—till they have caused their parents great anxiety and sorrow. And children never can or do repay gratefully what parents do for them. No, never, or very rarely! The love of children is so selfish compared to that of parents and husband and wife. Parents' love is always giving out which as a rule is not the case with children. I must end now with tenderest love to Fritz and the dear children and with renewed expressions of warm love and affection ever your devoted loving old Mama.

From the Crown Princess

SANDOWN, AUGUST 23, 1874

We went this afternoon to a little church at Brading which is very pretty—and where the singing is beautiful. The service was particularly well done. You say the love of parents is far more unselfish than that of children—and in most cases I think so, but that makes it so blessed—"the more I give, the more have I"—in Juliet's words—which are differently applied.[1] If my children grow up with the same love to me as my heart is full of for you I shall think myself amply repaid for all I have tried to do for them, but I do not expect it, nor can I.

From the Queen

BALMORAL, AUGUST 25, 1874

I send you here the copy of what I wrote to Bertie which please return. On the other subject you mentioned I wrote to Sir William Knollys saying that I did not believe it at all. I had heard from several people that there was a large sum owing to Sir A. de Rothschild. Had he ever heard of it? You shall hear the result.[2]

---

[1] Act II Scene 2:
"My bounty is as boundless as the sea, My love as deep; the more I give to thee, The more I have."
[2] Probably borrowing money about which there was much gossip at this time. See *King Edward VII*, by Sir P. Magnus, pages 128-9.

From the Queen

I enclose my letter open for Willy—which I would wish you both
to read, then stick down and give him—with two kisses from his old
and loving Grandmama, and to ask Bertie to give my gifts in my name.
I can only repeat what I wrote in the Bible of which I send you here a
copy and translation as I should wish the Emperor to see what I wrote.
Truly sorry am I that I cannot be present on this eventful day—but you
know how little up I am to any excitement or fatigue or representation
and that it is all I can do, to go through any of it at home even. But my
thoughts and prayers will be with you all.

I told Bertie I hoped he would take the sacrament with you all; it is
right all Protestant Churches should do it.

From the Crown Princess

NEUES PALAIS, AUGUST 29, 1874

Many thanks for letting me see the copy of your letter to Bertie.
You were so right to say something about playing high for it is a great
danger, which often makes me tremble. About the other report no
doubt you will soon hear, and I trust only what is satisfactory.

We are so busy about Willy's confirmation and the boys' subse-
quent departure to a school, but the difficulties we have with the
Emperor are very great. If we were to carry out his wishes William
would be ruined and all his education undone! The Emperor wishes
him to go out altogether and now appear in the world on all occasions.
There would be an end of all study at once, and an end too of all hopes
of his becoming a steady and serious man, so we are determined to
fight against him to the last. But the Emperor became very violent and
we had most unpleasant scenes. I must say the Empress took our part,
but this seemed only to pour oil into the flames.

From the Queen

BALMORAL, AUGUST 31, 1874

I send you here in confidence Bertie's answer to me—and also Sir
William Knollys' answer to the other subject both of which I should be
glad to have back. Upon the whole both are satisfactory.

My thoughts and prayers will be so much with you tomorrow when
I will finish this letter.

1st September   May God bless protect and guide dear Willy and may he ever put his trust in Him and His blessed son—and neither swerve to the right or to the left but fight a good fight. I am so sorry that you have so much difficulty with the Emperor about the dear boy. It would be utter ruin to let him go out into the world at 15 and a half!! You must be firm upon that point. I am sure the Empress would support you but the Emperor's age makes him no doubt very difficult to manage on these points.

From the Crown Princess

NEUES PALAIS, SEPTEMBER 1, 1874

Dear Bertie is all kindness, so considerate, so amiable and affectionate—so kindly accepting all that we can do for his comfort or entertainment which alas is not much! He is as amiable a guest as he is a host and this is saying a great deal! It is a great comfort and happiness to have him here as I felt rather lost at having no one of our family present. Fritz and I drove with Willy and took him into the vestry to wait until the Company had assembled and taken their seats in the church. We received the Emperor and Empress and the *few* members of the Prussian family who were here, outside the Friedrichskirche in the cloisters you may remember—and then all went in. For the members of the Royal Family there were two rows of chairs; the rest of the company in the nave stood; (I fear they must have been very tired as the ceremony was very long). William behaved very well—was not at all either shy or upset and showed the greatest sangfroid. He read his confession of faith off in a loud and steady voice—and answered the forty questions which the clergyman put to him without hesitation or embarrassment. I do not think he was touched or much impressed! My heart was very full! I thought of the different occasions I had stood on that very spot, the one awful one never to be forgotten. I thought of you absent, of darling Papa—dear bright angel—and I felt it cruelly that the dear boy's two young grandparents should not be there to give him their blessing—though I know you were there in thought. For indeed none except ourselves can take so loving and sincere an interest—so enlightened and experienced an interest—as dear Papa would have done and as you do! This I hope and trust he will feel some day! The Emperor's interest is warm but alas! his influence on the child's education whenever he enforces it is very hurtful! The Empress means most kindly! She was deeply moved and so was the Emperor. Charlotte, Henry and Vicky cried the whole time. The clergyman's three long addresses might have been better and shorter still they did not spoil the ceremony—the Communion followed directly after; dearest Bertie took it with us and

Willy, and no one else receiving it except three ladies and two gentlemen of our household. The Emperor and Empress remained as spectators.

From the Queen

How well alas! can I enter into your feelings, and into the terrible wrench which it is to part with one's sons—and to see them slip out of one's grasp. If you feel this now with the father by your side think of me who had four (though poor Leopold for his health has never really been taken from me)—alone growing up around me—obliged to submit to many things which I highly disapprove and dislike and I know that beloved Papa could not have prevented them—I feel thankful that I should have to bear alone much that would have hurt and distressed him so deeply. But I think you will, as time goes on—and your large family grows up find what difficulties try and always weigh you down. This is far more the case in the higher classes and especially in the Royal Families where—unlike in the poorer classes (where the children support and help their parents) the parents have to help and support them and screen them from difficulties. Royal children never therefore sufficiently feel what they owe to their parents.

From the Crown Princess

Dear Bertie's visit was such a pleasure, I have never known him more dear and kind and nice—so considerate and so quiet. I was so grieved to part with him and miss him so much! I had quite an unexpected opportunity of speaking on the subject which frightened me so much—as he showed me an article on that very report, in a back newspaper—so that I could then say it was a widely spread and very firm belief; he laughed and said exactly the same as Sir William Knollys has written to you. Heaven be praised that it is so,—for I own it tormented me more than I can say. My fears are now quite at rest. Still I am glad you asked Sir William the questions.

Dear Bertie won all hearts here by his kind, amiable civil manner. He looked so handsome at the Parade in his bearskin cap.

We have carried the point with the Emperor of sending the boys to school for three years and now he cannot force William to appear at Berlin on all occasions and go out into the world—it was the only way of stopping this preposterous determination on the Emperor's part—

which we could not have shaken had the boys stayed here. But it is a hard sacrifice to give them up. I hope they will some day know how much their Mama has striven to do all she could for their good against so many difficulties.

From the Queen

BALMORAL, SEPTEMBER 8, 1874

Many loving thanks for your dear letter of the 5th received today with all the cuts from the newspapers which will interest me very much. But I am much distressed that no drawing has been made. Could not one be done from recollections? How wrong to take anything down without photographing it before. Here that always is done.

I am certain Willy and Henry will see in this and feel how much they owe to you, and I am truly thankful that the Emperor has given way to let the boys go to Cassel for 3 years. Is the school a very good one there?

I am very glad Bertie answered you so satisfactorily[1]. I only grieve for the Baden races.

Let me ask you again—always to ask me straight out whenever you hear anything whether there is any truth in it. I will tell you at once—whether it is about the brothers and sisters or about me.

How dreadful is this perversion of Lord Ripon's. I knew him so well and thought him so sensible.[2]

From the Crown Princess

NEUES PALAIS, SEPTEMBER 11, 1874

I certainly will avail myself of your kind permission to speak openly whenever I hear strange reports about anyone or anything at home, but you know how difficult it is to trust such things to paper and how much mischief an imprudent word may do. I hear very little gossip and believe none, but when people speak to me of such things I am always very glad to be prepared with an answer which shall effectually stop their mouths.

---

[1] General Ponsonby wrote three days later to Sir Arthur Helps, the Clerk to the Privy Council, about the Prince of Wales's supposed debts and said "The *World* has published three leading articles stating that his Royal Highness owed £600,000, that he applied to Mr. Gladstone to bring the matter before Parliament and that he refused, that Mr. Disraeli was to be asked to do so, and finally that the Queen had paid off these debts. There is not a word of truth in any of the above statements." *Letters of Queen Vicoria*, Second Series, Vol. II, p. 352.

[2] The Marquess of Ripon 1827–1909. He was received into the Roman Catholic communion at the Brompton Oratory on September 6.

From the Crown Princess

I am not in spirits just today for all that is going on and that I have to take part in! It is a very painful feeling to me to be here, as you can understand! If we had to come at all, this is a good opportunity as there are so many people on account of the manoeuvres! They have received us wonderfully well here, but this I am not surprised at, as since the year '70 they would receive us well in any German town be it in or out of Prussia, under the eyes of another sovereign or not. The parade was very fine yesterday, and the manoeuvres very interesting today.

I found the boys well at Cassel, the house in which they live is old, ugly and cheerless and looks out on a dull street but the children do not care for this sort of thing! We visited the school and classrooms, which are very rough indeed, and saw the Director, a very nice man, and some of the masters. Willy enjoys the thought of it very much, I do not know that he will like the reality half as much when it comes. Henry cried very much dear boy when he went away, and I am afraid I did no better—it seems such a breaking up! The Emperor is wonderfully well and in the best of spirits—as young and strong as ever—riding about, never tired and always in good humour.

Are you not shocked at the cruelty of the Carlists; really I do think it too bad to allow them to go on in their barbarous way. What a monster Don Alfonso's wife must be if all the stories told are but half true.[1]

From the Queen

I can quite enter into your feelings on parting from your boys though I dislike big boys in a house very much. But it is a break in their life—and the beginning of a totally different life to what they are used to, and I don't think boys are ever as nice again when once they have mixed with others! I have thought and I know others have too, that Waldy is much more fit for the Navy than dear Henry who is not very strong and who does not seem to me to have much disposition for it. Has that never struck you? You don't perhaps know that we never wished Affie to be in the Navy—but in the Army—and Leopold (long before

---

[1] Reactionary supporters of the male line of the Spanish Bourbons. Don Alfonso was grandson to the original Don Carlos: his wife was daughter to Dom Miguel of Portugal. A German officer, acting as a newspaper reporter and when a prisoner, was shot by the Carlists.

we knew he was so delicate) to be in the Navy? But Affie would go into the Navy, which has not been good for his character and after long resistance we gave way! Waldy looks to me so like a sailor. But be that as it may I only just mentioned what entered my mind.

She [Marie] is the most even-tempered kind person I ever saw and very amusing; both my daughters-in-law are never cross, *elles n'ont pas de mauvaise humeur*, and are satisfied with everything which is such a blessing in daily life, but in Marie's case I should think more remarkable as she was such a favourite. But I think her mother was very strict.

From the Crown Princess

NEUES PALAIS, SEPTEMBER 19, 1874

The visit to Hanover went off very well, Marie Münster, the Count's eldest daughter rode with me. I had no idea that Hanover was such a hopelessly dull, tiresome, uninteresting town, as it has a reputation of being a very nice place! Perhaps it was my melancholy thoughts and all the associations which made it appear so to me, but I was heartily glad to get away again. The people of the town and those who came to court were very nice and civil, and I hope the visit of my father-in-law pleased them and may do good in many ways.

The fables about Bertie's colossal debts, with many a rude comment and a disagreeable remark, are since several days filling all the German newspapers (purporting to have copied these reports from English ones) and you can imagine how annoyed and how angry one feels for him and for you to have all these disagreeable things read and talked of by everyone in Germany! It does so much harm to our family, and is grievously unpleasant for those of us who are obliged to live in Germany. I suppose there is nothing to be done. People invent wicked reports quicker than one can contradict them and contradiction is often not believed.

From the Queen

BALMORAL, SEPTEMBER 23, 1874

I enclose a short paragraph which has been inserted contradicting these infamous lies—and I think you should get it put into some of the leading German papers.

Affie and Marie left us on Monday. I have formed a high opinion of her; her wonderfully even, cheerful satisfied temper—her kind and indulgent disposition, free from bigotry and intolerance, and her serious, intelligent mind—so entirely free from everything fast—and so full of occupation and interest in everything makes her a most agreeable companion. Everyone must like her. But alas! not one likes him! I fear that will never get better.

From the Crown Princess

NEUES PALAIS, SEPTEMBER 25, 1874

I hear Lord Odo Russell is coming back soon—and I am busy painting some flowers on a large looking glass which belongs to him and Emily, and which I hope they will like. I am sure Emily will like better being here than at Berlin, and that it will be better for her health.

I hear that a protégé of Triqueti's has photographed all the details of the Wolsey Chapel, and wanted to dedicate this work to you.[1] You have not accepted it and now Mrs. La Childe wants to know whether it may be dedicated to me, and I should certainly accept it if you have no objection or wish to the contrary. Would you mind dear Mama letting me know as soon as possible if it is not disagreeable to you and I should give an answer in the affirmative?

From the Crown Princess

NEUES PALAIS, SEPTEMBER 29, 1874

Our German press is one of the worst there is, and scandal is what they particularly choose to feed on. It annoys me too much, and gives our darling Bertie such a name on the Continent as he certainly does not deserve! I do not know what one can do against this. Lord Odo Russell would be able best to tell—it is not good to rake things up again when they are once forgotten. Either our family must be very interesting or very much hated in Germany, for they are always picking holes in us— if not in one way then in another. You, Alice, I, Bertie, Affie, Lorne, Christian, all come in for their share and often some nasty little bit in some paper or other gives ill-natured people occasion to make rude remarks. Dear Uncle Ernest does us all a great deal of harm by his odd ways and uncontrollable tongue with his very lively imagination. Our dear brothers have often been (though they are not now) horribly imprudent; I am a stranger here which is a sin in itself. Still other families who I fancy have more weak and attackable points than we have are not run down so much. Be this how it may one ought not to attach more weight to all these stupid things than they are worth and it

---

1 The walls of the Wolsey Chapel were decorated by the Baron Triqueti.

is very difficult to know what to do whether to defend oneself actively
—or to let ill nature go by unnoticed.

From the Queen

What you say about the shameful lies about out family is indeed
very disgraceful—but whoever is in a conspicuous position—even only
attached faithful servants to Royalty—are abused and attacked! It is a
very shocking trait in human nature,—and one cannot but hope in time
it will cease. But it is almost always jealousy—perhaps of some one
obscure individual who puts in a lie and an invention—sometimes and
generally a pure invention and at other times founded on some facts
which are distorted and misrepresented. When a thing is actually false,
it should be at once contradicted, for I have seen the necessity of it—by
the mischief caused when it is not done, and the good effect when
it is done. It should always be done at once and in the shortest way.
I think Lord Odo, or Mr. Morier could help in getting something
put in.

From the Crown Princess

All Berlin is in a state of extraordinary agitation at Count Arnim's
being arrested and put in prison—for (it is said) having unlawfully
taken possession of certain despatches written to him while he was
Ambassador at Paris. He refuses to give them up! It is clear that he
meant to publish a sharp attack on Bismarck, who having heard this, is
determined to render his enemy harmless—and thus crush him. It is
an awful scandal and I am very sorry—for though I never had the
slightest sympathy for Count A., nor a good opinion of him—still I
feel very sorry for a man in such a high and official capacity.

We have also heard that Marie of Bavaria has turned Roman
Catholic! Though I am not one of those who thinks such a step a crime,
still I am very sorry! But she is very much alone—her sons neglect her
—and she has no one to turn to—and always lives among Catholics.
She is very good but not very bright, and always a little cracked on
religion—so I can't be surprised and only hope she feels happier now
poor dear! For Elizabeth of Darmstadt it is very disagreeable. Fritz and
the Emperor are much shocked.

We have again terrible difficulties with the Emperor about the boys,
he will meddle and interfere in everything and we have a hard time of

it! Now he retracts his given permission of their going to school, but of course we shall try our utmost with all duty and respect—but still adhere to what we consider right and necessary for our children.

From the Crown Princess

NEUES PALAIS, OCTOBER 10, 1874

There will be no occasion to put anything about dear Bertie's affairs in the newspapers. Our newspapers have brought a short extract of the excellent article in *The Times*, but I fear no one has read it, and the lies have made a noise which is quite incredible, everybody was talking about it and it made me so savage.[1]

The affair of Count Arnim goes on creating the greatest excitement. It may have been very necessary to have the papers he was in possession of—and to make him give them up, but the proceedings I think unheard of! It only shows how little liberty there is here! I cannot understand Harry Arnim's conduct. He was always an ambitious and unprincipled man eat up with vanity,—he most likely wanted to compromise Bismarck. Why not do it? He had plenty of time, why announce his intention and wait until Bismarck has him taken up!

---

[1] The first leading article in *The Times* on October 1 made several interesting points. It stated that people on the Continent believed that the debts of the Prince of Wales amounted to £600,000.

"It need not be said that the rumours of serious debt and embarrassment have no substantial basis. They have arisen from misapprehension of the real facts." The writer then went on to say that immediately the Prince married "he was called upon to assume a relation to English society and to foreign Royalties which does not necessarily, or even usually, fall to subjects however near the Throne." This of course was a reference to the seclusion of the Queen which threw additional burdens of representation on the Prince. "To meet all these calls the Prince has an income which, at the time of settlement, was estimated at £100,000 a year." The writer contrasted this with the income of "our leading nobles". They had been heaping up money for years past from coal and iron, houses and docks. The nearly fixed income of the Prince can not enter into competition with the enormous wealth possessed by the highest section of English society.

The writer went on to point out that the accumulations from the Duchy of Cornwall during the Prince's minority had not been exhausted by the purchase and embellishment of Sandringham and that this fund was used to bridge the gap between the Prince's income and expenditure to between £10,000 and £20,000 a year. The writer concluded by saying that "the Country will learn with satisfaction that the rumours so long prevalent have no foundation and that the Heir to the Throne is content to draw on his own resources".

The Editor [Delane] was on terms of private friendship with the Prince of Wales and the article was evidently not written without knowledge.

From the Queen

This affair of Count Arnim's is indeed a great scandal, and the great man seems a real tyrant.

I am so sorry that you have all this trouble about the boys' education. I have to answer the Emperor and shall just say that I think it so good for them to be at a school, and to remain children as long as possible. He wrote to me very affectionately and nicely about Willy's confirmation and what I had written to him and into the book and I can easily say something as from myself—if you think it would do good. Just telegraph to me if you don't wish it "Think you better not write that." For I wish to be of use—and not to add fuel to the flames which one does sometimes.

Regarding the Queen of Bavaria I must say I am greatly shocked for it is a complete surrender of your intellect—and individuality to another—and when one thinks of what the confession is (which our people want to reintroduce into England) one can't understand anyone who has been a Protestant ever submitting to this. Tell Fritz that I share his and the Emperor's feelings being as dear Papa was—a fervent Protestant and hating all that approaches Catholicism which unfortunately is what people are so fond of here. But I know you don't feel as I do—and have not that love for the very simplest, purest faith as near to our Saviour's precepts as possible.

From the Crown Princess

I think it would be very kind if some day but not directly perhaps, you were to say both to the Emperor and Empress that you were glad the boys were at school and were to be kept at work, and how hurtful it would be for them to be steeped in Court life and given to the world at the early age of 15 or 16.

I do not quite see with what right you say that I do not care for a pure faith approaching the precepts of Christ as I fancy it is the very contrary—the purer the teaching from these precepts is, the better I like it—but one of them is tolerance, and if other people are not of my way of thinking I can regret it, and think them difficult to understand but I do not blame them.

From the Queen

In a former letter of yours you said that there was an excellent article about Bertie's supposed debts in *The Times*; now I think you must have overlooked the great untruths it contained, of a dangerous nature, in which it tried to make out that B.'s expenses were caused by me, which is an abominable falsehood, which made Sir Thomas and my Government very indignant and as we have talked and corresponded so much about it—I think you should see the enclosed statement which Sir Thomas drew up which I sent to Mr. Disraeli who says it shall and must be set right. Pray return to me, but let Fritz see it.

With respect to the Queen of Bavaria and the purest faith, I expressed myself wrongly I fear. I meant more the very simplest form—and I think you hardly like that as much as I do. I am for toleration, but then it must be mutual—and the R. Catholic is a religion which is so aggressive, so full of every sort of falseness and uncharitableness and bigotry (unlike any other) that it must be resisted and opposed. Papa was against the great liberties which have been given the R.C. and with right—for they only take them and become more aggressive and dangerous. And I do blame those who go from light to darkness!

From the Queen

I will shortly write to the Emperor—but I enclose the extract of a letter from the Empress to me—written early this month in which you will see she entirely agrees with you, for I had at the time said how necessary it was the dear boys should remain as children and that both should go to this school at Cassel.

I regret Bertie's going to France but the Bisaccias are very nice respectable people.[1]

There is a most indiscreet book of Mr. C. Greville's (the Duchess of Richmond's uncle, former Clerk of the Council) published. It is Mr. Reeve's intense indiscretion to publish it—and shows a nasty, and most ill-conditioned disloyal disposition towards my two Uncles in whose service he was and whose hospitality he enjoyed. And I am most indignant that I should be praised at the expense of my poor old Uncle and predecessor, who though not dignified or very clever—was very honest—most anxious to do what he thought was right and always very

---

1 Sosthènes, Duke of Bisaccia 1825–1908.

kind to me. But the accounts in many ways are very full of truth—and the one of my first Council wonderfully exact. Also the greater part—though exaggerated—of that unfortunate dinner in '36 at which the poor King made such an unlucky speech.[1]

From the Queen

She [Marie] has not had any drawback—and is as well and strong as possible and shows a very healthy constitution which is a great thing is it not? She nurses the child—which will enchant you. As long as she remains at home—and does not publish the fact to the world—by taking the baby everywhere and can do it well—which they say she does now—I have nothing to say (beyond my unfortunately—from my very earliest childhood—totally insurmountable disgust for the process).

I am glad that you understand what shocked my people even more than me, for I felt it was so utterly false. Bertie certainly is kind and dutiful but to defend his own little extravagances he has once or twice hinted at this which is very wrong—for it is utterly false.

From the Crown Princess

I read an extract of the memoirs you mention in the *Edinburgh Review*. I can quite understand their having made an unpleasant impression on you.

What a good thing that dear Marie's constitution proves such a good one. To have strong nerves is a blessed thing indeed. Mine were strong once and perhaps she will know one day after she has seen more of life, when she knows what sorrows and anxieties are,—and has had more children, her nerves will not be what they are now! No one's can be I think, though there are those calm, happy, placid natures who are always the same and they are to be envied indeed! What thin-skinned, sensitive, imaginative people suffer mentally and bodily is not to be told—and only to be understood by those who are so organised—for to others their sufferings appear all as mere caprices. The old Napoleon once said *"heureux sont les phlegmatiques intelligents"*. How true that is and what would I give for a little of it!

The boys are getting on very well at Cassel I hear and there are some

---

[1] Trusting that his life would be spared till his niece, Queen Victoria, was of age so that the Duchess of Kent did not become Regent.

nice boys at the school amongst others one of the Battenbergs. Willy has to work very hard which is very good for him.

From the Queen

I thought I told you Leopold had to my great regret gone back to his beloved and I think very odious Oxford, where it is wet and muggy and where he cannot attend any classes but he can have lessons and as he was so unfortunate in the spring I did not on this occasion like to oppose his wish to try and study, which in itself is a good thing. But he must not be tired. I do hope your boys are not overworked, I have such a horror of that.

From the Queen

Your letter crossed mine telling you how glorious our weather was. And I can't think why you always write how cold our weather here is! It is quite mild now again, since yesterday—and is as variable almost as England only always nice, fresh and crisp. And there is so much pine and fir wood that it never looks dreary like the awful broomsticks in England, and the birches even when nearly bare keep such a pretty little tinge which relieves against the blue and ever varying hills; and the lights of an evening (on the frosty evenings) are indescribably beautiful —such lights and colours. Then trees keep on their leaves and look very brilliant mixed with the firs of which I plant a good many about here, as I come early and go away late and prefer to have some green trees.

You had not good nerves as a child and young girl, which is natural as I always was very nervous, an inheritance of my family, and which I am sorry to say from my hard work and early and many trials, anxieties and sorrows have certainly become greatly worse and are very bad now, and have no chance in my position and with that enormous family of getting better. I am sure if you were in my position you would feel, as I do, the comfort of being quiet with my sweet-tempered, ever-cheerful Beatrice and some two or three kind and pleasant ladies.

That book of C. Greville's, which you would like I think to see, shocks everyone—even far more than me—for I have not my mother's and father's names dragged up to be abused to scandalise the world. The Duke of Richmond (whose wife is Mr. C. Greville's niece) and who is here is quite horrified; for he says that to go and speak of your Sovereign in whose service you are as "a beast", to accept the hospitality of people you call your friends and then to write every ill-natured thing you can think of them is really too bad! And he rakes up mere gossip which is of no importance to anyone, and shows a diabolical nature, which shocks everyone; but Mr. Reeve, who has published all without, as is generally done, leaving out names, is still worse! In short it is a perfect scandal.

From the Crown Princess

Yesterday evening we had another rehearsal of the Dettingen Te Deum which is going to be performed on my birthday. It is one of Handel's most beautiful pieces I think. But so difficult. We are about 45 amateurs, and only have the help of a piano.

The whole of the German press with few exceptions, and almost everyone one speaks to at Berlin, think the proceedings against Count Arnim quite right and just; and I remain in the minority—for to me it savours of despotism, violence and everything that is bad.

I deeply regret the business at Trier,[1] but fear that this open warfare between the Catholic Church and the Civil Authorities will go on for very long! The Government cannot retreat nor can the Church, therefore in our lifetime I see no chance of amicable relations between the two.

I forgot to congratulate you on the Fiji Islands—how glad I am that England has them. We now form a belt right round the globe which is a proud thing for us and a blessing for civilisation.

People are very angry here about an article in the *Blackwood Magazine* about our "manoeuvres" written by Henry Knollys who was here; they say English officers are kindly treated and received, and show themselves ungrateful by abusing everything in our army in the English Press and many find a fresh excuse to vent all their bitter feelings against England and Englishmen, which is very painful to me.

From the Crown Princess

How charming is the letter of which you sent me a copy! I wish you could give me a copy of it, for after our uncles and aunts have been abused in so many books and have got such a name it is so pleasing to

---

[1] Where one of the expelled priests was arrested by the police at the altar.

hear a word said in their favour.[1] The Greville Memoirs are indeed too bad—as ill-natured as anything can be.

I am going to trouble you with a request to which you must simply say no if it is inconvenient. We are so very anxious to improve the breed of our pigs and our sheep in our farm at Bornstädt. Would there be a possibility of our buying from Windsor at not too high a price—three of each, i.e. a hog and two sows and a ram and two sheep. (The latter not for the wool, only for the meat.) Would you be disposed to give us one of them? I think dear Papa gave Uncle Ernest some at one time. Could we get someone's advice about it, and some hints about what they might be fed on, and exactly how they ought to be fed, as that is so different here! You will laugh at this I am sure! But our mutton is very indifferent, and I think the pigs could not be worse. I have never seen a good pig since I have been in Germany and they are by far the most profitable animal to keep here.

From the Queen

BALMORAL, NOVEMBER 16, 1874

Mr. Gladstone's pamphlet has set all the world by the ears.[2] What an incomprehensible man he is! First of all coming in to office to destroy (which thank God he has not done) the Protestant Church in Ireland, and doing all to flatter and cajole the Catholics—and now attacking them most violently. Old Lord Palmerston was not wrong when he said to me; "he is a very dangerous man." And so he is—for he is continually changing and acting contrary to his former principles though not from the intention to deceive.

From the Queen

BALMORAL, NOVEMBER 18, 1874

Accept my warmest and most loving good wishes for many, many happy returns of your dear birthday, and for many, many more in health and happiness, and growing yearly in wisdom, unselfishness, humbleness and trust in God's love and mercy in all things. Your position is, as every Royal person's is, a very difficult one for they have not their position to earn, and yet surrounded by flatterers, who are the first to abuse you behind your back!

---

[1] In her letter of November 10 the Queen said that she enclosed the copy of "a most curious letter" from America. This has not survived, but it was evidently a defence of the Royal Family against Greville's strictures.
[2] "The Vatican Decrees in their bearing on Civil Allegiance; a Political Expostulation." This was a criticism of Papal Infallibility and its effect on the loyalty of Roman Catholics to their own states. It sold 145,000.

About dear Charlotte I must repeat that you are really not doing her good by forcing her on with her lessons for she will not get stronger and not grow if she is overworked. I assure you that it is of as much importance as the bodily treatment and believe me that education is very much overdone in all classes.

I am very sorry indeed about this article in the *Blackwood* by H. Knollys. It is very mischievous! People should really be careful. I hear he speaks very gratefully of the treatment he received.

From the Queen

WINDSOR CASTLE, NOVEMBER 25, 1874

You will get a letter from the Duchess of Atholl describing the christening which though interesting was neither pretty or impressive. The room was not tastefully arranged and though very large not disposed so as to admit of people seeing well; and there was naturally no music or singing. I would have arranged all differently had it been possible, but the Bow or '53 room was used as a passage room for the Empress and some of her people stood there, so I could not arrange it as I wished. Then the Archbishop[1] got nervous and confused and christened the child which I handed to him before asking me to name it!! It is very good and is a fine child, large and fat and fair while Affie was dark; I (and Lady Fanny[2] thinks the same) think it will become very large and like its enormous Russian uncles. It seems very good tempered, but is greedy and takes more than Marie can I think afford. He is fed besides.

I thought her [the Empress] very ladylike and *Grande Dame*, with remains of good looks—far more than Marie who certainly is not pretty and graceful (and will I fear age early) and very kind and amiable. We were at ease at once, but she has a sad expression and looks so delicate. I think we should get on very well together. Poor thing I pity her much.

I am now going to tell you of my Christmas presents to you both; as they cannot be surprises or put on the table,[3] viz: the three pigs and three sheep you wished to have. They are beauties all bred at my farms and the latter Southdown and the four ladies in a hopeful state which will I am sure commend them to you. I wish only to know now when they shall be sent to Hamburg and to ask you to send a man for them. Also to whom Mr. Tait, who manages my two home farms, is to write

---

[1] Archibald Tait, 1811–82.
[2] Lady Frances Baillie, youngest daughter of 7th Earl of Elgin. Lady-in-Waiting to the Duchess of Edinburgh.
[3] Meaning the table on which presents were arranged.

about them. He knows McKay. Should he write to him and could he translate and explain to the proper people about their food etc.?

The Empress reminded me in her *tenue* and manner of dear Queen M. Amelie! How very rough and wanting in respect her gigantic sont are towards her! So rough and unpolished.

From the Crown Princess

I must say the children have a very comfortable home—such as they will not find again so easily on the Continent. I only hope that it may inspire them with ideas of neatness, order and taste, so that when they once have homes of their own to arrange they may know as much as possible what a tidy house should be like!

From the Crown Princess

Fritz was much satisfied with his visit to Cassel; he found the boys well and the masters satisfied with William. He says Willy looks pale and pasty and his face very pimply; this has been the case for two years or more to my despair; he will have a horrible complexion, and his features have grown very thin perhaps that will improve again later on. At his age almost all boys here look like that, I have not observed it in England and often thought how fresh and rosy the Eton boys looked.

From the Crown Princess

Many thanks for your note received yesterday evening and for the copy of the Emperor's letter which we are very grateful to have. It is just like him! He has not the faintest idea of education, nor of the requirements of the present day. How should he, he was completely neglected as a child and is one of the most ignorant men alive! He cannot judge of what is necessary, besides he has the most obsolete ideas of what princes and especially Prussian princes ought to be! But it is no use discussing things with him. If we by dint of persuasion and begging and even of stratagem, can get him to allow us to do what we want it is all we can hope for. In one thing I agree with him that it is to be wished the boys should early learn civility etc. etc. I can only wish them to be as charming, amiable and polite and chivalresque as their Grandpapa is in society, for he is a perfect *grand seigneur* in the best sense of the term, and it is that which captivates everyone so much.

I am afraid Willy will be very awkward and uncouth in his manners; his figure and way of speaking are much against him poor boy—and he is very shy which often makes him appear very rude, he is very touchy and sensitive, and will not bear a single word said about his manners so I always fear they will make an unfavourable impression on strangers. Whereas Henry is at his ease with everyone,—but such an *enfant terrible!*—Of course it would be much nicer if one could keep the boys in the house, and nothing but the most profound conviction of the absolute necessity of sending them away from a Court over which we the parents have no control, could have induced us to part from them so soon! But how right the step was I see more and more every day.

You need not be afraid of their being overworked—my children take good care not to overtax their brains or over-exert their fingers; if anyone is overworked it is the teachers and not the pupils who are really very lazy, and make no effort of their own unless they are forced to do so! Willy's health is very strong as you know, and Henry has no more lessons than he had at home and is very backward in every way. The masters are all well satisfied with William excepting in mathematics where they find him much behind hand. He is very happy at Cassel and very proud of being at school and having more liberty! The masters are all struck with his fondness for conversing and associating with older men, and with his always selecting the nicest and steadiest boys for his friends! This is a sign which gives me great hopes for the future! He is not the clever, gifted boy, I once thought he would turn out, but he is not wanting and I am sure will develop and come out later. He will take more after the Prussian family in tastes and character and in intellect than after ours,—and is already a regular Hohenzollern.

From the Queen

WINDSOR, DECEMBER 9, 1874

Poor Addy I pity her very truly.[1] Could you not say so some day? I am, as you know, no great advocate for marriage for marriage's sake; unless there is real attachment it is too dreadful, and I think all young girls should be taught not to look at it as the one only object in life! I feel this more and more every day.

The poor Empress Eugénie, who dined and slept here quietly on

---

[1] "The old Grand-Duchess of Schwerin is here, which bodes no good to poor Addy's affairs; they will try to force her to go back to her horrid husband." Crown Princess, December 4.

Monday, mentioned to me the correspondence of Marie Thérèse with Countess Mercy d'Argenteau and I will get it at once. But there are so many things to read, I never know how to get through them.

I have had such work choosing and ordering presents for Christmas though I began doing so in Scotland already. It increases every year beginning with 9 children—2 daughters and 4 sons-in-law and 23 grandchildren and ending with the school children at Osborne.

From the Queen

WINDSOR CASTLE, DECEMBER 12, 1874

I am sorry I was not more successful with the Emperor but at his age and with his peculiar views it is difficult to expect. I hope though that you will not have much more difficulty. Civility to high and low is of the greatest importance. Abroad they think too little (at least many do) of friendship and kindness to those below them, though I was pleased to see that this was not so with Willy. But the young people now are not taught *égard* and consideration and small attentions to others in society and in general which gives such pleasure. It ought to be constantly repeated to them. Dear Grandmama and your Grandpapa of Coburg had this to the greatest degree, and Bertie has.

Poor Bertie has had a great blow—his good Major Grey—the only child of dear old Sir G. Grey (who is very ill), who dear Papa placed about him—died at Sandringham of congestion of the lungs on Thursday—having only really been in danger since the evening before, though I fear he neglected a cold for some time! This happening just at this time of the year and at Sandringham is most distressing and painful. Dear Alix was there with the poor wife to the last.

From the Crown Princess

BERLIN, DECEMBER 12, 1874

I will say nothing about the Arnim trial which occupies everyone here very much! He is a man for whom little is to be said, but I think from beginning to end the affair a disgrace to us, to our Government, our Foreign Office and above all to our taste and good feeling! But I stand almost alone with this opinion. Stockmar and M. de Normann, the Empress and one or two more are the only ones who agree with me.

From the Queen

Poor Bertie is travelling down to the North, where they have had a great deal of snow, to attend poor Colonel Grey's funeral which takes place tomorrow. All his Gentlemen go—and one of his equerries went down with the remains. I feel quite anxious about him for he looked so ill and was alone and shaken, that I was quite afraid he may catch cold and get ill. Dear, sweet, excellent Alix looked so distressed and shaken from all the heart-rending scenes they had witnessed! She is so simple, and so good, so truly pious and so full of sympathy for others. I could but be struck by the difference between her and M., who is very good, and sensible and cleverer, and more serious in her pursuits—but seems to me to know little of the sufferings of others. At present they are too much engrossed with the baby and the nursing which is a most important affair and, for which reason, I think in this cold weather she should not pay visits and think of anything else.

From the Queen

Beloved Papa's life is received with great interest and pleasure and its pure spirit has an admirable effect in contrast with that disgraceful and lying book of Mr. C. Greville's who seems merely to have recorded the passing scandal and gossip of the day which as we know dies away so quickly and is not hardly noticed after a few months more. But to publish it—with all the near relations alive is monstrous. It is very inaccurate, and many people can contradict the assertions and will do so. Besides he only got numbers of the stories third hand—and re-tells them! The whole thing has raised a burst of indignation and nothing more than the base and wicked calumnies—the result of party spirit, which was far worse then than now—against the good and excellent Queen!!¹ I will send you a very good review on it in Macmillan's. I hope you will write to Mr. Martin soon as everyone of your brothers and sisters have done so.

I quite share your opinion about Count Arnim's trial. Count Münster says it is the Emperor's doing more than Bismarck's!

---

¹ Adelaide.

From the Queen

I made Beatrice read Doctor Hallzendorff's speech to me tonight which is admirable. Mr. Sahl (who is a perfectly blind adorer of the bad man who is all powerful with you) did not at all like my reading it.

1875

From the Queen

OSBORNE, JANUARY 2, 1875

You have not once mentioned your beloved Papa's life which is read with such delight by all parties and ranks here. Mr. Gladstone says it will be one of our standard books, and many others that it will do such good to young men to read.

From the Crown Princess

BERLIN, JANUARY 2, 1875

I had a letter yesterday from General Ponsonby written by your order. I never mentioned to you all the rumours which I was obliged to hear about the Emperor of Russia's visit, as they were so ill-natured and made me so angry that I thought it would be quite useless to tell you, and only cause you needless annoyance and pain. I suffered more than I can say at all that was said, but treated it as what it was "foolish gossip" contradicting it with vehemence wherever I found an opportunity, though I fear I was not believed as all these stories were told by the Russians here, of which a great many passed through from London and Paris. Of course to hear your Court and dear Alfred blamed for things that could not be true was too irritating, particularly as the Russians seemed to make a semi-political grievance of it. The abominable articles in the *Ruski Mir* not one of our German newspapers have reprinted. But the Russians have been at particular pains to spread these reports here in Society in the diplomatic and in Court circles. The Empress refuted them with as much energy as I did.

From the Crown Princess

BERLIN, JANUARY 5, 1875

Yesterday I had a rare treat, as the Musical Academy under Joachim's direction performed "Hercules" of Handel—it was most magnificent and was very kind of the Emperor and Empress, as it is not in their line at all, but I begged so hard that they might have it done— as the work is so incomparable and the Academy had never been heard by the Emperor, and being a government institution I thought they ought to have this encouragement and Joachim also. His wife[1] sings too beautifully and he certainly is the very first violinist in the world—and a thorough musician; he conducted very well. I should like to recommend a young man to you who often plays with me, and is now going to settle completely in England (at Harrow). Leopold has heard him at Oxford; he plays the violin and is called by the funny name of Herr Peiniger. He is a pupil of Joachim's. I should be so very glad if he could be heard at one time or another when you want a little music. He is a deserving young man and began as a schoolmaster in Westphalia.

You ask me about dear Papa's life. We have both read it with much interest and are very glad that it pleases so much in England.

From the Queen

OSBORNE, JANUARY 6, 1875

I am sorry dear child that you did not at once tell me of the shameful abuse and lies of the Russians, as it would have saved a good deal of trouble if it had been at once contradicted. And you promised me you would always ask me; for I think your gentlemen hear a great deal of malevolent gossip which is not the case in England. The *Corps Diplomatique* here are a nest of lies and gossip, and I do not except entirely your Ambassador.[2] As regards the thing itself it does not worry me in the least because the complaints are so groundless but it shows what people these Russians are. I have told Affie my opinion of them, and he has as much reason to complain as I have.

No one here but one paper thinks Serrano has made this *coup d'état*, and Alfonso is not his son. But it is a great thing he should be proclaimed King and everyone praises the boy.[3]

The Emperor of Austria has kindly sent me a very fine copy of that beautiful picture by our unequalled and ever to be lamented Winterhalter, of the lovely Empress with her hair down! I never saw a lovelier picture and so like. All these great artists Angeli, Richter etc. cannot throw that life and lightness and animation into a portrait that dear old Winterhalter could.

---

[1] Amalie Weiss.

[2] Count Münster.

[3] Francisco Serrano, Duke de la Torre, 1810–85, a successful general and president of the Executive of the Spanish Republic throughout 1874. The restoration was accomplished through public opinion and by the Army and some Ministers and not by Serrano. Alfonso XII was 17, and a cadet at Sandhurst. The irregularity of Queen Isabella's private life and her attachment to "the handsome general" (Serrano) in earlier times explain the Queen's allusion. (See *Spain 1800–1939*, by Raymond Carr.)

Today is Affie's and Marie's wedding day. I am afraid from what I have heard since that he, by the way in which he managed things, brought a good deal of this Russian abuse on! This is very unfortunate.

From the Queen

OSBORNE, JANUARY 27, 1875

I hear but little of Affie and Marie who are entirely absorbed in themselves and their wonderful baby, and hurt me much by taking hardly any interest in poor Leopold's illness all along. She never once enquired! One feels deeply want of sympathy at such moments and people I hardly know have enquired. At last A. got very much frightened and has been more attentive.

From the Crown Princess

BERLIN, JANUARY 29, 1875

How excellent M. Rousselet's book on India is which you sent us for New Year, it interests me so very much.[1]

From the Queen

OSBORNE, JANUARY 30, 1875

Are you not sorry for Kingsley's death? He is a great loss—so energetic, noble, warm-hearted, chivalrous and loyal and did so much good amongst the poor and amongst young people. You used to admire his books.

From the Queen

OSBORNE, FEBRUARY 18, 1875

I have not yet answered your letter of the 14th January relative to your coming to England. It came just when Leopold was so very ill and I could form no plans and settle nothing. I will now however go into your letter and your proposal. First of all let me ask you if you have well considered the expense of a journey to England with the whole large family and the expense of a season in London—which is ruinous to almost everyone who is not rich? You are always complaining of great poverty—and last summer declared you could not make the ends meet hardly, and that you could not go to the sea for your

_____

[1] *India and Its Native Princes.*

health and then I offered to help you as the doctors said your health required it. Have you reflected well on this? If people complain so much of poverty they should live accordingly and not spend in another direction. I am bound to tell you this before I agree to your coming in the spring and part of the summer. Would not the beginning of November when you could go to Bertie, and come to me when I come back from Scotland and just staying over Christmas have been better?

Then the very large family would be really too much for me at a time. It is bringing all the children which makes such a difficulty. If you came together or even alone with two or three the thing would be much easier. I put this all before you and wish for answers before finally deciding how it should be managed.

One thing let me state besides relative to your visit, whenever it may be, and that is that the time of its duration agreed on, should be strictly adhered to, and not prolonged beyond that, afterwards. It is a bad plan and leads to difficulties and inconveniences.

From the Crown Princess

BERLIN, FEBRUARY 20, 1875

I left darling Alice and Louis at Frankfurt yesterday shortly after 6. I ought to have been here this morning at 7 but only arrived at $3\frac{1}{2}$. We were snowed up for 5 blessed hours not far from Börsum, and had to be dug out with shovels and 6 engines dragged us along at a very slow pace. You never saw such a snowstorm, such a hurricane of wind and hard frost besides. Of course we could get nothing to warm the carriage as no station could be reached nor anything to eat, and it was very miserable. The eau de Cologne in my bag in the bottle was frozen to a hard lump! The wind rattled through the railway carriage till it seemed a sieve.

From the Crown Princess

BERLIN, FEBRUARY 28, 1875

Everyone here is wondering whether Prince Bismarck is going to resign or not. I hardly think so; it seems to me only to be a threat of his to get different things he wants. His family of course would prefer his resigning—so his wife told me again last night. He now goes to Constanz more, so one hardly ever sees him. His irritability is very great indeed, he will not allow the slightest contradiction from anyone or in anything, his nerves no doubt have suffered but I cannot believe he means to leave, though I dare say he is beginning to see that it is not so easy a matter to fight the Church of Rome as he fancied, and that he has underrated her power of resistance and overrated the power of the government in the strife which he has purposely brought on; why I do not know.

Rubinstein is here, and plays too marvellously.[1] It is too great a pleasure to listen to him.

From the Queen

I went with Baby to see Aunt Cambridge who really in her face looks unaltered as to expression and mind—only so venerable and nice in a little white cap, her hair quite white and the dark eyebrows also very nearly so—so that the severity of expression is all gone. She is quite helpless and one arm all but powerless.

I do think with you that the Great Man has gone too far in this quarrel with the Catholics though they are dreadfully aggressive people who must be put down—just as our Ritualists, and he may wish to resign in order not to be beaten. Is that your opinion?[2]

From the Crown Princess

BERLIN, MARCH 6, 1875

Give her [the Duchess of Cambridge] my love, Fritz also enquires with much interest after her, but I fear she will not care to hear that considering the way in which she has cut him of late years.

It is just possible that Fritz and I may take a little incog: tour in Italy in April and May and then we shall leave the children behind here. But we have first to get the Emperor's permission and see that there are no difficulties in the way. We should not go further than Northern Italy, the lakes etc. as there is so much I want to see, draw, and study and much information in art and history I want to pick up, having a special interest in the period of the early Italian renaissance, which was so beautiful in the North.

You ask about the Great Man. The Emperor and several of the ministers have most positively declared that he has no intention of resigning, and this I had begun to look upon as the truth, though with

---

[1] Probably Anton Rubinstein (1830–94). Born in Russia, he played extensively in the capitals of Europe. His brother, Nicholas (1835–81) was a composer.
[2] In Prussia the State provided the stipends of Bishops and clergy. By 1874, 8 of the 12 Prussian Bishops had their stipends withheld as part of Bismarck's anti-Catholic policy.

him who can tell? He has certainly gone too far with the Roman Catholics, but he seems to intend going further and further still, and I think will certainly not allow himself to be beaten! I think things in the most unsatisfactory state; though croaking is no use, and a bad habit. Still I must say I think much that is now being done very injudicious. I shall see the Russells this evening I hope; it is always a pleasure to me. We are very sorry Mr. Gosselin is going away, as he is very nice and so popular here.[1]

From the Queen

Angeli is getting on wonderfully, and Baby's will be lovely; mine very like though excepting for the pencil sketch on Thursday I have only sat once! It is quite *en face*, hands crossed before me as I generally stand; my usual evening cap—and a black satin evening dress cut square as I wear them in the winter. But what an odd man he is; saying everything and anything about everyone! A little *enfant terrible*. But a great talent undoubtedly, though not greater than our dear Winterhalter whom he too much despises.

From the Crown Princess

BERLIN, MARCH 27, 1875

Willy and Henry are enjoying their holidays very much—and Willy is as nice as possible, so affectionate, good and dear to me, which I used always to fear he would never be.

From the Crown Princess

BERLIN, MARCH 30, 1875

Nothing is as yet decided about our journey to Italy, we have not spoken to the Empress about it, only to the Emperor who is not sure whether he will go or not; he has not had courage to mention it to the Empress as she will be so much averse to any of us going.[2]

A. [Angeli] is a very funny man, but really an excellent creature,

---

[1] Sir Martin Gosselin. Second Secretary at Berlin 1872–75. British Ambassador to Portugal 1902–5. Died from the effects of a motor-car accident. Joined the Roman Church 1878.

[2] The Emperor went on a state visit to Milan at the end of the year. Bismarck, ostensibly for reasons of health, did not go with him. The Empress, with her Roman Catholic sympathies, disliked the association of the Emperor with the temporal power of Italy.

generous and charitable, so noble-minded about money matters, which alas you know is not the way with many artists. I wish so much he should see Sir Richard Wallace's collection to be able to judge of Gainsborough and Sir Joshua Reynolds—of which I have told him so much. I do not think there are better specimens. Has he seen the portraits in the Audience Room?

From the Queen

We were so pleased to see him[Arthur] and he to see Leopold able to walk about a little, and dear Alix was here and all seemed so nice when a terrible thing happened which has upset us all. Arthur's sweet little dog so attached and gentle a little fox terrier—whom he was so fond of as she was of him, was driven over and killed!! It had been left behind and taken the greatest care of—he only saw it yesterday morning again and most foolishly and unwisely wished it to run with the carriage for which it was far too small and quite unaccustomed— and which is always frightfully dangerous, for you know Leopold killed his in the same way, and both brothers were in the carriage close to the door when this happened. It is a thing not to be forgotten and we all were quite upset! It was a darling—and he is sadly distressed! It might all have been prevented and such an ending to a dear attractive pet is too dreadful!

Angeli is most successful—and a really dear and sensible man. Beatrice is quite lovely, and mine absurdly like.

From the Crown Princess

The Emperor has bought that charming bronze statuette of Thomas Carlyle by Böhm which I suppose you have seen. I think it beautifully done.

From the Queen

I subscribe to what you say about Angeli, and I like him very much, and what I like is his honesty, total want of flattery, and appreciation of character and expression in countenances. His talent is evidently quite extraordinary; he catches the likeness at once, and draws most beauti- fully; and his flesh, in painting young people, I think quite as soft and round as our dear old friend Winterhalter. But his taste is different to Winterhalter—and therefore he does not care or even like the beautiful light, white dresses and extraordinary elegance of female attire—nor the occasionally rough and broad touches and unfinished state of some of Winterhalter's most successful pictures which we delighted in. Angeli dislikes white and won't paint it, if he can help it—and also not light sky backgrounds. He in fact told me again and again how little he cared for positive beauty or great youth—but rather paints older people with character and expression, which is very pleasant. But as he won't flatter in the least and paints every peculiarity I could not advise the Empress to be painted by him. I think it would not be pleasant for either—unless she herself wished it. I shall speak of my portrait to her and then we can see. I really have sat less than to any other artist except Mr. Böhm. And I must say it is a marvellous likeness—as if I looked at myself in the glass. The face is finished in fact and I shall only sit again to bring all into harmony. Beatrice's face and neck (equally successful and quite lovely) are finished but not the dress or arms. He has taken them to B. Palace where I have given him a room to paint. He is going to do Lenchen's now and Louise's and Lorne's heads for me. But he is first going to Sandringham to paint the group and returns to Windsor when we do.

From the Crown Princess

BERLIN, APRIL 8, 1875

It has only just been settled an hour ago—after a great deal of discussion that the Emperor does not go to Italy and that Fritz does not represent him, that we make no official visit—but leave on Monday to make a little tour as we had originally intended! Prince Bismarck came this afternoon to tell us the decision that he and the Emperor had come to, and the Emperor afterwards sent us a note to the same purpose.

From the Queen

OSBORNE, APRIL 10, 1875

I am glad we so entirely agree about Angeli for unfortunately I think we do not very often agree, in matters of taste etc., though in many we do. Certainly not in the passion of going about and seeing things in which you seem to me to rival the Empress in. As Angeli is pleased with England he is sure to come here again when he can paint Arthur and Leopold; neither of them is handsome—though Arthur has a dear, honest, kind face and beautiful eyes and a pretty smile. If he did not keep his hair so short, and shave off his whiskers his head would not look so small.

I am very glad that Marie of Flanders has got a second son as it is of great importance. But it is a trial to poor Leopold and Marie. Philip has most amiably named the child after dear Papa—Albert—which shows such a nice feeling.

From the Crown Princess

BERLIN, APRIL 12, 1875

The Emperor and Empress dined with us yesterday. The Empress is so much distressed at the state of politics with regard to the Roman Catholic Church; it makes her so unhappy, is such a grief and a blow to her that I really feel for her from my heart, and only wish I knew some way of comforting her and calming her fears. The aspect of this question is not one at present to be of any relief to her I fear. The strongest measures are being taken everyday! This warfare is being carried on with energy—and who can tell where and when it will stop? The poor Empress's heart and soul as it were is wrapped up in the Catholic institutions of the Rhine,—and I fear she had for years nursed many an illusion, such as bringing about the most perfect harmony between Protestant and Catholic authorities, etc. And this so far from being realised is in her eyes being cruelly and wantonly destroyed. I have never seen her so much cast down. I feel the deepest pity and sympathy for her. For though I have no particular affection for the Catholic Church yet I hate anything like violence, and people's feelings are being most cruelly *brusqué* but the Government having begun this course can not but continue it—it would be useless and very wrong for Fritz to interfere in any way.

From the Queen

OSBORNE, APRIL 16, 1875

I did not enter into your remarks about the seaside because neither Sir William Jenner or I thought it very advisable—with the long journey and sea voyage at this time of year and that Vevey or Montreux would have been much better. Since that I had offered one of the houses to the Biddulphs and I could not divide my establishment anyhow further as some of Alice's children are at B. Palace.[1]

---

[1] The letter about the seaside does not seem to have survived.

You ask if I don't approve of your trying to improve your stock of knowledge? To a certain amount yes;—but I think that when one has seen so much as you, one does not require it—especially should not carry the artistic culture too far, and not make it a chief object in life.

What you told me about the dear Empress grieves me, because it is very distressing. She has never mentioned the subject to me, perhaps because she knows how very anti-Catholic I am. But with all that I think persecution very wrong and a great mistake and I think the Great Man has made a great mistake and has entered on a great struggle which he will not be able to carry through and yet he can't give it up—and how is it to end?

From the Queen

You are in your usual ecstasy about Italy which I suppose I shall never see. The papers speak of Fritz going to many places alone.

Little Alix[1] is the most lovely child I ever saw. Her colouring—excepting that she has blue (and what glorious!) eyes—reminds me of poor Charlotte and also of Clotilde—who had fine blue eyes—but she was smaller and the eyes smaller!

From the Crown Princess

It is charming here, we see all we can and find I know and remember wonderfully little of all the beauties and glories of art heaped up together in this delightful town. As you say, so it is. Art cannot be our chief object in life—in a position such as ours. But it may be, and I think ought to be, its chief recreation. Living as we do in a place and a country so singularly devoid of artistic collections one enjoys it doubly when one sees so much before one! And I own that it is only as one grows older and more thoughtful that one can really value the treasures Italy contains!

I say nothing of museums, galleries, churches, pictures and statues —because I know it bores you and my enthusiasm would weary you, but for those who love these things and see them so rarely, it is a perfect paradise.

---

[1] The future Czarina. The Grand-Duchess, her husband and children were staying with he Queen.

From the Crown Princess

FLORENCE, HOTEL NEW YORK, APRIL 27, 1875

There is another painter at Vienna who is much the fashion called Lembach, people usually prefer him to Angeli. I think him awful a sort of "Turner" in portraits, if such a thing can be imagined. I have seen the most terrible daubs pronounced to be wonderfully clever, original and beautiful; to me they appear simply crazy.

From the Queen

WINDSOR CASTLE, APRIL 28, 1875

You will truly share our sorrow at the unexpected loss of our dear, kind, excellent, devoted Lady Caroline which Alice telegraphed to you.[1] In my last hurried letter I did not mention her illness as I then hoped she was getting better and we could not realise her loss!—You have all lost a dear and attached friend, who really loved you like a mother, and I have lost one who had been with me since I was 18, and who was so wonderfully devoted to her duties. Under a somewhat irritable and sharp manner at times, there was a fund of warm love and tender affection, and she was so safe, so reliable and very clever and agreeable. I parted with her just as I left for Osborne on the 2nd— quite well—thinking I should see her on Friday last and never dreaming we should not meet in this world again! Life is a hard struggle and these separations are terrible! Few have lost so many kind friends and props as I have and few feel the need of them more!

From the Queen

OSBORNE, MAY 13, 1875

Only think that poor Jane Churchill has had her dressing case with all she most valued, and the few good jewels she had, stolen and is in perfect despair! She has lost £600 worth of things! Her orders, your wedding gift (your miniature in a bracelet) and Fritz's handsome diamond and enamel eagle brooch! Would you not both give her something to replace what of course was so valuable to her? I could have the same photograph of you repainted and set as nearly like what it was for you to give her. It was a simple setting and perhaps Fritz would give her a brooch. I shall of course do the same.

---

[1] Lady Caroline Barrington, widow of Captain the Hon. George Barrington, R.N., daughter of Lord Grey "of the Reform Bill"; Woman of the Bedchamber to the Queen.

From the Crown Princess

After ecstatic descriptions of Venice the Crown Princess writes:

We have very pleasant society here, Countess Bernstorff with her eldest son and Victoria, the director of the Berlin academy (H. von Werner) and a very amiable man (a painter from Vienna who usually lives at Berlin and is related to the Mendelssohns) called Pasini, perhaps you know his lovely watercolours considered the first in Germany.[1] We have known him for some years. It is in his studio that Angeli paints when at Berlin.

From the Queen

BALMORAL, MAY 18, 1875

I have never heard of Pasini or seen his watercolour drawings; in what style are they? Venice must indeed be beautiful—but I fear I shall never see it—though one can't tell—circumstances change.

Alice, Louis and the four children went with Bertie and Alix to Sandringham on the 15th. Victoria and Ella are charming girls, and Ella very lovely; so natural, intelligent and so well behaved. They are delighted with every little trifle. Dear Charlotte is grown so pretty. She is I think changing her figure and I think you should lengthen her dresses a little. She would look taller even—and is really too old to be dressed like Vicky who is not quite nine.

Little Alix is indeed splendid, and so very beaming and always cheerful, and very clever and amusing. She is quite the same sort of child as Ella was—only handsomer, much livelier and brighter and still larger.

From the Crown Princess

MUNICH, MAY 24, 1875

You ask about Pasini's style. Of late years he has painted only mountain scenes—and studies of Italians which are most highly esteemed but he is just as clever at interiors and architecture and at portraits. He is a very amiable, agreeable, quiet and gentlemanlike man, who goes into society a good deal both in Italy and at Berlin—formerly the Empress of Russia used to order a great deal from him. Some of his pictures are in England, and a great many in Russia and several in Germany. He is very anxious to see England once.

---

[1] Alberto Pasini (1826–99) chiefly known for his Venetian and Oriental paintings.

From the Queen

Dear Beatrice, supported by dear Victoria and Ella of Hesse were the only ones to greet me personally[1] but we were as quietly happy as suits me now in my old and widowed days when recollections of the once very bright and happy past will make me very melancholy. But I try not to give way and to be grateful for what is left.

From the Queen

BALMORAL, JUNE 1, 1875

I can imagine that you regret your pleasant tour in your beloved Italy—though to me dirt, insects and absence of many comforts (not luxuries which are the bane of the present day) would destroy all pleasure! You say pleasant things seem to come to an end much sooner than disagreeable ones. It certainly often does seem so, but don't you think it is because one longs for the ending of the latter and vice versa with the former?

I can't understand your returning to fur;[2] I think there are certain things which belong so entirely to another season—that though one may wrap up thickly—fur should not appear after the 1st of May when leaves are on the trees. The French formerly used to laugh at us English wearing velvet in summer as quite out of place; just as mad as wearing muslin in winter, when we often have it very mild which looks very odd.

I am having Queen Louise's life read to me.[3]

From the Crown Princess

NEUES PALAIS, JUNE 1, 1875

The Queen of Sweden left yesterday and I am perfectly exhausted with the life I have been leading these last three days between Berlin and here! I was in attendance on the Queen from 11 every morning till half past 9 or 10 of an evening, changed toilettes nearly a dozen times a day. The Empress had settled what was to be done, and I had the carrying out of it. I think the poor Queen of Sweden who has very poor health was ready to drop by the time she left! I call it killing our guests with kindness, and making an official visit the greatest fatigue

---

[1] On her birthday.
[2] To meet the cold of Berlin after returning from Italy.
[3] A German book by F. Adami.

and bore in the world, but so the Empress will have it. The Queen seems a very excellent person. She was not difficult to get on with. She has some likeness with Nicholas of Nassau but on the whole reminds me more of her sister Princess Waldeck, though she is not like her in face. She is also very plain, but has an amiable expression. The King is just the same as you knew him as Prince Oscar. They seem to be a very happy *ménage*. The Berlin public received them very well indeed.

The irritation and rage against England is very great here and abuse of all kind is poured upon us. The nasty horrible *Kladderadatsch*[1] is a specimen of it. Why all this is I really do not understand. The whole time we were in Italy I never looked at a newspaper, and was thankful to hear as little as possible of politics which poison one's life at home. So this all seems to me rather uncalled for.

From the Crown Princess

NEUES PALAIS, JUNE 10, 1875

We had a very interesting person here to tea yesterday, the celebrated Dr. Nachtigall[2] who has tried to explore unknown countries in central Africa. He was most interesting to listen to and is a pleasant man. He will go to England in August to be present at a meeting of the Royal Association. I am sure it would interest you to see him.

Prince Bismarck is gone to his place, where not a paper or an employee is allowed to follow him; he wishes to be completely free from ·all business,—the other ministers have to plod on—but if any question of importance arises he alone is to decide.

From the Queen

BALMORAL, JUNE 14, 1875

I am delighted that you can give so good an account of the dear Emperor, but I hear that his memory is much weakened. Is that so? He has written me a long letter which I will send you a copy of. It is a little far fetched to write me a letter (but it was only a kind pretext) to thank me for my telegraphic answer to his telegraphic congratulations!

---

[1] A satirical journal of the time.
[2] Gustav Nachtigall (1834–85). In the 1880's he was to pave the way for the formation of the German Colonies in East Africa.

It is however important and I will answer it and take note of the pacific declarations.[1]

From the Crown Princess

I am sure you were sorry to part with Angeli as he is really so pleasing and nice. Fritz has just seen the one he did of the Emperor of Russia and says the Emperor Francis Joseph does not like it. I get quite cross when people find fault with his things! I have often heard the remark "they are so hard; the details are done with too much care. His pictures look like coloured photographs!" This is too bad I think. I am very glad that Mr. Gladstone admired them, as I know he admired Lembach, and sat to him. Lembach is much more the fashion and more admired in Germany by all who profess to understand art (not by artists). I think most of the things mere daubs with a striking little bit now and then, but more tricks than art, and very unsatisfactory. Will you not ask Mr. Gladstone to show you his picture so that you may have an idea of the difference of the two? There is a tremendous jealousy of Angeli, though he has so many friends! His picture of my father-in-law, is I think the best portrait I ever saw!

The Empress is to spend the whole month of August here, the Emperor too, so Potsdam will cease to be a quiet place.

From the Queen

BALMORAL, JUNE 15, 1875

The Queen asks the Crown Princess to send a photograph of herself to

old Wrangel with many thanks for his photograph which shows how little altered he is since '58 when I saw him and he was very kind to me. Might I send it back to ask him to write his name under it—as it would be such a curiosity?

---

[1] See all this correspondence in *Letters of Queen Victoria*, Second Series, Vol. II, p. 391 ff. In a letter which is published in Monypenny and Buckle's *Disraeli*, Book 5, chapter xi, the Crown Princess writes to her mother "To us and to many quiet and reflecting Germans, it is very sad and appears very hard to be made an object of universal mistrust and suspicion, which we naturally are as long as Prince Bismarck remains the sole and omnipotent ruler of our Destinies". In her reply, *Letters of Queen Victoria*, Second Series, Vol. II, p. 406, the Queen says "Bismarck is a terrible man, and he makes Germany greatly disliked; indeed no one will stand the insolent and overbearing way in which he acts—and treats other nations".

From the Crown Princess

Many loving and grateful thanks for sending me the copy of the Emperor's letter. It contains exactly what he always says; and it is touching and almost melancholy to see how much he is "*de bonne foi*" and what illusions he lives in. He knows hardly anything of what Bismarck does—and of course must be very much astonished when he hears of excitement in the world caused by things of which he knows nothing. As for the newspapers you know he never reads one by any chance! He receives little extracts everyday from all the newspapers, pasted on paper—from the president of the police done at the police office but cut out and arranged so that of course it gives no adequate idea either of the tone of the press or of public opinion. As the excitement against England and *The Times* in particular was very violent (instigated of course by Bismarck) and our press very violent the Emperor draws his inferences from these. I saw nothing in *The Times* that was not moderate, just and reasonable. But everybody was furious here. One thing however is certain—and the Emperor's letter again confirms it—that he wishes for peace, and that Bismarck would have the greatest difficulty in pushing him to war if he (B.) wanted it, and this is always a safeguard and comfort and something to work upon—as the Emperor is very stubborn as you know in certain things —which is very awkward in many things but has more than once under this Great Minister—proved a very great blessing. The Emperor is such a thorough gentleman, and so honourable, and so conscientious and full of good feeling in general that there are things even Bismarck cannot push him to do—so he usually tries to avoid the Emperor.

From the Crown Princess

NEUES PALAIS, JUNE 16, 1875

I went to the Royal Observatory yesterday evening to see the moon through a large telescope which magnifies it 700 times. It was a most interesting sight and I could have stayed all night looking at the moon and distinguishing the mountains and valleys and listening to the explanations of Dr. Forster, a very clever and learned man. We give a large dinner today and have invited an American admiral which I do not exactly like the thought of as I hear he is very odd. We have thirty guests to dinner.

From the Queen

I see that the poor Emperor is kept quite in the dark. Do you think the letter is his own? I send you today the copy of mine to him, which I sent the day before yesterday to Ems.

All you say about Angeli interests me very much but he is too honest and independent to be popular with the fine or the merely rich people. I hope and think he is not tiring himself too much. His likenesses are wonderful, and the painting so splendid. I quite admit I was not taken with your picture (of which I only saw the copy) as I disliked the costume very much and thought it fanciful. But here he has painted us all just as we are and the pictures are lifelike.

From the Queen

How are all your dogs? I feel so much for animals—poor, confiding, faithful, kind things and do all I can to prevent cruelty to them which is one of the worst signs of wickedness in human nature!

From the Queen

I took leave of Angeli yesterday quite *à regret*! He has done marvellous things. Mr Gladstone, the Dean of Westminster and Mr. Disraeli, who all have a feeling for art, were in ecstasies and Mr. Gladstone said, as indeed many others, that it was me—and no difference. This is what Mr. Gladstone said.

Two or three—not Ladies[1]—were not pleased at its not being flattering and no sort of weak, generalised, green complexioned daub —which is what they are accustomed to here.

From the Queen

I am trying all I can to get some better and more eminent persons added to this list[2] which I send you, as I promised, but the difficulty is very great and I fear dear B. has a number of stupid, *soi-disant* friends

---

[1] Meaning not members of the Court.
[2] Of those who were to accompany the Prince of Wales on his tour of India in the winter.

who put all sorts of ideas into his head. The whole thing is very full of difficulties. You say that Bertie's breakfast must have been charming. I myself think them dreadful and very fatiguing bores, walking and standing about and seeing fresh faces in every direction—but it don't last long and pleases people and so there it is and easily done.

I saw the Abercorns on Monday—and the Duchess is very unhappy about Albertha, who is miserably unhappy for he, Lord Blandford, not only neglects her dreadfully but behaves brutally to her and she is so good and gentle. The parents were foolish about that marriage which ought never to have been—and she bitterly regrets it now, good mother as she is. The Duke's coronet was the foolish attraction. How can people be so weak?

I saw the Crown Prince of Italy for a quarter of an hour on Monday and thought him quieter and pleasanter than I expected though very plain and like the King as to the eyes.

From the Queen

OSBORNE, JULY 24, 1875

I was greatly relieved to hear that my picture had safely arrived as I felt very nervous at letting it go.[1] I see you admire it as I knew you would. I have now got Louise's here and I own it is most exquisite. It is wonderfully, marvellously like, and there is a depth of feeling in the eye and mouth which are Louise herself and (as with all Angeli's pictures) you can look at it quite close by as though it were enamel—which is really what the surface is like. Lenchen's may be more striking as a picture, but I think there is much more to look at in this. The only unworthy person about it is good and very odd and obstinate Leopold. I cannot understand it—for it simply is Louise. Lorne's is very good too and equally characteristic. I have kept Louise's on an easel in my room for a little while as I enjoy so to look at it.

There are two marriages which may interest you. Lord Leicester —who has five daughters married and two grown-up ones unmarried but is only 53—to a niece of Mary Lascelles, Lord Chesham's daughter 29 years younger than him; and Mr. Gladstone's eldest son to the youngest daughter of Lord Blantyre and grand-daughter to my dearest Duchess of Sutherland.

---

[1] The Queen had sent her painting by Angeli to be photographed at Berlin so that the Crown Princess could see it, but the picture was on no account to be shown to the public or any photographs sold.

From the Crown Princess

NEUES PALAIS, JULY 24, 1875

Your beautiful picture has arrived and is safe in my room. How very like it is and what a marvel of painting; the surface is like enamel. If I had anything to object in so fine a portrait I would say that it has not all the charm and loving-kindness that light up your dear face so softly when you smile and speak; that it looks a trifle stern and set, but then who can give two expressions at once, and the one I wish to see almost comes out when I look at the picture longer.

The old Grand-Duchess of Schwerin is at St. Petersburg, where no doubt she will make as much mischief as she can, for she is made of malice and malevolence as we have too much reason to know; she is furious against Fritz and positively hates me—there is nothing she does not say against me—all because we take poor Addy's part, and not her son's in this unfortunate affair.

From the Queen

OSBORNE, JULY 28, 1875

I was sure that you would greatly admire my splendid picture. I think that for a picture to represent the Queen it was necessary to have it serious—and I constantly begged him to make it so.

From the Crown Princess

NEUES PALAIS, AUGUST 3, 1875

There is a very beautiful lady here at the English Embassy, a Mrs. Mordaunt. I rarely saw so pretty a face; everybody admires her.

From the Queen

OSBORNE, AUGUST 4, 1875

I am afraid I am very troublesome about my ugly old face and my picture, but as they failed so entirely here, and as I don't know when it will be engraved I am anxious to get several sizes of good photographs. The picture however I hope they will not long detain.

I shall burn your letter directly. As for Countess Redern I know nothing and you may be sure I shan't say anything but will remember the character. I fear some other *aventurier* has been taken up and that there is more of that playing now. But it must be stopped.[1]

D.V. I am going to Inveraray at last this autumn but not till after Bertie leaves. He is grown so large—and nearly quite bald. Dear Alix is very thin but seems well and very dear as ever. The children are well and in high spirits. The little girls come every morning to breakfast out of doors.

From the Queen

OSBORNE, AUGUST 7, 1875

I went yesterday with Beatrice, Leopold and the little children to the Regatta but it was half over and very bad. We took a little sail afterwards. I admire Tennyson's *Queen Mary* immensely excepting the coarseness which ought to have been omitted.[2] It is very powerful I think—and adheres very strictly to history. Beatrice read it (with all those parts omitted) with Bauerlein[3] and greatly enjoyed it. What a dreadful time it was!

Angeli, I understand, varnishes his pictures early. Winterhalter wished it to be done after a year but not before—Landseer not for much longer and certainly it is often very much too much done in England, and gives the pictures a "teabordy" look which is dreadful.

From the Queen

OSBORNE, AUGUST 11, 1875

You will be interested to hear about Augustus of Portugal the youngest and sole surviving brother of Louis, who came here for one night yesterday. His face is wonderfully like Antoinette and the Coburg family and he is pleasant and good humoured and immensely

---

[1] In her letter which the Queen destroyed the Crown Princess was probably repeating gossip current in Germany about the Prince of Wales.

[2] For example the following:

Queen Mary   As to myself
             I am not so set on wedlock as to choose
             But where I list, nor yet so amorous
             That I must needs be husbanded; I thank God
             I have lived a virgin, and I noway doubt
             But with God's grace I can live so still.

The play was produced in London on April 19, 1876, and the Queen would not have liked the pointed and noisy applause with which the audience received the line "I am English Queen not Roman Emperor", marking the unpopularity of her title Empress of India.

[3] Familiar name for Fraulein Bauer the German governess.

tall, but has a very awkward figure and his legs seem weak—with very large thighs and he walks very badly. Otherwise he would be very good looking and he is like all the cousins—his father to begin with, Leopold and Philip Flanders, etc. One likes to see it. He has blue eyes and looks younger than 27; he has come to see his sisters whom he has not seen for 16 and 14 years.

I wanted to mention to you that awful trial of Colonel V. Baker!!¹ Was there ever such a thing and such a position for a poor young girl? And what a disgrace to the Army. No punishment is severe enough. Sir William Jenner knows the brother who is a distinguished doctor and she is a very nice girl—though some officers and people tried to excuse him by abusing the poor, unprotected girl but the country are furious with him and he will be disgraced for life. The articles in *The Times*, *D. News* (especially) and *D. Telegraph* were excellent. What is to happen if officers, high in position, behave as none of the lowest would have dared to do, unless a severe example is made. I own I feel most indignant. Should you care to see the two last-named articles I will send them for you and Fritz to see. Colonel Baker has a very bad moral character and Sir S. Baker his brother also does not stand very high in that respect.

From the Queen

OSBORNE, AUGUST 14, 1875

On Thursday I received six beautiful horses or rather more four horses and two ponies which the King of Italy has most kindly sent me; they are beautiful but not little Sardinians. He sent his Grand Ecuyer Count Castellengo, a very tall and very ugly but gentleman-like old man, over to present them. The ponies are grey and the horses are chestnut—half Arabs.

A young lady, a governess, travelling alone first class on the Portsmouth line of the South Western Railway, was assaulted by Colonel Valentine Baker of the Tenth Hussars. Unable to use the communication cord she got out while the train was moving and travelled for five miles on the step, till her plight was realised. Her assailant was tried and sent to prison for one year. Dismissed from the Army he served under the Sultan of Turkey and was known as Baker Pasha. His brother, Sir Samuel Baker, to whom the Queen refers, was the African traveller and explorer. Both brothers were friendly with the Prince of Wales and it was of Sir Samuel that the Queen wrote to the Prince "If you ever become King you will find all these friends most inconvenient". Sir Philip Magnus, *King Edward VII*.

— *189* —

From the Crown Princess

The story of Colonel B. is indeed most distressing and makes one shudder, it is terrible to think what a slur such conduct throws on a whole existence—and one feels so shocked and so ashamed at a gentleman being capable of such a thing. I am happy to say I have never heard the subject mentioned and certainly I never allude to it, as I feel so vexed it should have happened in England. I have read the articles you mention, they seemed very just.

From the Queen

BALMORAL, AUGUST 21, 1875

I can still write and think of little else but this dreadful catastrophe on Wednesday evening and send you here the copy of my letter to Louise giving an account of it![1] Please send it at once to the Empress Queen to see. The evidence you will see in *The Times*. Nothing will ever efface from our minds the horror of that scene; I hear the crash now and feel the shock—see the poor lady in her calm, silent despair and the poor dying old man![2] One can now realise a collision at sea and the disappearing in a few seconds of a large ship!!

No blame can I feel sure be attached to my people on board the *Alberta*. They behaved admirably and had it not been for their promptitude I am sure no one would have been saved.

From the Queen

BALMORAL, AUGUST 24, 1875

I told you I think the relations of the Peels are strange to say living near here. The funeral was to be today! The poor man is not found! There are ten of the Peel family.[3] Poor Miss Annie who was drowned was much beloved, an excellent person and very handsome! And had charge of the children of a sailor who had died who were also at Ryde. The poor old mother travelled all night to Portsmouth and saw the

---

[1] On August 18 the Royal Yacht, with the Queen on board, was in collision with the *Mistletoe*, a schooner belonging to Mr. E. S. Heywood of the Manchester banking family. The Captain of the *Mistletoe*, the mate and Mr. Heywood's sister-in-law, Miss Peel, were drowned. A fine description of what happened by the Queen is on p. 417 of *Letters of Queen Victoria*, Second Series, Vol. II.
[2] The Captain who was 70.
[3] A Lancashire family of the same stock as Sir Robert.

remains of her poor daughter. The poor drowned old Captain and mate have left widows and children.

I hope and pray this Herzogovinian business may not lead to complications but it makes one very anxious.

From the Queen

You did not telegraph yesterday for the first time that you omitted it![1]

The inquest was only over yesterday evening; and we expect the verdict today. I hope you will read all the evidence. Ernest[2] is very angry and says in a letter I got yesterday dated the 24th "as you already know by telegram the inquest has once more been adjourned till Thursday. In fact it is now no longer an inquest but a trial of a most delicate, professional, naval question, by a set of prejudiced and ignorant men. The spirit which animates them they show on every occasion, and so does the rabble which fills the room. They think it a fine chance of being able to throw dirt at the Navy and at the Royal Yacht. The coroner, who knows this well, Mr. Harvey, and who is a gentleman, insisted on sending for a naval assessor from the Board of Trade to have the opinion of one man of professional experience in cases of collisions. I should think that unless they again adjourn, the verdict will be given the end of this week. God alone knows what it will be though in reality no blame can be attached to us." All this makes me very anxious. If, what I must call a "wrong verdict" should be given, there will be a Naval Inquiry which will satisfy my officers. Mr. Heywood behaves extremely well. Alas it is terrible that three lives were lost. Poor Miss Peel, she suffered so much.

You ask when and where I will take leave of Bertie? Where could it be but here?[3]

From the Queen

This very distressing affair which all who are at a distance judge rightly, has ended for the present in a most extraordinary and I believe unprecedented way and the very painful part is the abominable and

---

[1] The anniversary of the Prince Consort's birthday.
[2] Prince Ernest of Leiningen, Captain of the Royal Yacht.
[3] Unless, as the Crown Princess was hinting, the Queen had left Balmoral earlier than usual to wish Godspeed to the Prince on his important tour.

unstraight-forward way in which Mr. Heywood has behaved (unlike what we thought at first) and the nasty spirit shown at Gosport and Portsmouth. But those seaport towns are known to be very low indeed, and always very disagreeable.

Let me now answer your dear question about your coming to see me in November; you know how dear you are to me, how impossible it is that you could ever become a stranger to me and how gladly I should see you. But this winter I fear it is impossible. Dear Alix will be here with me a good deal, and I believe her parents will come to her and stay with her, and would come and see me—and this would prevent my seeing you at all quietly. D.V. next year that would do— and we might besides meet for a day or two in the spring at Coburg— if I can get there—which I hope to do. So I fear we cannot think of it this year, which I grieve to say, darling child!

From the Queen

BALMORAL, SEPTEMBER 3, 1875

The ordering of a Naval Inquiry seems a mistake and a pity. Unfortunately Captain Welch[1] and Ernest are both very unpopular and very abusive in their language, and I fear that this is going against them. The funnel on board the *Alberta* may be in the way, but that is the fault of those who built her, not of the officers. The new inquest will I hope clear matters up,—but you can't think how worried and annoyed I have been and am. Such writing, telegraphing, etc. I assure you I wish I could avoid ever going on the seas again which as we happen to be an island, and Osborne is on one, is impossible.

From the Queen

BALMORAL, SEPTEMBER 7, 1875

This dreadful business is going again, but they hope to finish it tonight. Ernest is in a dreadful state of anger and irritation which is very natural but not very prudent. He however is in no way responsible. This dreadful collision between the two Ironclads has created a great sensation![2] Thank God no lives were lost.

You are quite wrong in saying you are "unwelcome"; that is a very wrong word, and I am extremely sorry to have to refuse you— but this year I cannot help myself, as I told you—for reasons which I explained.

---

[1] Staff Captain by whose orders the vessel was steered.
[2] The *Vanguard* and *Iron Duke* off the Irish coast; the former sank.

I am, as I told you, having Queen Louise's life read to me, and think it very interesting. What a charming, kind woman she must have been!

From the Queen

BALMORAL, SEPTEMBER 11, 1875

I telegraphed to you yesterday to say that the inquest was over and the verdict given. It is a great relief that it should be over, but the impression of the disgraceful conduct of Mr. Heywood and of the Portsmouth mob continues to be very unpleasant and painful. As regards the former we think he must have gone off his head—for he promised the Admiral to set right the bad impression he had given at the first inquest and then went and publicly made it even worse. As for the low Portsmouth people—they are a big, low and bad population and must have been incited to behave as they did.

I am as proud of the British Navy as you can be; but that has nothing to do with my dislike to go on the sea—which, after an accident like the present, is but natural and moreover it really is not safe during the summer with the enormous number of yachts there are now—which has trebled in the last few years.

I was much surprised and I must say pained to see that Arthur went to Hanover!! If I had known that this was intended I should have remonstrated against his going. It is too soon,—and hurts our feelings; and it is unkind to poor King George and his family. Bertie is furious and Uncle George will be equally so.[1]

From the Crown Princess

NEUES PALAIS, SEPTEMBER 18, 1875

It may possibly interest you to hear that a very choice and valuable though small collection of antiquities has passed into my hands, through the sudden death of an old gentleman, a lawyer called Herr Robert Jornow; he was a nephew of the celebrated Rahel von Ense who I am sure you must have heard of as one of the cleverest and most gifted women that ever existed.[2] We made the acquaintance of this interesting and clever old gentleman a few years back. He was a friend of Winterhalter's but quite peculiar in his ways and lived the life of a

---

[1] The Queen was mollified when she heard that Prince Arthur had not stayed at Hanover.
[2] 1771-1833, married Varnhagen von Ense. She was a powerful influence on the leading intellectuals of her day. Carlyle described her as "a kind of spiritual Queen in Germany". She was, he said, "a woman equal to the highest thoughts of her century".

hermit in his house at Berlin, into which only very few people were admitted. He was always most kind and civil to Fritz and to me, and took a fancy to me. In the endless, dreary, wretched winters at Berlin it used to be one of our chief pleasures to go and pay him visits; we stayed hours listening to his clever talk and admiring his collection; he used moreover to assist us on all occasions; he lent us things for our ball, etc. Three or four days ago he went out shooting as usual and fell down dead in a fit of apoplexy. In his will—in a few kind and touching words he leaves his collection which was his only happiness in this world to me. The funeral took place yesterday and I only learned the fact yesterday afternoon. His death shocked us very much as he was so kind to us.

From the Crown Princess

NEUES PALAIS, SEPTEMBER 25, 1875

I hear your pretty charming Lady-in-Waiting, Lady Clifden, is going to be married. You will be sorry to lose her I am sure.[1]

I was over at Berlin yesterday to be present at an examination for young girls, which was quite excellent; it was at the institution called Letterhaus which you may perhaps have heard I was instrumental in founding. The pupils gain their living in different professions, book-keeping—as clerks at telegraph offices and insurance offices. The result is most satisfactory. We have a dress-making and a sewing school there and have had successively six hundred pupils.

From the Queen

INVERARAY, SEPTEMBER 27, 1875

I was much pleased to hear that you have had this interesting collection of antiquities left to you, although I grieve for you to have lost the agreeable old gentleman.

We arrived safely here on the 22nd after a prosperous journey and the drive over here from Tyndrum by Dalmally and Loch Awe was quite beautiful. The position of the house and the magnificent trees of all kinds with the fine loch and beautiful mountains make it a very beautiful place—though the climate is not pleasant. Too muggy, and—excepting the first day—a great deal of rain though it held up in the morning and the afternoon. But today which was much brighter was

---

[1] Eliza Seymour married 3rd Viscount Clifden 1861. Lord Clifden died in 1866, and his widow married Colonel Sir Walter Stirling in October 1875. See also page 234.

fearfully showery. The country looked lovely between, and this afternoon we drove up to the very head of the Loch—up Glen Fyne. I have walked in the grounds and driven about to the finest spots including the Dhu Loch and Glen Shira. In the house are dear Louise and Lorne, six daughters (the three youngest live at the factor's house) Sir J. and Lady Emma McNeill, J. Campbell (of Islay)—3 clergymen (!!) one of whom is gone and two of whom are very charming and distinguished people; and others[1] have come to dinner. There was one great Tenants' Ball on the 24th but otherwise nothing. We leave at a little after nine on Wednesday and shall not reach Balmoral till eleven that night. We shall go by Loch Lomond way.

From the Queen

Lady Clifden has left me some time ago and only did occasional duty once a year or so as extra Lady. But now she will naturally not do any. She is quite throwing herself away on an insignificant young officer six years younger than herself and not very recommendable. But dear and good as she is; she does not show much discrimination in her choice or she could not have married Lord Clifden.[2]

From the Crown Princess

Is it not curious that Prince Adalbert (funny fat man) should have died. You know there is a superstition in Bavaria and especially in the Royal Family that if one member dies, that same year two must follow. Princess Alexandra died in spring—Prince Charles in the summer and now Prince Adalbert. They will believe this nonsense more than ever. The only thing that might break the spell would be to consider the ex-Queen Amelie of Greece as one of the Bavarian family, as she too died in April.

I really do not know what you could give Fritz for his birthday. He has many little wishes but they are all for curiosities which he has seen in one place or another. Any trifle of old silver, an old salt cellar, or cruet stand, or sugar basin, or knife and fork and spoon, provided it be real old English would give him the greatest pleasure.

---

[1] Meaning people not clergymen. Both the Queen and the Prince Consort were somewhat apprehensive of the society of the nineteenth century clergy.
[2] He died from softening of the brain when he was 40.

From the Queen

Let me say how sorry I am to hear of the bad neuralgia. Have you never tried the application of aconite and of a new application which never affects the skin, oleate of morphia? If you have none I could send you some. It should be rubbed in, in small quantities but for some time.

Poor dear Bertie is gone! Dear Alix went over with him to Calais and we heard the passage was good. He was very low at going. God grant all may go well!

I send today to you my gift for dear Fritz which I hope he may like and use—as it is really old English Silver. I am no great amateur of old things—but sometimes they are very handsome.

From the Crown Princess

Nothing makes me feel so wretched as a very heavy cold followed by this most violent and with me uncontrollable neuralgia. I do not know the oil of morphine, but have a salve of morphine which I suppose answers the same purpose, aconite, bella donna, and veratrine salves have all been tried. Aconite irritates instead of soothing. Even smelling salts I cannot use as everything a little sharp seems to set it on. The only thing I take inwardly is bromide of potassium but I do not perceive that it has any effect.

Dear Arthur must be gone by this time—dear kind boy. I hope he will have a good passage. The charming climate of Gibraltar will be sure to do him good.

Charlotte's figure is alas! not quite straight—one shoulder and one hip a little larger and higher than the other. (I suppose inherited from the Empress who has that defect though it shows very little.)

From the Queen

You know that I have *unberufen* derived such immense benefit from taking the Carlsbad waters in the summer. I hardly (*unberufen*) suffer at all now from rheumatism, etc. I only took 2 small wine glasses of it. I have taken it now for 3 summers running for 5 or 6 weeks.

I send you a bottle of the oleate, which is rather a new thing and

Top: the Duke and Duchess of Edinburgh with their son, Prince Alfred, July 1875
Below: Princess Sophie and Princess Margaret of Prussia in a goat cart, August 1875
Reproduced by gracious permission of Her Majesty Queen Elizabeth II

The group photograph of the Royal Family in the Green Drawing Room at Windsor Castle
made by McLachlan. Left to right: Prince Leopold, Princess Louise Marchioness of Lorne,
Princess Charlotte of Prussia, Alfred Duke of Edinburgh, Prince William of Prussia, the
Prince of Wales, Prince Arthur, Princess Alice, the Duchess of Edinburgh, Princess Helena,
Prince Christian of Schleswig-Holstein, the Crown Prince of Prussia, Princess Beatrice
(holding bouquet), Queen Victoria, the Crown Princess of Prussia, Prince Louis of Hesse
(with beard), the Marquess of Lorne, Prince Christian Victor of Schleswig-Holstein (seated
on floor), Princess Louise of Wales, Princess Elizabeth of Hesse, the Princess of Wales,
Prince Albert Victor of Wales. *City Art Gallery, Manchester*

Queen Victoria with, left to right, Princess Louise Marchioness of Lorne, Prince Leopold the Marquess of Lorne and Princess Beatrice, September 1878. *Reproduced by gracious permission of Her Majesty Queen Elizabeth II*

certainly soothes and never irritates the skin. Another thing which never hurts the skin or does more than redden it, which I have found an immense relief, is to put ginger, like a poultice, on a piece of brown paper and lay that either on your chest or arm—or behind your ear— especially when you go to bed, and it is a great relief. It gets hard and stiff when it gets cold but a hot sponge takes that off. With me smelling strong things always relieves.

From the Queen

BALMORAL, OCTOBER 23, 1875

Leopold left this on the 4th and is now at Oxford. I can't say anything very satisfactory about him I am sorry to say. Dear Arthur had a fair passage. I think it is a great mistake to complain so much of one's own climate especially with the English or British. Unless you are really very delicate you ought to be able to live in your own home and undoubtedly nowhere is this found better or the climate more moderate than with us.

I was present at a solemn and touching funeral here on Thursday— the father of my faithful Brown—an old man of 87; as usual the simple service was at the house. The dear excellent old wife of 76—nearly blind—stood at the door near me, and was much affected—but listened most attentively to the minister's fine prayer; but she was quite overcome and so were the good sons, when she knew the coffin was being carried away by her five fine, tall, strong sons—themselves deeply affected and so devoted to her! The small cottage stands high above the road on the hill-side and the scene was solemn and striking to see the large procession, for there was an immense attendance, wending its way down to the road and on to the churchyard!

From the Crown Princess

NEUES PALAIS, OCTOBER 28, 1875

I quite agree with you that it is ridiculous, besides being very ungrateful, to attack the British climate; it is such an excellent one. Never the heat we have in summer, never the long, long winter from December till May—where it is impossible to take much exercise out of doors and often one cannot set one's foot down in the melting ice and snow. Here one has a right to complain, but in England where you can ride almost all winter, and go in an open carriage most days— where the houses are so comfortable and the food is so excellent no one can complain except those who are very delicate—consumptive or rheumatic, etc.

From the Queen

The accounts of the Arctic ships is indeed extremely interesting and so is the death of poor Captain Goodenough, at the Isle of Santa Cruz. He died, as Bishop Patteson, and many others—only that the Bishop was killed at once by a club whereas poor Captain Goodenough died from tetanus the result of those dreadful poisoned arrows.[1]

From the Crown Princess

Our time of peace, liberty and comfort is up; and we must pack up for the town which I always do with rather a heavy heart. I see so little of Fritz at Berlin, and we have so much illness always during the long, and trying winter!

Everyone here is much excited about Count Arnim's pamphlet, which perhaps you have heard about. Sahl could show you extracts from our papers, which would give you an idea of the sensation created here. The poor ill-used man must have quite lost his head as he could have done nothing more ruinous to his own cause, he has made it almost impossible to take his part, and it will now make people approve of the harshness with which he has been treated, and forget how unjust it was. He is so very vain, but he does not understand that this has been cutting his own throat.

What a nice speech Leopold made at Oxford,[2] and what a very good one Mr. Gladstone made on Art in Education; it interested me very much.[3]

From the Queen

Captain Montagu's accident is serious. I pity any one who has an accident to their eye—else I could not feel very sorry if the great O.

---

[1] The inhabitants of Santa Cruz were subject to kidnapping to work in the sugar plantations of Fiji. A naval squadron was sent to check this practice, but the people of Santa Cruz—as was also true of their neighbours on Nukupa where Bishop Patteson was murdered in 1871—remained suspicious of all white men.
[2] At the Oxford School of Science and Art, where with many references to his father, he showed how English designers were doing work which was formerly exclusively foreign.
[3] At a distribution of prizes to science and arts students at Greenwich.

had a good lesson and was shaken a good bit—for he is an odious individual who annoys B. very much—often.[1]

Angeli's picture of me is hung up in the Oak Room and looks very well, only we must arrange lights to show it off at night—ugly as the old lady is to behold.

From the Crown Princess

NOVEMBER 26, 1875[2]

Yesterday we could not walk about the town because of the snow and sleet, but we went over the beautiful collections and the Picture Gallery also over the old Church and down into the vault where it made a most moving impression on me to see the English coffin containing the remains of unfortunate Queen Caroline, resting by the side of her ancestors.

From the Crown Princess

BERLIN, NOVEMBER 27, 1875

I think as you do about O. Montagu.

I am very glad you thought of me on my birthday and that my health was drunk, as I often think I have quite slipped away out of the memory of those at home, and a sign of remembrance is always very pleasing and gratifying to me.

From the Crown Princess

BERLIN, NOVEMBER 30, 1875

I must congratulate you on the newest deed of your Government, the buying of half the shares of the Suez Canal; it sent a thrill of pleasure and pride, almost of exultation through me. It is a delightful thing to see the right thing done at the right moment. Everybody is pleased here and wishes it may bring England good—even the Great Man B. expressed himself to Fritz in this sense yesterday evening. Willy writes from Cassel "Dear Mama, I must write you a line,

---

[1] Captain Oliver Montagu was the third son of the 7th Lord Sandwich. He subsequently was Colonel Commander of the Royal Horse Guards. See *Queen Alexandra* by Georgina Battiscombe, Constable, 1969, for further particulars of this somewhat swashbuckling soldier. In the Prince of Wales's family he was affectionately known as Tut-Tut.

[2] The Crown Prince and Princess were staying with the Duke of Brunswick.

because I know that you will be so delighted that England has bought the Suez Canal. How jolly!!!"

This will mark in History among the many great good and useful things done in your reign, and that makes me so proud and happy. I am sure Mr. Disraeli and Lord Derby must be quite delighted at the accomplishment of so important a measure, and at its popularity.

From the Queen

You are never forgotten and the dear, devoted Highlanders of all people remember when you were carried by them and a friendly merry "lassie"! If I had an observation to make—I should say I thought it was more you who forget them!

The accounts of dear Bertie are good and satisfactory but he does too much!—and in that heat. Today is our beloved Alix's birthday! She is in very good looks. The Queen,[1] I think a good deal aged, she stoops so and is so shrivelled but most amiable. Poor Thyra is terribly plain, though she has fine eyes, but I never saw so hideous a mouth with no chin and a thick flat nose. The eyebrows are too thick—and though she is straight and élancée the figure is angular and she moves ungracefully. She seems a remarkably nice, good girl but certainly very plain.

From the Queen

WINDSOR CASTLE, DECEMBER 4, 1875

I received your dear letter of the 30th the day before yesterday and copied out the part about the Suez Canal for Mr. Disraeli as I knew it would please him so much. He did it, not Lord D. I am so pleased to see how pleased Willy is at the Suez Canal affair.

From the Queen

OSBORNE, DECEMBER 29, 1875

Darling child let me begin by wishing you a very, very happy New Year and every blessing which this very uncertain world can bestow! May God bless, protect and guide you and yours in the path of wisdom and duty—ever trusting to Him,—for many many a long year.

---

[1] Of Denmark.

30th   I could not finish my letter last night and therefore do so today. Many loving thanks for dear letters of the dear children, Charlotte's and Vicky's are very well written. Willy's is a little peculiar as to the English which Henry's is not—but what I grieve over most is the handwriting of both which is bad like their uncles', whereas the girls' is very good. Do watch over that with the dear boys.

Leopold who had enjoyed his Christmas very much is laid up with a bad knee again since yesterday morning which came on suddenly the night before last without any reason that we can think of—but I fear he stood too long in the wet grass and excited himself playing at golf—which his naturally very weak and susceptible legs will not bear.

1876

From the Queen

One word to thank you for your long letter of the 2nd received yesterday which I will answer *au long* another day—but I must scold you very much for the extraordinary way in which you speak of my not being interested in your children when (excepting the two eldest) I saw them continually only 18 months ago—and that you would have written volumes to Papa which means that he understood it and I— who have had quite as much experience and whom he consulted upon every single point—do not!! I feel this, but know it always was so.

But you will find as the children grow up that as a rule children are a bitter disappointment—their greatest object being to do precisely what their parents do not wish and have anxiously tried to prevent.

From the Crown Princess

We have been doing our utmost here to persuade our Government authorities to send things to the Exhibition of Scientific Instruments to be held this year at Kensington, and I hope we have succeeded. I do not know whether you take any special interest in the undertaking, which seems to me a most excellent one. Mr. Owen was here to meet our professors and officials. What a pity that he has resigned for the Exhibition of Philadelphia. He is really so excellent in his special branch.[1]

From the Queen

Dear Augusta[2] . . . continues the same—one day weaker and one a little stronger—very suffering from restlessness giving the most

---

[1] The loan Exhibition of Scientific Instruments was opened by the Queen on May 15 following, and included exhibits from most European countries and the United States. Francis Philip Cunliffe-Owen (1828–94) was Director of the South Kensington Museum with particular responsibility for the British side of the then fashionable international exhibitions. He started as English Commissioner for the Philadelphia Exhibition, which was held to mark the centenary of the Declaration of Independence, but, owing to personal difficulties, resigned.
[2] Lady Augusta Stanley, wife of the Dean of Westminster.

touching and beautiful messages and directions about everything—wishing Fanny should take care of "her Arthur" and live at the Deanery; then that her "darlings" should wear her things, so that she might feel she should be among them—in short too beautiful and touching! I own I feel it dreadfully! For since darling Aunt F.'s death she has been, as it were, the last link[1]—and her unselfishness was and is so wonderful. Alas! the present generation are so terribly selfish.

Poor old Lord Russell's eldest son Lord Amberley is dead. He is no loss but it is terrible for poor Lady Russell whose second son is mad! The old Lord is past feeling it much I hear. Still it is very sad to think of.

From the Queen

OSBORNE, JANUARY 19, 1876

I feel and enter into all your anxieties and troubles about your dear children, but Papa and I felt the same. But experience has taught me alas! that youth is so wayward and foolish that all one's wish to make them do what is for their good and what is the best is useless! One must try and pray for them to be guided for the best—and must leave them to learn by experience what they will not do from confidence in and affection for their parents. But how it hurts oneself it is difficult to express. It is a great, great trial. But as one goes on in life, one learns to bear this better. Most extraordinary it is to see that the more care has been taken in everyway the less they often succeed! And often when children have been less watched and less taken care of—the better they turn out!! This is inexplicable and very annoying.

I can assure you that, though in each individual grandchild I can't take the same interest, I do in the anxieties of each of my children about their children and yours—especially the elder ones—the very greatest. How I wish you would send Willy and Henry before they are older to come and see me. To Scotland, how nice and how good for them that would be.

From the Crown Princess

BERLIN, JANUARY 25, 1876

I shall ask Uncle Ernest and Aunt Alexandrine to let me come to them during your stay at Coburg so as to be there should you wish to

---

[1] With the Queen's mother to whom Lady Augusta was Lady-in-Waiting.

see me; and at Baden I can be near too, but you need not fear my being in your way—or taking up too much of your time and leisure. You do not know what the effect would be in Germany if I were not allowed at least to be in the same place as you are, but of course I wish in no way to be a *gêne* or a burden and would only come when you wish to have me. I trust this will not annoy you, you see me so very seldom that I trust these few days will not be too much.[1]

From the Queen

OSBORNE, FEBRUARY 2, 1876

Bertie's progresses lose a little interest and are very wearing—as there is such a constant repetition of elephants—trappings—jewels—illuminations and fireworks.

Pray say everything kind and civil to the Grand-Duke and Grand-Duchess[2] on the occasion of the marriage, offer my good wishes to the bridal pair. Can you send me photographs of them and of the younger sister? If the Grand-Duke and Grand-Duchess should ask about my coming abroad and say they wished to come and see me—say positively that I must decline every visit but the very nearest relations, as I only come for a very few days quite privately and could make no exceptions. For this reason pray come as quietly and with as few people as possible —and as my daughter and not as the great Crown Princess of Germany —for it would be quite out of character on such an occasion.

Poor dear Henry, I am sorry he gets on so slowly but he is so good and amiable that will make up for learning.

From the Queen

WINDSOR CASTLE, FEBRUARY, 9, 1876

I am terribly pressed for time and can only write very hurriedly but I must just observe that it is very strange and not right in you to take all my observations about your meeting me or coming to see me always amiss. You may not at all be aware of it—but your people already in '65 showed at Coburg how completely they were above the people there and of course now these feelings can hardly be improved. You I think also hardly know with what a suite you always move about—which makes everything difficult. This is not said to offend

---

[1] The Queen replied that she thought she could have the "pleasure of getting a glimpse of you . . . it would look strange indeed if you did not meet me". 29 January.
[2] Of Saxe-Weimar; their daughter married Prince Reuss on February 6. The Empress was sister to the Grand-Duke.

but as the truth. To see you both is always a pleasure, but you hardly know how tired and fagged I am, overpowered with work, and how easily I am knocked up and tired, I never get to bed till one—and with the greatest wish to see those I love I must have time to rest—not because you are in my way.

From the Queen

You ask who I bring; Baby, Lady Ely, Lady Churchill, General Ponsonby, Colonel Byng and Sir William Jenner. Leopold made such a point of going to the South that though the doctors think it not at all necessary and I had wished him to go with me abroad as I had put off my going till this year and moreover as I thought one[1] might remain in England when all are away his usual self-will and great selfishness made him wish to go—and so he goes away on the 2nd of March and he will stay away three months.

From the Queen

I have been giving several dinners—yesterday Count Münster and his daughter dined, and the Duke and Duchess of Somerset (she grown perfectly enormous), Lord and Lady Salisbury, and Lord and Lady Grey (grown very old) and Sir Garnet Wolseley. And on Monday we had the French Ambassador and Madame d'Harcourt (very charming people), the Lord Chancellor and Lady Cairns, the Dalkeiths etc. and on Wednesday Count Beust, Lord Malmesbury, the Bedfords, Lord Granville, Lord and Lady Bradford etc.—on Monday Count Schouvaloff (if the poor Grand-Duchess Mary does not die before),[2] Lord and Lady Halifax, Lord Hardinge, Lord Carnarvon and Lord and Lady Ilchester dine.

From the Queen

That singular dear Lady—the Empress of Austria—is really coming over here to hunt!!! I think it very unbecoming as well as

---

[1] i.e. One prince.
[2] The Russian Ambassador; the Grand-Duchess died on February 21. She was the Emperor's aunt, and had married first the Duke of Leuchtenberg and then Count Strogonoff. She frequently visited Torquay and the Isle of Wight.

dangerous and have told Count Beust so—who quite agreed and promised to warn the Emperor but it was too late.

You will be shocked to hear that we have not yet done with the Misletoe[1] and it is really most disgraceful. The tone held by many people including, I am sorry and surprised to say—Count Münster, is most offensive to my Officers.[2] I continue my dinners which is very praiseworthy as they are very tiring.

From the Crown Princess

I wish with all my heart Affie and Leopold would stay at home, because then I could get 2 letters a week from you! which is impossible when they are away! As it is I cannot imagine how you can find time to write so much and so often and often fear it must be fatiguing and cannot be good for you!

I am very sorry to think that you should have fresh annoyance about that unfortunate Mistletoe, and that people should speak unkindly specially that Count Münster is said to have done so, it is not at all like him, and I cannot help thinking that a remark he may have made has been exaggerated in being repeated to you, which after all so easily happens with the best intentions.

It does seem rather strange that the Empress of Austria carries her passion for hunting so far, but I think it is less astonishing to wish to hunt in England than to follow the hounds on the Campagna at Rome instead of looking at the museums, monuments, churches and gardens, but tastes differ in this world and I daresay she thinks it just as absurd for anyone to sit down and draw old houses or dirty looking people!

From the Queen

BUCKINGHAM PALACE, MARCH 6, 1876

Alas! Alas! our beloved Augusta is gone to a happier brighter Home—but we shall miss her terribly. I shall only see the dear coffin when I go there today. The feeling of love and respect and sorrow is very, very great. To me the severance of this tie with the past is a very great pang—and the loss of one so devoted is terrible. I am going there this afternoon after the Levée to see the poor Dean and poor

---

[1] One of the few occasions where the Queen's spelling is at fault.
[2] After the Coroner's inquests an Admiralty minute was published exonerating Prince Leiningen but reprimanding Captain Welch. There was a somewhat acrimonious debate in the House of Commons over this on April 10.

Fanny who is there and will live a great deal there. On Thursday at noon in Westminster Abbey the sad ceremony takes place and I shall see part of it from a private seat or pew at the Deanery which over-looks the Abbey.

From the Queen

BUCKINGHAM PALACE, MARCH 8, 1876

I have ordered a wreath for you for tomorrow. Lady Ely walks representing me, and all the family,[1] male and female, Christian and Lorne go. The pall bearers are I believe to be the Archbishop of Canterbury and Bishop of London, the Dukes of Westminster and Argyll, Tennyson, Principal Caird of Glasgow and two others. She is to be laid in Henry VII's Chapel. You shall hear all later.

Yesterday everything went off admirably in the East end.[2] The day was fair enough though very windy. The crowds immense as great and quite as much enthusiasm as on the Thanksgiving day—and with such pretty decorations and really touching inscriptions in the very poorest parts—several to the "Queen and Empress" and "Empress of India", I have been called so for twenty years and everyone thought I was nearly[3]—only the style was not taken. The title is one easier to compre-hend by the Orientals and very popular in the country, only made use of, as alas almost everything is, as a party thing, not knowing I cared for it really.[4]

From the Crown Princess

BERLIN, MARCH 10, 1876

I see that your title is just what I supposed wished and hoped, i.e. Empress of India added on to the rest, which you have in fact had for 20 years without always using it. I was only afraid it might be other-wise changed. But how about the objection made that the Colonies ought to be named also in your title?

From the Queen

WINDSOR CASTLE, MARCH 22, 1876

I am so overwhelmed with work that I can hardly write properly and I fear this will be the case all this week. There has been a really

---

[1] i.e. the Queen's children.
[2] The Queen was opening the new wing of London Hospital.
[3] Meaning "nearly everyone thought I was".
[4] The Liberals disliked the title of Empress as indeed did the Prince of Wales.

most disgraceful opposition and misapprehension (which did not exist till Mr. Lowe's and Mr. Forster's speeches) against the legalising of my title of Empress of India and my name has been discussed and dragged about in a way which I feel deeply and shall not easily forget.[1] They were so delighted to annoy the Government that they did not think how offensive it was to me and this after I had taken care that they should know it was my wish! I hope however it is now past and that there will be no more annoyance.

I hear constantly of the poor dear little Dean and from Fanny B. The sermons are very touching, fifteen thousand people passed before her open grave filled with flowers during the few days that it was not closed up!

I can now tell you Leopold's address—Baron Balmoral, Hotel d'Angleterre, Florence. My address will be Countess of Kent, Villa Hohenlöhe, Baden.

From the Queen

WINDSOR CASTLE, MARCH 25, 1876

Just a word to say that I have nothing to add to my letter beyond the perfectly disgraceful and mad conduct of the Opposition on this Bill.[2] I am utterly disgusted with everything and with the wickedness of party which in this instance is carried rather too far.

From the Queen

Prince Albert
On my way to England
APRIL 22, 1876

The Queen is describing her long journey from Coburg, where she had been staying for a few days:

La Villitte is a dreadful, enormous junction with coal depots and all sorts of manufactories like our Clapham Junction and here where there is no *gare*—the Marshal had come out in his carriage as well as Lord Lyons to see me. They were all in plain clothes. Marshal McMahon got

---

[1] In the House of Lords the Duke of Somerset, who was a Liberal, said that the title was merely a trick so that the Queen's children might gain a higher standing in the Courts of Germany. The Queen described this language as ungentlemanlike and unusual. (*Letters* II, 451–2.)

[2] The Royal Titles Bill. Led by Lowe in the House of Commons, 134 members voted against the Bill. In the Lords, Shaftesbury's amendment that the title of Empress should not be used was only rejected by 46 votes.

in and sat a few minutes with me on the sofa and is a very friendly, plain, little old gentleman with quite white hair and a florid complexion.

I was so much pleased to have seen dear Willy, such a dear, amiable boy. And now before concluding let me say a few words about Count Seckendorf who I am sorry should be offended and aggrieved. It is impossible for me to disbelieve Bertie's word. And I think you have only heard one side of the story.[1]

From the Queen

I know that you have many great difficulties—and that your position is no easy one, but so is mine full of trials and difficulties and of overwhelming work—requiring that rest which I cannot get. The very large family with their increasing families and interests is an immense difficulty and I must add burthen for me. Without a husband and father, the labour of satisfying all (which is impossible) and of being just and fair and kind—and yet keeping often quiet which is what I require so much—is quite fearful. You will one day have to encounter this though never like me; for you will not be the Sovereign and please God will always have your dear husband to guide and help you. Dear Willy seems a dear, amiable, good and natural boy. May he ever remain so! I shall always take the warmest interest in him.

Writing of Princess Beatrice the Queen says:

She well deserves being loved, for a dearer, sweeter, more amiable and unselfish child I never found and she is the comfort and blessing of my declining years. 'Benjamina' as Aunt Alexandrine calls her.

From the Crown Princess

BERLIN, APRIL 29, 1876

I see Bertie and Arthur are at Madrid.[2] Is not Louis Battenberg's rank a trifle overdone when he travels with Bertie? He is such a very nice young man that one cannot wonder at Bertie taking him up so much, perhaps more than may be quite good for him.

---

[1] He was a member of the Crown Prince's Household, and this possibly refers to an overbearing manner in the German retinue to which the Queen alluded in her letter of February 9.

[2] On his way back from India the Prince met the Duke of Connaught at Gibraltar. Together they spent 3 weeks in Spain and Portugal. Prince Louis of Battenberg (1854–1921) was promoted lieutenant at the end of the Indian tour.

From the Queen

I quite agree with you about Louis Battenberg and so does Alice. His parents are distressed at it.

From the Queen

WINDSOR CASTLE, MAY 6, 1876

The Empress's visit is passing off extremely well. I am unfortunately suffering with headaches and not feeling very well—and tired—but she is most kind and discreet and it is a great satisfaction to talk to so old and kind a friend of near my own age (though she is seven years older). Aunt Alexandrine being the only other very intimate friend I have left besides, who is of my own rank and age, and I never hardly see her.

From the Queen

BUCKINGHAM PALACE, MAY 10, 1876

The dear Empress seems to enjoy being here—but I think (and she says so herself) she cannot do as much and is more easily tired than formerly.

From the Crown Princess

NEUES PALAIS, POTSDAM, MAY 12, 1876

We had a love of a Dackel, which I told you about, such a beauty and quite like a member of the family—a darling thing and Waldemar's pet, he was quite wrapped up in this dog, his only playfellow upstairs. The day before yesterday a carriage went over it and killed our dear dog. I cannot say how poor Waldy feels it, he would not eat, he sobbed all night and his tears flow fast whenever any allusion to his poor pet is made. I am very sorry as I was very fond of the poor dear thing!

From the Queen

WINDSOR CASTLE, MAY 16, 1876

I took leave of the dear Empress with the greatest regret on Saturday evening at B. Palace. She was so kind to everyone, to my people—Ladies, Gentlemen and my good servants a friendly word to all, which gives such pleasure. Her kindness towards me which, ever since '51, has never varied, only increases with years and I know that it is a great comfort to her to be with me. She spoke most kindly of you and yours—and Fritz.

Bertie's arrival and the hearty reception he met with and I also met with, which was very striking and of which I sent you an account in the *Daily Telegraph* as *The Times* did not condescend to notice—was a proof of the immense loyalty of the country in spite of the attempts of the Opposition (not all) and of their very radical supporters as well as of the Press to agitate and rouse them against the Throne in which they themselves say they entirely failed, is very remarkable and very gratifying. When I appeared at the window—though Bertie with Alix and the boys were just driving away—the whole immense crowd turned round and cheered and waved their handkerchiefs without ceasing—then I led the Empress forward and then I had to appear again alone.

From the Queen

WINDSOR CASTLE, MAY 18, 1876

You speak only of the enthusiasm for Bertie! That for your own Mama was I thought much greater.

From the Crown Princess

NEUES PALAIS, POTSDAM, MAY 20, 1876

Dearest Bertie's safe return is a great and auspicious event, and the sympathetic and loyal greeting which you received on that occasion must have been most gratifying to you. No people are so truly loyal as the English and that is why you are the happiest among all sovereigns on this earth! Of course difficulties, murmurs, complaints and many a thing that gives one pain you are not spared alas! but still there is more light than shadow—thank God!

From the Crown Princess

POTSDAM, MAY 22, 1876

The lovely Collie has arrived all right and is very friendly to me and to the others—his companion our old Collie, seems more excited to see her new mate. Many thanks for sending him, of course they are quite unknown in this country, but will be all the more admired.[1]

---

[1] The dog had come from Norfolk Farm at Windsor. The Queen said that he had had distemper, and that he should not be given much meat.

I have put on a very slight mourning for poor Lenchen's little one, and we shall have no child's dance on your birthday.

From the Queen

The Oriental affair is very disagreeable. But we could not accept the proposals though we have in no way advised the Porte to reject them or to count on our support if they did so. Our wish would be to act with the other Powers but we feel that the proposals are such as cannot be entirely accepted as they are impracticable. But we hear that modifications will be asked for by the Porte. It was wrong to exclude us from these Conferences as England has more to do with the East than with any other country.[1]

From the Crown Princess

The Oriental Question does fidget one in the extreme! Every wish is shown here to go with England, and the fault does not rest with our Government that England did not take part in the Conferences—I think they would have been only too glad here for such to have taken place. England ought to propose surely, what is to be done, and Germany to second these proposals—which to me our Government seems in every way disposed to do.

From the Queen

The Eastern Question still looks very threatening. I fear Ignatief[2] has done all the mischief but there will I have no doubt be a Conference.
Poor Bertie is laid up with his old bad leg and can't move. I felt sure beforehand that if he tired himself so much when he came back,

---

[1] At this time the Balkans, except for the southern part of modern Greece, were under Turkish sway. In the previous summer (1875) the Bulgars rose in rebellion against the Turks. The three powers most nearly concerned—Russia, Austria and Germany—conferred together in Vienna, and in a document known as the Berlin Note urged that Turkey should agree to a two months' armistice with the rebels. The conferring powers also asked for the support of France, Italy and England. The two former agreed but the English Government, under Disraeli, declined though privately urging moderation on the Turks.
[2] Nikolai Pavlovich Ignatiev (1832–1908), Russian Ambassador at Constantinople (1864–77).

he would break down. And so it is. He tired himself too much, added to cold and a strain and this is the result. Bertie is strong but not as much so as people think and he wears himself out.

From the Queen

BALMORAL, JUNE 6, 1876

Alas your fears as to the poor Sultan's death are realised—only not I believe certainly by other hands than his own.[1] Having seen and known him I can't help feeling sorry for him. Ignatief is the one cause of mischief.

With respect to the Collie as he is only seven months and not very strong it would be better not to try to have a family quite yet. It is often very dangerous and kills a dog. Forgive this explanation but I am so accustomed to have to hear and know about farming and other breeding concerns with the simple, good, pure-minded people who are concerned with them, that I don't scruple to say it to you.

From the Crown Princess

NEUES PALAIS, POTSDAM, JUNE 10, 1876

I feel so sorry for the poor Sultan, and think it such a horrible tragedy! Do you remember my saying that I thought it would happen? I suppose there is no doubt that he was really murdered, on the day of his abdication and that the story of his suicide &c. is only an invention! I think it too cruel and terrible! I am sure the poor man meant no harm. I feel very unhappy about this Oriental Question—as I am so afraid of England and Germany being estranged by it, and really it is not necessary and can be easily prevented. Our Government cannot be more desirous than it is of going with England, and having a thorough good understanding on all the points which England wishes. The Press on both sides does a good deal of harm. The Court here—and a large Party—are very Russian and not well disposed towards England, whereas Bismarck and most sensible people are thoroughly desirous of an English alliance. One cannot trust the French or the Russians, though of course it is very desirable to be friends with them and to

---

[1] Abdul-Aziz, the Sultan who visited the Queen in 1867—see *Your Dear Letter* pages 140–4. His deposition strengthened Anglo-French influence at the Porte and diminished that of Russia. Shortly after his deposition he committed suicide with a pair of scissors. He was succeeded by his nephew Murad V, who had developed a strong attachment for champagne and old cognac and was himself deposed in the following August. He was succeeded by his brother Abdul-Hamid II, who was long known to Englishmen as Abdul the Damned.

keep out of war. If Ignatief goes—there will always be many others of the same kind, found to replace him!

From the Queen

BALMORAL, JUNE 13, 1876

The Oriental affairs do cause much anxiety. There is here also every wish to act with Germany—but we don't want to be doing anything, only to encourage Turkey to carry her own reforms and not to cause endless difficulties by demands, etc., and not as Russia does (though I believe not at this moment) to encourage the Principalities in their insurrections. This is really our only wish. But we cannot be excluded from all councils and discussions and then be asked to join. Affie has sailed to join the fleet at Besika Bay.[1]

From the Crown Princess

NEUES PALAIS, POTSDAM, JUNE 13, 1876

Are you not shocked that the poor Sultan's wives and his old mother (the Sultana Valide) were thrown out of the window and killed, or threw themselves out of the window?[2] Fritz had a long conversation with Prince Bismarck two days ago, and I was to tell you, that Prince Bismarck said it was his wish that England should entirely take the lead in the Oriental Question, and that he was quite ready to follow and back up whatever England proposed. This I thought very nice, and hope that the opportunity may be seized of the two countries acting in concert, England making proposals for what is to be done.

I read with mournful interest the description of the transferring to Dreux of all the coffins from Weybridge, but why not dear Aunt Victoire.[3]

---

[1] At the entrance to the Dardanelles. The Fleet was sent after disturbances at Salonika.
[2] This was a rumour. On June 24 the Queen wrote:
"The Sultana Valide is not dead." What gave rise to the rumour was that the brother of one of the Sultan's wives, having maddened himself with "bang", killed the Minister of War and wounded two other Ministers.
[3] On June 7 the coffins of Louis Philippe, his wife and children—ten coffins in all—were moved at 3 a.m. from Weybridge to Dreux in Normandy. Aunt Victoire, who was the Duchess of Nemours, Louis Philippe's daughter-in-law, was the only Protestant among the party. Probably for this reason it was rumoured that she had been left behind; in fact her coffin was the first to be moved and the first to be landed in France.

From the Crown Princess

What you say about England's attitude in the Oriental Question
we can quite understand. It is curious that Montenegro and some of
the other Principalities should so implicitly obey Russia, that a telegram
from the Emperor Alexander (not Gortchakoff)[1] telling them to be
quiet, completely stopped the fresh outbreak they had planned, and
which was expected at Whitsuntide! We hear the Emperor of Russia
is very angry with England and bitter against it, which I am sorry for;
he is decidedly a man of power and very upright, and it is a pity there
should be ill will! As for the rest of his subjects they are not to be
depended upon in any way. We alas! hear the Empress[2] is very violent
against Turkey and for the insurgents from a religious point of view.
I think everything seems to look peaceful enough now but I fear the
evil day is only put off. Turkey is too far gone to be patched up by
any reforms for long—and the present Sultan is not very different from
his unfortunate predecessor I fear!

From the Crown Princess

Poor Henry does not get on with his lessons, he is terribly hard to
teach, being so lazy, so slow and so utterly indifferent. His spelling and
handwriting do not improve one bit, and he never reads—of his own
accord! He gives a deal of trouble, and as his character is so weak, I
often fear he will be led away when he grows older—to many a thing
which is not right—and it makes me very anxious. Whereas I cannot
help hoping and thinking that Willy will be steady and conscientious,
but one can never tell.

From the Crown Princess

Many many thanks for the few lines I received yesterday; I gave
your letter to Fritz instantly, but he did not wish it translated.[3] He

---

[1] Prince Alexander Gorchakov (1798–1883), Russian Minister for Foreign Affairs
(1856–82).
[2] Presumably of Russia.
[3] The Crown Prince had evidently written to the Queen in the sense of the Crown
Princess's letter of June 13. Before replying the Queen sent the Crown Prince's letter to
Disraeli. In his reply Disraeli said that the British Government was ready and willing to
work closely with Bismarck, though regretting that Bismarck joined in the Berlin Note

thanks you very much indeed, and will tell the Emperor and the Chancellor, and will also ask to see the Despatch you mention. It seems sad to think does it not, that before one can intervene in Turkish affairs a deal of blood must be spilt and many lives lost which might have been saved by timely interference.

From the Crown Princess

NEUES PALAIS, POTSDAM, JUNE 27, 1876

The day before yesterday we went to see the stud at Graditz, which was very interesting and then visited the old town of Torgau on the Elbe, which has an old castle—(former residence of the Electors of Saxony, especially of Frederick the Wise) called Schloss Hartenfels; it has a splendid courtyard, in the Renaissance style! So picturesque. Luther's wife is buried in a church close by, and he often preached there and lived in the town.

May I just say that our vice president of the Council and Minister of Finance (the next in rank to Bismarck) Dr. Camphausen,[1] will be in London almost immediately, and should you give a Garden Party, or a Concert &c. would be immensely flattered if he could get an invitation or be presented to you. He is a great, fat man with a red face and spectacles, rather vain and pompous and I cannot recommend him as amusing or agreeable, but he is a good and honest man. He comes from Cologne, and has the funny accent from there; he has not been in England for more than 20 years. I fancy dear Papa knew his brother—who is a very distinguished man.[2]

From the Crown Princess

NEUES PALAIS, POTSDAM, JUNE 30, 1876

Waldy learns so well, and is such a nice boy to teach, with such a good memory. He is by far the most gifted of the boys, and has the most spirit and energy, he is very unruly sometimes—and headstrong, but he has such an open honest nature, and is so sensible and independent, that I trust he will make a real man someday, if he is spared. He and Fritz Carl's little boy have their gymnastic lessons together—and walk out together, little Fritz Leopold is a most gentle, amiable, tract-

---

without insisting that England should be included. See *Life of Disraeli* by Monypenny and Buckle, Disraeli's letter of June 18.
[1] Otto von Camphausen (1812–96), Prussian Finance Minister from 1869–78.
[2] Ludolph Camphausen (1803–90), Cologne banker and leader of the Rhenish Liberal Party.

able little boy—but shy and delicate and brought up in the most approved orthodox old-fashioned way—which is considered the right thing for a Prussian Prince—luckily the child has such a good disposition that it does him no harm whatever. I think he will grow up very nice, and in temper the very reverse of his Papa. He is very plain and small for his age.

From the Crown Princess

HOTEL D'ORANGE, SCHEVENINGEN, JULY 4, 1876

We are in a pleasant hotel on the sea side. I think the air very delightful in spite of many terrible smells around. The coast is about as ugly as you can imagine—but I am so delighted to see the sea that I do not mind the total absence of trees or grass—or any growing thing! I fancy I feel better and stronger since I am here already. The boys have arrived from Cassel and are very glad to be here. We cannot see as much of them as we should like, as they are obliged to devote a good deal of their time to their school tasks. The Hague is a very pretty little town, so clean and gay looking, and the Dutch are so particularly clean as regards the outside of their houses, for the inside one cannot say as much! The caps and head-dresses the women wear here are very quaint, picturesque and becoming. We went to Leyden yesterday, and saw what was to be seen, not much, but still it was interesting to see a thoroughly Dutch town. The Queen[1] is most civil and amiable to us! I think she is looking ill, however, poor thing. We have begun to bathe in the sea. I look with longing look and melancholy feeling of homesickness across the water, in the direction where dear England lies, and think how different, how far far nicer in every way it is across there, and how much I should wish to be there.

From the Queen

WINDSOR CASTLE, JULY 6, 1876

I had an hour's talk with Lord Odo yesterday which was pleasant and interesting as it always is. I never saw anyone so grateful for kindness or of so little sensitive and touchy a disposition or so fair. We lamented over the state of society (especially in England) of the very bad tone of the young men and I fear young ladies too—and such want of all respect.

---

[1] Queen Sophie (1818–77), wife of King William III of the Netherlands from whom she was separated. Her advanced views gave her the name of La Reine Rouge.

I remain here for another week—that is till the 14th—when I go to Osborne which I do with little pleasure this year as the recollection of last year's misfortune and of the disgraceful behaviour of the yachting people which has made Ernest L.'s and Captain Welch's position —but especially the latter—most disagreeable. Of course I shan't go on the water at all—but I must go there and back by water!

From the Crown Princess

HOTEL D'ORANGE, SCHEVENINGEN, JULY 8, 1876

We dined with the Queen of Holland the other day, and Fritz has been to the "Loo" to see the King;[1] Prince Frederick and Prince Henry are in town, but we have not seen them yet. Prince Alexander we have seen several times, and he has not increased in beauty, poor man. The Queen has a tent here on the sand, where the whole of the *beau monde* of the Hague, and all the people staying here at the hotel, sit out and walk about listening to a band, and displaying their smartest toilettes. This amusement we rather avoid, and prefer a quiet walk on the sands. It is a dull sea, as one sees no ships except a few herring smacks, and no one goes on the water, there is not such a thing as a pleasure boat to be seen, not a sailor anywhere, and of course no pier or harbour of any kind near, only a lighthouse.

From the Crown Princess

HOTEL D'ORANGE, SCHEVENINGEN, JULY 12, 1876

I saw the King of Holland yesterday, for the first time since 1849 at Windsor! I remembered him quite well, but thought him altered of course, very stout and grey! He was most cordial and civil, but the most uncomfortable *"relations de famille"* on all sides, makes it rather difficult what to talk of! The Prince of Orange I never have heard mentioned by anyone. I do not think people quite know where he is, or when he is coming back.

I am so glad you saw dear Lord Odo Russell, he is certainly a pearl not only among diplomatists but among men, and dear Emily is quite his counterpart in every way. They possess universal respect, confidence and good will which is such a pleasure to see, as alas! it is not always the excellent and the worthy who succeed in the world, and who are liked by all.

As for the Oriental Question—I think it is as serious as possible!

---

[1] Castle of Loo, where the King lived, was near Amsterdam.

I fancy my father-in-law is alarmed at England's feeling towards Russia, and thinks it quite unjust, but I do not think this is quite Bismarck's view of the case. So long as England takes and keeps the lead, inviting the three Emperors to join whenever necessary, I think all will go well but vice versa—it will never do.

From the Queen

FROGMORE GARDENS, JULY 13, 1876

Bertie and Alix brought Willy down with them here yesterday and I gave him the Garter here in the house! He looks very well and unaltered.[1] Bertie I don't think very well. And he certainly is absent and preoccupied and not in spirits.[2]

I believe the telegraphic accounts of the horrors committed by the Baschi Buzuks[3] are greatly exaggerated and that nothing is said of the horrors committed on the other side. But I have sent message upon message to ascertain the truth and to remonstrate most strenuously.[4]

Arthur left Liverpool on Tuesday for Edinburgh with his regiment and will take nearly three weeks to get there.

From the Queen

OSBORNE, JULY 17, 1876

The heat is so terrific since the twelfth I can hardly do anything—86 to 92 in the shade and 140–150 in the sun. Upwards of 70 at night! This is too dreadful for anything and quite stupifies me; it is great suffering to me and many—though there are those who don't mind it. Happy people! That accident is too awful 15 poor people killed at once—three died going up to the hospital and 15 more since.[5] Out of seventy injured only twenty are expected to survive! and they were and are in such agonies—it is too terrible to think of! Were it not for this frightful, awful heat I would go over there but I could not face

---

[1] The King of the Hellenes.

[2] Probably because of a personal quarrel with the Churchill family over Lord and Lady Aylesford's matrimonial affairs. See *King Edward VII* by Philip Magnus, Chapter 8.

[3] Turkish irregular troops responsible for the Balkan atrocities. Generally spelt Bashi-Bazouk.

[4] These atrocities threw the nation back "on our rather forgotten humanity" (Gladstone) and opened the door to that statesman's great campaign against the Turk on behalf of the Eastern Christians. To Disraeli, the Queen wrote, "I have been horrified by the details of the massacres in Bulgaria." *Letters* Second Series, II, page 474.

[5] H.M.S. *Thunderer* was undergoing engine trials off Spithead before going to the Mediterranean. The boilers exploded and more than 40 men were killed.

this heat without almost having a fit! I have sent Colonel Gardiner and Dr. McEwan of the *V. and Albert* over there in my name this morning and shall see them when they return.

That war in Serbia is awful.[1] But both sides are as bad. The Sultan is said to be very unwell, others say he drinks dreadfully.

From the Crown Princess

HOTEL D'ORANGE, SCHEVENINGEN, JULY 22, 1876

Admiral Sir Edward Harris[2] is most civil and kind, and his wife also. They allow the children to play lawn tennis in their garden. They have five pretty daughters, and seem much liked and esteemed here, at Court and in Society. I do not know whether you know them? The "relations" in the royal family here are most sad, and yet the Dutch are so loyal and so devoted to their dynasty! The Prince of Orange behaves too terribly. He has been away at Paris, only with a valet, now for more than a year, has quarrelled with his father, and a complete bankruptcy threatened him a little while ago—when Prince Henry most generously paid an enormous sum of money for him, *"pour le tirer d'embarras"*! Does it not seem too bad?

Is it true that Carlo Hamilton has turned Roman Catholic and become a Priest; that would be too strange, I suppose it is a mere invention of the newspapers.[3]

From the Queen

OSBORNE, AUGUST 15, 1876

You will have been surprised at Mr. Disraeli's well-earned elevation to the Peerage—but it was entirely on account of his health which at 72, and not robust, cannot stand the anxiety and responsibility in addition to the lead of the House of Commons and the late hours. Sir S. Northcote succeeds him in the lead in the H. of C. while he takes it in the H. of Lords. He is immensely popular in the country.

---

[1] The Serbs and Montenegrins, commanded by a Russian General, were openly at war with Turkey.
[2] British Minister at the Hague.
[3] Lord Charles Hamilton (1847–86) son of the 11th Duke of Hamilton and Princess Marie of Baden. His behaviour caused much scandal in Germany at this time. He joined the Roman Church in 1885.

From the Queen

I send you today an Edinburgh newspaper with full accounts of what took place though descriptions can hardly give the impression of the very enthusiastic, warm welcome which I received and which can only be seen in dear Scotland.[1] The decorations were most tasteful and beautiful in that beautiful town. The ceremony—touching, simple and well managed—and I send you the music sung most beautifully on the occasion. Professor Oakley is a fine composer and very fine organist, himself a relation of the Duke of Atholl's and the Drummonds and well known to dearest Augusta. He was dreadfully hurt by being overturned in Switzerland some years ago and is still lame. The whole effect of the statue and group is good—but I do not quite like the statue especially not the horse which is not good—but Sir J. Steell is such a kind, good man with a good deal of talent, that I would not like to have this repeated publicly. Dear Arthur rode by my carriage the whole time, and would not get off even for the ceremony.

From the Queen

BALMORAL, AUGUST 31, 1876

I hope the mediation which all seem anxious for may put a stop to this too awful war.[2] I dare not think of it. But fear the Russians have stirred it up and set it going.

The Sultan is to abdicate or be deposed immediately. He is quite hopelessly stupid or mad from drink, etc. They say he is haunted by the death of his uncle and that his brother does not like to succeed him unless he is sure that his brother cannot recover.

From the Crown Princess

NEUES PALAIS, POTSDAM, SEPTEMBER 4, 1876

Alas, you say right, I fear, when you suppose that the Russians have stirred up the war; one can almost say—it has been the Russians fighting in Serbian dress! There is no doubt that it is all due to their influence, though the Emperor Alexander is personally much against it. He is supposed to be much irritated at this moment against us also,

---

[1] The unveiling of the Albert Memorial at Edinburgh on August 17.
[2] The invasion of Serbia by the Turks. On the 24th the Serbian Government appealed to the Powers to mediate.

because a Congress is not more strongly advocated from here, which Gortchakoff is so anxious for. It is a very critical and uneasy state of things! The war itself is too dreadful to think of, and one can hardly bear the descriptions of the way in which it is carried on.

From the Queen

BALMORAL, SEPTEMBER 9, 1876

You asked me if Sir S. Northcote was not very able. He is extremely so, and a particularly pleasant, amiable, good and conciliatory man who was employed in the Exhibition of '51 and whom dear Papa thought very highly of. He is staying here with us now and is extremely agreeable. Lord Beaconsfield never refused a peerage before—for there never had been any question of it. It was only when in June he said his health could no longer stand the fatigue of the House of Commons and that he could not go on that I pressed it on him, as his retirement would be a very serious calamity.

Eastern affairs occupy us continually and I hope and pray there may soon be a cessation of hostilities. We are doing all we can to bring this about with the other Powers. They made a great deal of noise and abused us very much but were not ready to come forward to press for peace as we are. The new Sultan is said to be fanatical.

From the Queen

BALMORAL, SEPTEMBER 12, 1876

Poor dear Miss Hardinge's death is too sad.[1] I call it butchery and hate these special surgeons who always wish to operate and cut.

The Eastern Question becomes more and more troublesome and those people here (with that incomprehensible Mr. Gladstone, that most mischievous—though I believe unintentionally so—of men at their head)—have gone mad and will not reflect on the great danger of furthering Russia!! It makes our task very difficult. The Russians set the whole thing agoing and it is we only who have been moving very earnestly in the line of peace! But the other Powers seem ready to join and support us. Turkey now is most obstinate.

---

[1] Emily Caroline, daughter of 1st Lord Hardinge. She was Lady-in-Waiting to Princess Alice at Darmstadt.

From the Queen

BALMORAL, SEPTEMBER 16, 1876

Pray send me what music is published of the new opera of Wagner —as I admire his operas very much. I should be very grateful if you would send it me—as Beatrice would play it. Lohengrin is our great favourite but I delight in Gounod too. His Faust, Romeo and Juliet, and *Mireille* and Joan of Arc are so lovely.

From the Queen

BALMORAL, SEPTEMBER 19, 1876

What you say about this dreadful Eastern Question is very true.[1] If the short armistice has been agreed on, *sans m'en vantée*, it is our doing, and not that of those who have so shamefully abused us. Mr. Gladstone's conduct is most reprehensible and mischievous—knowing as he does the difficulties of the government and therefore I call it shameful and unjustifiable in him and that horrid Mr. Lowe to try and make our difficult task more difficult. Affie's visit to the Crimea is unfortunate and I greatly fear he will become very Russian.

The Times has become most mischievous and stupid.[2]

Bertie has got Count Redern here!! I thought of what you once told me. I am more than ever anxious about the future in that direction. Matters are worse than they were.[3]

From the Queen

BALMORAL, SEPTEMBER 26, 1876

The dreadful Eastern Question looks better, but the mad delusion of the country here and the disgraceful conduct of that mischief-maker and firebrand Mr. Gladstone as well as of some (not all) others of the late Government makes our difficult task more difficult. It is very, very wrong.

---

[1] The Crown Princess wrote on September 16—"The Russians can not be trusted, it is they who urged on the Serbs."

[2] The great editor, Delane, was growing increasingly ill and as Disraeli said there was no "political head" in Printing House Square. *History of The Times*, Vol. II. 507.

[3] See the Crown Princess's letter of March 3, 1877.

From the Queen

Count Redern I was sorry to see here. The selection of friends is very distressing. Of affairs I really can hardly speak—it is very confused and critical and some of the former Ministers have really much to answer for and I feel, as dear Papa did, the great and lamentable want of patriotism.

From the Queen

The state of Eastern affairs is most critical—but as long as the Powers don't act separately, and keep together, there is no real cause for apprehension and if the Porte refuses to accept the propositions for peace which she made, which is possible as she has great difficulties with her people and the Mahomedans—we shall all have to force her, and how? If only Russia was honest—but she is not and that is the great difficulty. While she joins us in the negotiations the Russian Officers and soldiers keep pouring into Serbia to urge them to fight![1] Bismarck seems ready to act with us, France and Italy also. Austria is in great difficulties.

From the Queen

I am thankful to say that the country seems to be coming round to a knowledge and sense of the extreme danger of letting their just horror of the "atrocities" carry them away into a most dangerous policy of playing our interests into Russia's hands. The accounts today are more cheering and I hope our efforts for a real armistice followed by a conference may be crowned with success!

In a former letter you asked if I thought six Prussian Princes of the younger generation enough and seven Princesses. The former I think too much. Great many Princes without separate vocations I think a misfortune.[2]

---

[1] On September 16 the Porte had agreed to a suspension of hostilities but negotiations were hindered because Prince Milan of Serbia, influenced by Russia, allowed himself to be proclaimed king with all that title's implications of independence.
[2] The Crown Princess is limiting the point to her own children and the descendants of Frederick William III.

From the Crown Princess

The Russians are so clever and so sly that they will end in turning all to their own account and when a settlement is come to they will have gained a great step towards their real design—i.e. possessing Constantinople, and the folly of the Turks is playing the game into their hands! If the Russians do make formal war on the Turks, they will do so with the utmost cruelty! Their so-called Christianity is really no better than the Mahomedanism of the others and they are every bit as corrupt, both in the higher circles of Society and in their *employés* so I don't see their fitness to reform and to civilise from a moral point of view. The great thing is to prevent further horrors cruelty and bloodshed! Everything and anything ought to be done to prevent this surely!

We saw General Schweinitz[1] yesterday. He is gone to Varzin today! I hear that Bismarck is determined to be on the English side! There are many influences at work to drag the Emperor[2] on the other side, but it really does not much matter, except that it is annoying.

From the Queen

Just two words to say that affairs look better—as an armistice of six months would seem to promise so well. But there is always a hitch. The unfortunate thing is (and of that I verily believe there is no doubt) the poor Emperor Alexander cannot to a great extent prevent the Russian movement and that the state of Russia is very alarming.

Next messenger the second volume of dear Papa's life will be sent you which is particularly interesting and important at the present moment as it brings in so much about the Crimean War.

From the Crown Princess

I have not heard a word about Prince Bismarck's views but know that many people are working at him to get him to take the Russian view of the matter, by exciting his distrust of Austria (which I think a misfortune). England, Austria and Italy are our safest and best allies.

---

[1] German Ambassador to Russia, and an old friend of the Czar.
[2] The German Emperor.

Here there is great excitement about the Paris Exhibition, whether or not Germany is to take part. I for my part, wish sincerely she should, for many reasons, but opinions are much divided on the subject.[1]

From the Queen

Two words as I am rather hurried and wrote on Friday—thank you for your dear letter of the 14th. Alas matters *se sont empirés* and I think it looks critical. Still with patience and perseverance united with firmness, all may yet come right. Only Germany should keep firmly with us. Austria too,—and then surely matters could be settled—if the poor Emperor Alexander can restrain his people.

What you said about poor Count Arnim in one of your letters I think most true. It is quite monstrous and shows how little safe one is abroad.[2]

Bertie, Arthur and Leopold are all very sound and strong on this Eastern Question. Affie is not.

From the Crown Princess

The Eastern Question seems just a trifle more hopeful now, a war would be too dreadful would it not? One can hardly contemplate such a thing! Prince Bismarck seems bent on strictest neutrality, but I hear is still very amiably disposed towards England! The Emperor's sympathies, and those of the public here, are quite with Russia. I think a firm alliance with Austria and England and if possible Italy, would be the best for us, and so unprejudiced and sensible people of liberal opinion think here also, but their number is small of course. It seems all dreadfully complicated, and each power to have a different interest of its own! How to reconcile all these wishes, sympathies and antipathies? What does Bertie think of it all, I wonder? Some think Austria may crumble to pieces sooner than Turkey. I hope not. The Russians, the Slavs, the Italians wish it. One feels anxious when one thinks of India and what Russian agents could set on foot there—not a Russian

---

[1] The Paris Exhibition of 1878. The German Government declined to contribute because of the insults and annoyances endured by German residents in France.

[2] Count Von Arnim had been German Ambassador in Paris 1872–4. He had been imprisoned for various short terms in 1874 and 1875 for removing official documents and then to 5 years at this time for treason. The Crown Princess said that he was the victim of Bismarck's "spite and revenge . . . People are so blind in their adoration of Bismarck that wrong appears right. This is a very wicked deed" (7 October).

Army, I believe that need not be feared by us, and we could easily get the better of it, but they are such a hand at intrigues, etc.

From the Queen

BALMORAL, OCTOBER 21, 1876

You had hoped things looked well and alas! they look very bad. And Germany is with Russia! What does that mean after all Bismarck's fine messages and expressions? If only the Powers kept together— Russia could do nothing. Now that Russia's attitude is so very threatening I do hope Germany will do all she can to prevent further bloodshed. It is a very trying, anxious time.

From the Queen

BALMORAL, OCTOBER 24, 1876

Matters look slightly better. It is really absurd for Bismarck to say (as Fritz writes in his letter) that he is ready to go with us—if he knows what we want!! That has been again and again told to the Powers and very clearly, and not a step was taken without their knowing. We want nothing for ourselves!! The six months was approved and supported—and only at the last when Russia and Serbia refused did Germany hang back! Italy behaves very ill. Surely if Turkey (as we heard yesterday she did) is ready to accept the six weeks the others will support her—if Russia in spite of all—tries to occupy any of Turkish territory.[1]

From the Crown Princess

NEUES PALAIS, OCTOBER 25, 1876

I have just received your dear letter of the 21st with many thanks! I have shown it to Fritz and am to tell you from him what he thinks, as he fancies you will prefer having an English letter to a German one, and I write our own dear honest tongue better and quicker than he can! You say "Germany is with Russia!!" What does this mean, after all Prince Bismarck's offers and messages and promises?" We have no

---

[1] This letter concerns the struggle between Serbia and the Porte. Though Russian led, the Serbians had been decisively defeated by the Turks. The Russians suggested an armistice for 6 weeks, but the Turks wished for 6 months. The Crown Princess told the Queen on October 12 that the Russians wanted the shorter term because it was "no joke for them" to have to keep their own Army on a war footing for 6 months.

precise information as to how Germany is supporting Russia but from what we can gather from different well-informed sources, we have perceived the German Government gradually leaning towards Russia, and not towards England and Austria. It is sorely against Prince Bismarck's will and liking I am sure, as he does not care for a Russian alliance—but an alliance he must have being in the disagreeable position of having always to be on his guard against France. This spring he would have given anything for a hearty response to his overtures! He wanted to know what British policy was going to be, and he would have backed it up,—he got no answer, or only what was so very vague —that he said to himself as indeed all Germany does, oh! there is no use in reckoning on England or going with England, she has no policy, will do nothing, will always hang back so there is no help for it but to turn to Russia, though it be only a *"pis aller"* for a better alliance and one more congenial to us and more in harmony with our interests! Austria is too weak, too unsettled, in too shattered and precarious a state to be any use as an ally; the only strong power—willing to stand by Germany when she is in a pinch, is Russia, therefore we must— whether we like it or no—keep on the best terms with her, and serve her—so that she may serve us, as she did in 1870. Surely Prince Bismarck is not to blame for this. It is only common prudence and good sense to make sure of having a strong friend when one is liable to be attacked any day! If Lord Derby had spoken out in the spring and if the Berlin memorandum had been accepted, matters would now stand differently. Bismarck wanted England alone to decide the Eastern Question, play the first part and have the *beau role* now taken by Russia to my intense disgust. I think it is not too late now to come to a satisfactory and close understanding with Prince Bismarck, as at any moment Russia may go even a step farther than Germany can quietly agree to. I hope that if no peace is come to satisfactorily now, and that the Russians occupy Serbia and Montenegro that then England will persuade Austria to occupy Bosnia, and England herself send Lord Napier at the head of the troops to occupy Constantinople and the British fleet into the Black Sea. I am certain this would be the very best thing! There would be no war, Turkey would carry out the reforms which were enforced, Germany could I am sure back up Austria and England—and Roumania which is dying to be supported by England and Austria, would add to counterbalance any overweight of Russia! At last some arrangement could be come to which would be satisfactory and lasting! Fritz is so very strong on the matter that he wished me to say all I could in support of this view! He has not seen Prince Bismarck lately! Could not a special letter, message, or person though no one could be so good as Lord Odo Russell, be dispatched to Prince Bismarck?[1]

From the Queen

With respect to your letter of today I can assure you that the Government are as alive to the great danger of Russia having her own way as possible and mistrust her to the greatest possible extent.[2] But we have such terrible difficulties first in the very unreliable conduct of the other powers—with whom we wish so much to act (Lord Beaconsfield especially being so anxious to act with Germany) who first agree to a thing and then turn round. And secondly in the stupid shortsightedness and really mad folly of the philanthropists in the country who have rendered all active support of Turkey impossible. Great distrust of Russia there is now and the feeling is changing— but the mischief has been done! I don't think you seem to understand this sufficiently—but all sensible Liberals condemn the conduct of Messrs. Gladstone and Lowe very strongly. Mr. Forster has acted very differently and honourably and I hear Lord Hartington has come back greatly condemning the conduct of the two mischief-makers. It is not a party question and the hands of Governments ought to be strengthened in every way. We are the only honest people and therefore our task of dealing with others who are not so is dreadful. There is however every intention and the determination to be firm and in case of Russia's attempting an occupation we should take care to prevent Constantinople becoming their prey. This is confidential to you but you may rely on that.

Affie is I am afraid quite Russian and I have had to warn him strongly.

From the Queen

BALMORAL, OCTOBER 31, 1876

Things have much changed since you wrote—Russia has made decided and more reasonable proposals, and the armistice is sure to be settled. As regards Bismarck's wish for an alliance, the sort of one he

---

[1] On October 28 the Crown Princess assured the Queen that she and her husband thought that on the Eastern Question Bismarck's views were "simple and honest".
[2] "What alarms me sometimes is the vague fear or feeling that Russia may get the better of everyone. Are people in England quite alive to all the danger?" The Crown Princess, October 23.

wished is simply impossible. No English Government could bind itself to support Germany beforehand. A moral understanding was also difficult for the reasons I have repeatedly given you—though Lord Beaconsfield is always most anxious for that and is so now. I hope and think matters will be arranged, for, once get into a conference and matters will take a very different shape. The feeling in England is quite changed and the Liberals condemn Gladstone and Co. most strongly. The anti-Russian feeling is as strong as ever.

You will have been interested in the account of the Arctic expedition. I hope to see the two Captains here.[1]

From the Queen

Thank God the armistice is signed. The day before yesterday was one of great anxiety. What caused that sudden ultimatum at the very moment when the armistice was being signed no one can tell![2] Probably the extraordinary victories of the Turks—and the feeling in Russia—for so many Russians were killed. The difficulties of a settlement will be very great.

From the Queen

Thank God that there is an armistice, and will be a conference. The great man has behaved very badly—and an alliance between us will I see clearly not be possible. He is now more Russian than English. Lord Odo can tell you this. The poor Emperor Alexander has given the most solemn—and I am sure as regards himself—truly sincere assurances that he wishes for no aggrandizement or territorial possessions.

Only think my horror that Bertie without even saying a word to me has invited the Prince of Orange[3] to Sandringham!! Oh what a contrast to the "noble life" which is now being universally admired

---

[1] The voyage towards the North Pole by *Alert* and *Discovery*. Sir George Nares (1813–1915) led the expedition in the *Alert*, and Captain Stephenson was in command of the *Discovery*. The Queen saw the Captains at Windsor, but warned the Prime Minister against encouraging a further Polar Expedition because of "the great sufferings occasioned by it". *Letters*, Second Series, Vol. II, page 356. "Captain Nares is I suppose the same one, who as Lieutenant wrote the best book on Seamanship that Exists." The Crown Princess, November 4, 1876. The Crown Princess is referring to his *Science and Seamanship*.

[2] On October 31 Russia sent an ultimatum demanding that Turkey should agree to the shorter armistice within 48 hours.

[3] William, 1840–79. A dissolute Prince for whom the boulevards of Paris were the limits of his ambition. See also page 220.

and looked upon as one of the purest and best! I often pray he may never survive me, for I know not what would happen.

From the Queen

I think you don't quite know or understand what has passed or you would see how unreliable Bismarck is.[1] The Russians we know well cannot be trusted—but it seems to me very strange that you say another time the Russians will take Constantinople!! as if we could for one moment (excepting Mr. Gladstone and a few more) tolerate or allow that!!

From the Queen

I have excellent accounts of Arthur. He is so universally respected and liked. He is called "the model Prince" for his wonderfully steady and perfect conduct. He at least follows in his beloved father's footsteps as regards character and sense of duty.

From the Queen

I can well understand your missing Willy and Henry though I am not very fond of boys, and the noise they make.

I hope Lord Salisbury's visit went off well. She is also a very clever and good woman a great friend of our poor, good, little Dean Stanley's.

From the Crown Princess

I can tell you a little piece of news about Coburg which will I am sure give you pleasure, and I have it on good authority. A certain horrid Fraulein Grone in whose power Uncle was, is on the eve of a marriage, and departure from Coburg. What a good thing! May she

---

[1] "I really do not think it is fair to say the great man has behaved very badly. . . . I see no obstacle, in him, to England's and Germany's going together.

I am certain they [the Russians] want to make tributary states of Roumania and Bulgaria, which will be as good as Russian—then they can cook up a fresh question whenever it suits them. The next time . . . the Russians will find the opportunity for taking Constantinople". The Crown Princess, November 11.

never have a successor, I am sure Uncle would be much happier, and Coburg would be another place again.

From the Crown Princess

He [Willy] is still so very childish dear boy, and I am thankful to say very fond of me, which I only hope may not diminish when he is out in the cold world which laughs at all genuine feeling and has a false standard of its own.

We are having very great difficulties with the Emperor just now about the children and unpleasant scenes. He is alas! very autocratic and tyrannical and very obstinate in these matters and Fritz takes it dreadfully to heart and it makes him very bitter and excites and distresses him very much. It is hard to be always interfered with and it does irritate one beyond measure to have one's children perpetually meddled with, and ridiculous, injurious, old traditions and prejudices forced upon one, when one tries to educate them usefully and sensibly and according to the requirements of the day, instead of according to the absurd old rules of 100 years ago, when a Prince was little else than an ignorant and useless doll, a puppet in other people's hands, and only there for show and make-believe. I hope we shall gain our point however, it is really very necessary and important.

From the Queen

Baby has written to you about that wretched Leopold—who has through constant carelessness—and absolute disregard of his doctor's advice to be careful and not tire and expose that much enfeebled leg—which had three attacks of swelling in it—got a most dreadful leg and is away at that place he would take—which is very much out of the way and where he can't have us with him! God knows how long he may be! This with all the anxieties we already have and the incredibly unpatriotic conduct of the Opposition, which hampers the Government as it does such incalculable harm abroad, really quite makes me ill.

I have no time to write long about politics tonight but never in my experience have I seen such behaviour—speeches and excitement tried to be got up and all in favour of Russia! If you only knew how it worries me for they act in a way to make Russia think we shall do what ever they wish! As for France wishing to attack you—it is really to me wonderful that you will believe that possible. On the contrary they are in the greatest fright that Bismarck, who is so utterly unscrupulous, will attack them, and are in the greatest dread of it. I don't think Bismarck will ever understand England, for England never could agree to the sort of alliance he wishes.

From the Crown Princess

BERLIN, DECEMBER 6, 1876

You say the French are in dread of our attacking them and do not dream of attacking us! Their present Government does not, but you cannot doubt that the idea of *une revanche* is always in the heads of the larger part of the nation and that a favourable opportunity is only being waited for. No sensible Frenchman desires this—but the wise and moderate there hope as we do—that time will soften this idea, and that a Government like the one they have now will succeed in lessening the desire for *revanche*, but that it exists largely no one doubts. However after years of peaceful intercourse it may yet go to sleep and become a thing of the past. It would be terrible indeed if we were never to be peaceful neighbours any more, each be afraid of being attacked by the other, and fearing that one another's strength was a menace. I trust this feeling will diminish. That our position is more precarious than that of the French one must allow! We are shut in on all sides by powers of whom we are not wrong in assuming that they would be glad to join any enemy of ours to crush us. Our great man is exactly what you say; but still the nation know their position and look to him for the best safeguard against the dangers I have named. The feeling is in no case a comfortable one.

From the Queen

WINDSOR CASTLE, DECEMBER 9, 1876

I was so very sorry to see by your letter of the 28th that you have so much trouble with the education of the children. I never mention any of your concerns to the Empress—though she is so dear and true and intimate friend of mine.

Leopold is of course quite laid up but free from pain and fever now. His wilful neglect of the advice of all near him really prevents one pitying him, for if he would only be just a little prudent he might have so agreeable a life and one of use to others, but he throws all away and the result is this severe attack which he has now got and will I am sure permanently weaken that leg which has had already five previous attacks within the year!! He will lose his Christmas and be very lonely and entirely his own doing.

Sir S. Maxwell the distinguished author got the Thistle today—a great distinction.[1]

I hope you have thanked Mr. Martin for the second volume. It has the most immense success and has raised Papa's memory in the eyes of the public who did not previously know all he was and did.

---

[1] Sir William Stirling-Maxwell; it was unusual for a commoner to be made a Knight of the Thistle.

1877

From the Queen

I received your letter of the 30th duly on the morning of the 1st and thank you much for it. It was a great day with you[1] and a glorious eventful one in India. Everything went off most admirably! I had two long telegrams on the 1st from the Viceroy which reached me that same evening. My health was drunk at our table and at my others in the house as "The Queen and Empress of India".

I will thank dear Fritz for his dear letter when I have a little breathing time. Let me however at once correct an impression, which as usual my letter seems to have conveyed. You both seem to think that the Empress has complained (which I must here state she does not to me—intimate though we are) of not having known anything about it before.[2] She never said a word about that; but I observed (as I know from various experiences that that is so often the case) that very likely she did feel that, though it was, as you say perfectly impossible as you yourselves did not [know]. Fritz and you have given me the probable key to the whole, viz, that the Empress never liked Bernard, though she never said this to me—but I have heard that he is not liked by everyone, though all think him clever and highly to be respected— which if he is kind and affectionate to dear Charlotte is everything.

From the Crown Princess

God knows I have no reason to entertain one kindly feeling towards Prince Charles, for he has always done me all the harm he could, but now his grief is so great that I cannot help feeling for him,[3] he cries all day long and sobs like a child and will not be comforted; he is really a pitiable object—as he has grown very old and broken of late— and wonderful to say, he and Aunt Charles always got on so very well together and were very happy and harmonious in their way. I cannot

---

[1] Celebrations to mark the 70th anniversary of the Emperor's military career; this began when he was 9.
[2] The engagement of the Crown Princess's daughter, Charlotte, to Bernard, Hereditary Prince of Saxe-Meiningen and grandson to Queen Victoria's sister.
[3] Princess Charles was dying.

say how sorry I am for her, she was always pleasant and amiable to me—and I think really liked me, after her own fashion, as I fancy that did not prevent her from often talking very differently of one behind one's back, still she was always very kind when we met, and very kind to the children. And I feel quite upset—and unstrung by the thought of her sufferings and all the sad scenes which are in store for us!

It is very likely poor Addy's sad affairs may finally lead to a divorce. Fritz has the whole business to manage, and it is a deeply painful and disagreeable one in every way.[1]

Adolphus Strelitz was looking so happy and proud of his engagement. His bride is a very nice, well-brought-up, good girl, with a beautiful head, an awkward ugly figure and a very small allowance of brains, but for this young men seem usually not to care, and on the whole one may say that unintelligent women are the happiest, if going through life as smoothly as possible really constitutes happiness.

From the Queen

WINDSOR CASTLE, JANUARY 6, 1877

I can't tell you how grieved I am at the sad accounts of poor dear Princess Charles. The Empress is too good and kind—in spite of the harm Prince Charles tried always to do her—not to be deeply grieved at her poor sister's sufferings. But I will say nothing unless she mentions it—of the nature of her illness. Pray say something kind on my part to both the Princess and Prince. Addy's affairs must also be a source of very great annoyance. How few happy marriages there are! And what wretchedness is unhappy married life! Nothing can equal it. Even indifference is bad enough.

I have not time to enter into all your dear letters today. You never even mention the great event at Delhi which exceeded anything that was ever known.[2]

From the Queen

WINDSOR CASTLE, JANUARY 13, 1877

I am much touched at poor Princess Charles being so pleased at my enquiry. Pray do so whenever you go and see her. I told the Empress

---

[1] Princess Alexandrine (Addy) of Prussia had married Duke William of Mecklenburg-Schwerin; he died two years later, and there was no divorce.
[2] On January 1 the Queen was proclaimed Empress and a Durbar, attended by the Princes and 100,000 people, was held on the Ridge, just outside Delhi, which was famous as the British base during the Mutiny.

also to do so. Alas! there never was any harmony between them and I think it is not desirable to have two sisters married into the same Royal Family. Poor Princess Charles was most particularly kind to me always, and always sent me such kind messages.

I wish now to ask you a question which pray answer quite openly and frankly. It is whether you would like me to give dear Willy the Grand Cross of the Bath (Civil Division) on the occasion of his coming of age. I have given it to many near relations—and I could not very well give him the Garter as he is not the Heir-Apparent—and I have never given it to any Crown Prince.[1] However if you think it is not enough pray tell me so and I won't do it, and shan't take it the least amiss if you would rather not. I am sure having so steady a future brother-in-law in the same country will be of the greatest help. My poor dear Henry (from whom as well as from dear Willy I had a very nice letter) will I hope remain steady—but Princes are so indulged and flattered in society—and people are so bad, that unless there is real good principle—religious as well as moral—and a strong sense of duty —it is impossible to resist evil.

On January 18 the Crown Princess wrote to the Queen a letter which was a model of tact, stating that nothing would make her so proud as to see an English Order "on my son's breast", but that as the Emperors of Russia and Austria and the King of Italy had already sent their highest order, Germans would misunderstand it if England sent only an Order which was not equivalent to the others.

From the Queen

WINDSOR CASTLE, JANUARY 20, 1877

It must have been a very sad scene, and one to make a deep impression.[2] How I wish it might bring all together! Oh! do think how short life is and how sad it is if comparative trifles cause heartburnings! I know the many trials and difficulties there are around you but try and bear them and above all let there be a kindly feeling towards the poor Empress who has never had a happy life! Especially Fritz should be loving and forgiving to her. He owes her so much! Papa knew that and she never complains (as you both perhaps think she does) and I do so wish there could be a little more harmony in the family.

I think it very dreadful that everyone was there. That I shall insist is never the case if I am dying. It is awful!

Poor dear Princess Charles she was very kind to me and Papa when

---

[1] The German Crown Prince was invested with the Garter after his marriage, but the Queen is clearly referring to those who were not members of her family.
[2] Princess Charles's death-bed.

we were at Potsdam and breakfasted at Glineke[1] pray do not forget
to say something kind and feeling to poor Prince Charles. I know they
were really in a manner happy together.

From the Crown Princess

BERLIN, JANUARY 20, 1877

Here we can think of little else than poor Princess Charles's death!
It is strange that the Empress will only wear a black silk gown—such
as one does when one is not in mourning occasionally, and no crape
or merino and only for 4 weeks!! Here people in private life wear
much deeper and longer mourning for a brother or sister.

About the order—there is one thing more, I would say. Louis
of Portugal has just sent his second order—the Torre a Spada—for
Willy.

From the Queen

OSBORNE, JANUARY 24, 1877

Only two words today (I shall write tomorrow) to beg you to give
this letter with the Inkstand to dear Willy on Saturday morning when
Lord Odo will bring the Garter to Fritz to invest him with! I need
not say how pleased I am to do it. He is such an exception. Lord
Beaconsfield was most amiable about it and greatly for it. I was at
first in doubt but upon reflection I thought it in every way right and
good.[2]

From the Queen

OSBORNE, JANUARY 25, 1877

As soon as I got your dear letter about the Order, I reflected on it
and thought, as Willy was my eldest grandchild as well as godson—
and was in a position unlike that of any other (excepting Eddie) that
the exception could be well made and I communicated with Lord
Beaconsfield, who has very large views on all these things as well as
the greatest consideration for my feelings, and he wrote "it appears to
me that there is every reason for Your M. conferring the Garter on
Y.M.'s princely grandson and not one reason against it. Such an act

---

[1] So spelt. But more usually Glienicke.
[2] In those days the Garter was given after consultation with the Prince Minister. The
Emperor and the Crown Prince were members of the Order; the Queen noticed that it
was very unusual for three generations of the same family to be thus honoured.

of Sovereign grace should and must from its nature be rare, but it should also be complete. The young Prince will never forget that on his birthday he received from Y.M. the most illustrious order of Christendom." This is so prettily said that I copied it for you.

I will not today dwell on the sad event of poor Princess Charles's death but I regret the short mourning and I am even more surprised at your not even having a black edge, which even for a cousin we would wear and which I have seen you use for less near relations. Perhaps you had none?

From the Queen

OSBORNE, JANUARY 27, 1877

I cannot resist writing a few lines again on this dear and eventful day—one which you can hail together—which was not my lot![1] But I don't repine for much there was and has been which beloved Papa could not have borne as I have! That I know—changes in public affairs for the last ten to twelve years which he would have resisted and could not, which might have done him harm.

All you say about the dear Empress and yourselves I understand. I only just always urge to try and overlook those difficulties. She has spoken kindly and sadly of her poor sister but strangely with no affection. It is better than to pretend it—where you don't feel it. I know that Prince Charles was the cause of this! and blood does not make affection. Friendship is far stronger than that! Happy is it when both exist.

From the Crown Princess

BERLIN, JANUARY 27, 1877

This must really be a letter of thanks—for you have showered kindness on us, not the least happy moment of this memorable day, was the one at which Lord Odo brought the Order of the Garter. Fritz invested Willy and my British heart felt much touched and elated— and involuntarily I felt the words rise to my lips—"God bless the Queen". William duly feels the honour conferred upon him.

You say you are astonished that I write without a black edge. It is so very rarely done in Germany. Only widows or people in mourning for their parents or children use black-edged paper and many even not then. The mourning is very short, and today we are invited to a large

---

[1] In fact the Prince Consort was alive when the Prince of Wales was 18, and came of age.

dinner at the Emperor's and are to appear out of black. Prince Charles was at the Investiture today. Dear Willy went through all the ceremonies today very well, and was neither too shy nor too forward. I trust he will not forget all the good advice he has received today and all the kindness shown him.

From the Crown Princess

BERLIN, JANUARY 28, 1877

Bernard of Meiningen will send his photograph very soon, one has been done on purpose for you but I think it very bad—and it does not show his nice, kind, frank expression, his fresh, healthy complexion and bright, white teeth, so rare in a German. He has very fine eyes and a very good well-shaped mouth though it is large. I am doing a head of him now but I get on very slowly and he is so extremely lively that it is quite a business to get him to sit still for one minute! His birthday is on the 1st of April, that will be Easter Sunday, and the day on which the betrothal will be declared. How kind of you it would be—if you have an engraving of dear Aunt Adelaide's picture by Winterhalter to send him one on his birthday! I am sure he would frame it and hang it up and prize it so highly.

From the Queen

OSBORNE, FEBRUARY 3, 1877

How entirely I do enter into all your anxieties about Willy! One can only do one's best—give good advice and pray to God to guide and help them—and the rest must follow. If (as in dearest Arthur's case) he has good, right principles he will go unharmed through the many temptations which especially surround the higher classes and Princes most of all. It is no doubt very trying to be prevented from doing all one feels right from prejudices and antiquated notions, but it is also very trying not to be able to influence parents in the right course as I feel so often to be the case.

From the Queen

OSBORNE, FEBRUARY 6, 1877

Let me thank you so very much for your dear, long and confidential letter of the third—which I shall destroy as you wish. I can so well enter into what you feel. It is very trying and very hard. Justice and gratitude are often met with, but not where and when one has a right to expect them.[1] You will understand many of my trials and heartburn-ings now, which you could not before and you will I think suffer perhaps more than I did and do. You will feel the change when Char-lotte is married very painfully; the real son-in-law with all his rights is very different to the fiancé. It will be a great trial you will see.

From the Crown Princess

BERLIN, FEBRUARY 10, 1877

Midhat Pasha's fate is a strange thing.[2] To me it seems as if Ignatief wanted to arrange a revolution at Constantinople and consequently used his influence to get Midhat Pasha, who seems to be a clever and energetic man—and one who really wanted to introduce reforms—sent away, and put Edhem Pasha in his stead because the latter is a con-servative and Turk of the old stamp, who will not hear of a constitu-tion and consequently may irritate the reform Party at Constantinople. As soon as Ignatief will have gained his point of disturbances at Con-stantinople I suppose the Russians will walk in to the Country and say —now the time has come to protect the Christians and put all this anarchy to an end. This would be a very clever game of the Russians —and very short-sighted of the Turks; and rather annoying to the rest of Europe that the Russians should manage to get their way in the end.

But this is all only a surmise of mine and I may be quite wrong, but it does not seem unlikely. As for the peace of Europe, it is England alone that can enforce it, by intervening between the French and the Germans, who are mutually suspicious of each other to an exaggerated degree! I do not fancy that there is a danger of a war—but I think England could alone take up the part of saying to each—you shall not fight—it is murderous for both of you, and neither can gain anything by it! As you cannot exterminate each other—you must learn to live as peaceable neighbours—and I will not let you cut one another's throats again. The guarantee of peace lies there—i.e. in England; and if the next 20 years pass without a war of *revanche* one may hope that it will be put off for ever, and trade recover the deep depression which

---

[1] Probably criticism of her daughter's behaviour on becoming engaged.
[2] On December 23, 1876, a Conference of the leading European Powers was held at Constantinople. On January 15, 1877, the Conference submitted two proposals to the Turks for ensuring that reforms were carried out. Midhat Pasha favoured the acceptance of these proposals but they were rejected by the Grand Council of Ministers of the Ottoman Empire, and Midhat Pasha fell and was banished. He was Grand Vizier and progressive.

this feeling of insecurity has occasioned. I think England could not have a more grateful or dignified or useful task—and certainly one which is more humane and wise.

From the Queen

I don't think there is any fear of the French wishing to fight now at all, but we must and shall try to warn as much as we can on both sides.

I send you and Fritz today two little medals (the exact miniatures of those given by Lord Lytton on the 1st at Delhi) which I had made to give privately away—which I hope you will wear on your watch chain in remembrance of the Empress of India.

From the Queen

I saw Sir H. Elliot[1] on Wednesday who is a strong liberal, but he is in despair at the way in which he says the Country has been humiliated by the line taken by that half madman Mr. Gladstone—whom he saw and says he found "quite wild", refusing to listen to or believe any facts and ready to hand over Constantinople to the Russians. What do you say to that?

From the Crown Princess

Have you seen in the newspapers a harangue which the Emperor held to William, and I cannot help thinking rather unnecessary and not quite to my taste?[2]

---

[1] Sir Henry Elliot (1817–1907) British Ambassador to Constantinople—possibly more of a Turcophile than the Queen admits. He was recalled after the end of the Conference and was succeeded by Sir Henry Layard (1817–94), the discoverer of Nineveh, who was also a Turcophile, see *Layard of Nineveh* by Gordon Waterfield, Murray, 1963.
[2] After introducing his grandson to his commanding officer the Emperor said:
"It may at first rather surprise you how insignificant many of your duties in your new career may seem; you must learn, however, that nothing in the Service is really small, and that each stone needed to build up an army must be properly shaped if the building itself is to be satisfactory and strong. Now, go and do your duty as it will be taught you. God be with you." *My Early Life* by William II.

From the Queen

The Opposition's attacks about the Eastern Question have entirely collapsed without even a trial of strength, which I hope will have had a very good effect abroad where the wild agitation during the Recess here—had done immense harm.

From the Crown Princess

BERLIN, MARCH 3, 1877

In Mr. Martin's book a letter of dear Papa's is mentioned as having been written to the King of Prussia in 1846 or 1847, on German affairs and Mr. M. says no copy of it has been found amongst your papers.[1] We had the arranging of Fr. W. IV's letters after his death—and I found many of dear Papa's—and Fritz has now hunted out this memorandum of Papa's and one of Uncle Charles Leiningen's which would perhaps be useful to have—either quoted in a later volume, or put into the German edition of this last volume, so we have had them copied for you and send them today.

Count William Redern's debts have amounted to over £50,000, for gambling at cards and on the turf; I think it too disgraceful as he has nothing of his own, nor his father either. Old Redern, whom you remember, has paid every shilling, but as he said: I do not ruin my fortune for my nephews—as for him I would not give a penny but for the sake of his excellent mother. The poor Countess has taken this so dreadfully to heart that she has taken to her bed, refuses to see any-one and cries all day and all night, and he old Henry Redern is so cast down at his son's behaviour that he will not show himself! The young man himself does not seem to see the degraded dishonesty of such behaviour—and thinks himself hardly used. You know how small fortunes are in Germany and how little people are accustomed to luxury and *train du grand monde*—therefore it is doubly wrong of this young man. It is making a great and just sensation here and people are much shocked.

From the Queen

WINDSOR CASTLE, MARCH 7, 1877

I was so much interested by seeing good old Jonah Henson—the original of Mrs. Stowe's "Uncle Tom". He is nearly eighty-eight—

---

[1] *Life of the Prince Consort*, Vol. II, p. 52.

and such a strong, fine, good old man—who has gone through such untold hardships. He was 46 years a slave and wished to thank me for all I had done for the poor, suffering slaves.

From the Crown Princess

BERLIN, MARCH 7, 1877

Yesterday evening we saw General Ignatiev and his wife. He talked without ceasing as he always does, though much he said was very interesting. Particularly the details of the murder of poor Abdul Aziz,[1] which must have been too horrible. The General's wife was so free and easy and so grand that you might have imagined some Empress (and not a very civil one) giving us an audience. I hardly ever saw anyone so cool or uncivil. To hear him talk one would imagine that he alone governed Constantinople and the Turkish Empire and that nothing was done without his giving his opinion. He spoke with a patronising sort of pity of all the Turks &c . . . I knew him in Russia —he is not a disagreeable man but has such a bad countenance and cannot conceal his ambition and vanity and his extraordinary activity —with a jovial and lively manner which I suppose is meant to make upon one the impression of *"abandon"*, *"franchise"* and *"bonhommie"*.

From the Queen

WINDSOR CASTLE, MARCH 10, 1877

Many affectionate thanks for your dear letter of the 7th with the interesting account of General Ig: and his amiable spouse.

I have had two large dinner parties but I have not yet had any diplomats on account of the extreme awkwardness of having the ambassadors to whom I don't wish to speak politics as I can't trust any.

From the Crown Princess

BERLIN, MARCH 10, 1877

I send another copy of a letter of dear Papa's which seems to me the very one which is mentioned as missing by Mr. Martin, amongst the copies you possess of dear Papa's letters. If this is published, which it certainly ought to be, would you kindly see that we are not men-

---

[1] See page 213.

The Crown Princess of Prussia, August, 1877. *Reproduced by gracious permission of Her Majesty Queen Elizabeth II*

Portrait by H. von Angeli of the Crown Prince Frederick of Prussia. *Reproduced by gracious permission of Her Majesty Queen Elizabeth II*

tioned as having procured the copy—as we have not been formally authorised by the Emperor to take it from the late King's papers?[1]

From the Crown Princess

I think Mr. Gladstone's newest Pamphlet very odd.[2]

From the Queen

And after all I shall see the Ignatiefs! Suddenly they came over and are being fêted at Hatfield—more than is wise. I can't say I look forward to seeing them. They will only have an audience.

I put off and off having the six Ambassadors to dinner—but I must now and so I shall have three on Wednesday and three on Friday but politics shall be carefully avoided. I hate it but it must be done.

From the Queen

I send you today the confirmation presents for Charlotte (a bracelet with my picture and a Testament) and for Henry (my bust and a large Bible). I am very sorry not to be at the confirmation—but you know I cannot now appear at other Courts—my own is almost too much for me.

I saw the Ignatiefs yesterday; he is vulgar-looking—she pretty and I thought unassuming. I fear matters are not progressing very favourably from what Lord Derby told me yesterday. He mistrusts the Russians as much as I do. I have a dinner today—which as there is no music or gaiety I felt I could not put off.[3]

---

[1] The Queen said on March 14 that the letter was most valuable and that she was particularly glad that the Crown Princess "had it copied in English characters as Mr. Martin can't read German written characters". The original letter written by the Prince would have been in German script. The letter in question is almost certainly the one printed on pages 108–13 in *Letters of the Prince Consort*, edited by Kurt Jagow, 1938.

[2] "Lessons in Massacre" which gave more detail of Turkish atrocities than was possible in a speech in Parliament. Mr Gladstone was disappointed in the sale—6 or 7,000 copies.

[3] Prince Charles of Hesse, father-in-law of Princess Alice, had just died.

From the Crown Princess

I was so distressed not to be able to write on Wednesday or Tuesday as I had meant; but when you hear how this last week has been scrambled and struggled through—with 72 German Royal Personages —you will understand it, and forgive me![1] I will not fatigue you with the account of receptions at the railway station at 10 at night, and at 7 in the morning after an asphyxiating soirée the night before, nor of the visits to be paid and received by each one, nor of the dressing and undressing, dinners, parties, &c. for I should make you feel almost as weary as I do myself! I can really say that I ache all over, and am ready to cry! However both Emperor and Empress are fresh and well—and do not seem to feel the frightful atmosphere in the Salon nor the late hours nor the standing, as we do!

The young Grand-Duke Nicholas (Nicolaievitch)[2]—who is here, is so particularly nice, so civil, steady—unaffected, well brought up— and unassuming—such a contrast to his cousins. He was brought up quite by his Mama, and I am sure she has every reason to be proud of the result.

From the Crown Princess

We are in the midst of a ministerial crisis here, that is to say; Prince Bismarck wants a long leave of absence, and the Emperor does not feel inclined to give it nor to make other arrangements to replace him so that it would remain left to the future whether he returned or not. How I wish with all my heart that this could be arranged, and his time come to a close, during the Emperor's reign and at this present moment when but few would regret it, I can hardly say! I should consider it as a godsend. I fear it is too good to come true, and Bismarck too fond of power ever to give it up—often as he may threaten with the intention of doing so.

If only the Turks could be persuaded to be reasonable and give way now, a war might be prevented. I set my hopes on Mr. Layard's energy in making them become sensible. M. de Gontaut (French Ambassador) also said to me yesterday, *"cette guerre serait une incendie—dont il est impossible de dire où elle s'arrêterait!"*—that is also my fear.

---

1 The Emperor's eightieth birthday.
2 1856–1929. Commander-in-chief of the Russian Armies 1914–15. His mother was a Duchess of Oldenburg.

We had a charming dinner yesterday at Lord Odo's, Charlotte and Bernard were with us. The Emperor of Brazil's[1] visit keeps us considerably on our legs! His power of seeing and visiting is something prodigious; but he is really so kind and amiable and agreeable that it is a great pleasure to be with him; the Empress too is so kind—and so good-natured, always satisfied with everything and in a good humour. How dreadfully tiring it must be to travel about like that, when one is no longer quite young.

H. von Angeli leaves tomorrow morning for England, I have unfortunately seen very little of him the fortnight he has been here. When he arrived, he was looking very ill and overworked, yesterday I thought him much better again. I have sent the little picture he did of me, a year and a half ago, to the Royal Academy for the Exhibition this year, so I hope you will see it; you will think the dress very fanciful and fantastic I am sure but it is not meant for reproduction and for the public but only for us, and it stands on Fritz's table. It is very like but also much flattered I am bound to say! It has a certain likeness with dear Grandmama, which perhaps will strike you. It is most beautifully painted. There is no one in the world who can paint like him!

Count Seckendorff also leaves for London for the purpose of making a copy or two in the National Gallery—or by permission of Sir R. Wallace, in his Gallery. I should be very glad if you would allow him to pay his respects some day to you when you are back at Windsor. He can also give you details of the confirmation, and betrothal ceremony, if you like to hear about it; and is anxious to be allowed to present the drawing of Calcutta he has done for you. I should look upon it as a great kindness and favour if he can be allowed to do a small copy in the Rubens room, and also to look at the Holbein drawings in the print room. I have also given him a little, curious, old case of miniatures to show you which belonged to poor Princess Elizabeth, Queen of Bohemia and has the heads of her children in it; there are three wanting and I thought they might be in the miniature collection, and he might be allowed to take down the names.

From the Queen

OSBORNE, APRIL 14, 1877

I feel very tired from the constant strain and anxiety (which seems only to increase) of this Eastern Question, and the disgraceful conduct

---

[1] Pedro II (1825–1891). A man of wide culture forced to abdicate in 1889. He married Thérèse, daughter of Francis I of the Two Sicilies.

of the Opposition which I really cannot understand! It is a terrible precedent for the future—and will make all negotiations with F. countries next to impossible! Mr. Roebuck an old radical but a very honest man has spoken out very strongly and rightly. The truckling to Russia of some of the Liberals is too astounding. I think it must make old Lord Palmerston turn in his grave! It is this, and not European difficulties which worry me so. As for your crisis—we felt alike I am sure but I still hope *he* may not return.

Today is my beloved Baby's birthday her 20th alas—and I can never thank God enough for the blessing of such a devoted daughter and child, who is like a sister as well as a daughter and my constant companion.

From the Crown Princess

BERLIN, APRIL 14, 1877

I hope that there is no idea in England that Prince Bismarck's intended resignation has anything to do with this war, it really has not. You know I look upon him as a misfortune for Germany and for the development of our liberties, our trade &c. and certainly a danger for the Crown, but I cannot shut my eyes to the fact that he is entirely for England, and has a sincere wish to be well with England, and that England's power should on all occasions rise superior to Russia's. He dislikes and distrusts the Russians, and feels that they are very dangerous neighbours for us; all of which the Emperor does not see, and is guided in his opinions by his almost blind affection to the Emperor Alexander and the Russians, and believes whatever they say, whereas Bismarck believes not a word. I hardly think we have one statesman in Germany half as anxious to be well with England as Bismarck is, as the others have not such large views (as he often though not always has) and are usually guided by a sort of curious jealousy of England, which he has not—at least since two or more years, certainly not. This you may rely upon as being the truth.

From the Crown Princess

BERLIN, APRIL 18, 1877

Is it not rather odd and uncivil of Augusta, to pass through here, have her dinner in the royal apartment at the station, send for Lord Odo Russell and never let me know, either that she is coming or that she would like to see me? This she does each time, and I think it so rude. Especially considering how kind we are to Adolphus whom Fritz had with him during the war. and also considering that she is a German Grand-Duchess, and lastly, that I have nothing to do with politics, nor am I responsible for any occurrence which is disagreeable to her feelings; and always remain her cousin! If she did not pass through here—of course one would not say anything. I must say it does hurt my feelings.[1]

The Duchess of Manchester is here, and still looking very handsome.

The Emperor and Empress of Brazil left yesterday. They really are so kind and good and amiable, that one cannot help getting much attached to them when one sees them often. And we saw a good deal of them, only my stupid cold prevented my going about with the Emperor as much as I had intended. The Emperor and Empress liked them very much indeed, and altogether they made a very good impression, except that everyone at Court (gentlemen and ladies) were horrified at the Emperor's persistently appearing at the Court soirées with a black cravat and without any orders, and all his gentlemen with black cravats. The society of Berlin turned up their eyes—with pious horror. I rather enjoyed (out of mischief) the shock this gave to their nerves! Of course it is rather funny—but in this case certainly not a crime. The Empress is really almost the kindest soul I ever saw. He owned to her *"je suis pourtant un peu fatigué"*—but for all that not an item is taken off the programme.

From the Crown Princess

HAMBURG, HOTEL D'EUROPE, APRIL 19, 1877

My cold and earache and sore throat were so bad yesterday evening that Wegner wanted to forbid my travel. But I felt I could not, without being rude, disappoint the people who had made so many preparations for our reception here; so I came away at 8 o'clock this morning. We passed by Prince Bismarck's place on the road and he came to the station to meet us and got into our carriage. He says he feels much better, and certainly looks the picture of health, only grown enormously fat. He cannot stand and looks to me very apoplectic, but they say he is in no danger of that kind.

From the Crown Princess

BERLIN, APRIL 28, 1877

Moltke must have alarmed the world by his warlike speech, but in reality it was only a military question in which the War Office could

---

[1] The Grand-Duchess of Mecklenburg-Strelitz: her dislike of Prussia, "the Enemy" as she called that country, was strong.

not make the Emperor give his consent to certain necessary measures, and they fancied that a speech in Parliament would force the Emperor whereas I fancy there were many other more harmless means of obtaining his consent than by crying on the housetops in a way to alarm one's neighbours—who are not annoying one in any way. But Moltke is no more a statesman than a baby! The first strategist in the world—an excellent soldier and an honest man, but rather dangerous in Parliament.[1]

The Empress and I are the subject of the rudest and most perfidious and lying attacks in the newspapers. They are either instigated by Prince Bismarck or evidently written to please him! I had thought of writing to him on the subject but I have now come to the conclusion that it is better to ignore it altogether, but should I have an opportunity of seeing him I should say exactly what I thought. I have been almost ill with annoyance but it is no use caring. Only it is an abominable system of his—trying to pull down the royal family in the eyes of the public to appear a martyr! It is wicked, disloyal and ungenerous especially to women who cannot defend themselves; and the German public are so blind in their adoration of Bismarck that they would believe anything bad of us, if it came from him or was sanctioned by him. Against me it is still more uncalled for than against the Empress— as I never even attempt to meddle or cross his plans—or interfere with anything or influence the Emperor in a contrary manner which some-times the Empress in the best of intentions (but prompted by her strong Catholic sympathies) thinks it her duty to do. Certainly she does no harm and it is absurd of him to exaggerate what she does to such a degree, but still if I were the Empress I would let it alone.

From the Crown Princess

NEUES PALAIS, MAY I, 1877

The children's very nice maid who has been with us 11 years is alas! now going to be married. She is a great loss as she was so excellent in every way—Mrs. Hobbs's niece, Penelope Hobbs. She is going to settle in London and the children are very sad to part from her, as well they may be; I wish she had waited till Charlotte's wedding.

---

[1] Moltke was a member of the Reichstag. His speech included the statement that in France "the Army was the spoilt child of the Nation".

From the Queen

We are here since yesterday. It is a very anxious time and we must and will take some marked line to show that Russia is not to have all her own way—which thanks to the most unfortunate and ill-judged agitation of last autumn and this spring has led Russia on to think she may do anything, and they are the cause of what is happening now![1] You never answer when I constantly tell you this—as if you thought the Liberals and that madman Gladstone must be right and the Government wrong! If you only knew how I have but one object—the honour and dignity of this country (of course the stopping of all acts of cruelty is as great an object to us as to anyone else) and it is the neglect of this which distresses and grieves me so much. The other party seem wilfully blind to the fact that Russia never would have dared to go as far as she has—had not they thought England not only would not fight but was with them. I know this is a fact from people who have been in Russia and yet the Liberals here, and I may name that good man Mr. Forster— is foolish enough to be pleased (I saw it in a letter of his) that the poor Turks are supposed to be beaten and rejoice in Russian success I could not have believed it!!

What a shame that you and the Empress should have been attacked in that disgraceful way. So cowardly. I this morning saw Angeli's little picture of you which is a real bijou; most exquisite. Like the old Dutch painters as to finish with the richness of colouring and the wonderful likeness which he so greatly possesses. It is worthy of Van Dyke and the greatest masters.

From the Queen

I will not dispute about Bismarck as you will not credit what I tell you—but I can only say that I know it from the person to whom he told it.[2] The Turks are getting the better of it in Asia, which may serve as a check. There are likewise risings in the Caucasus. The Government

---

1 Russia had declared war on Turkey on April 24.
2 The Crown Princess's letter does not seem to have survived.

had a very large majority on Mr. Gladstone's extraordinary Resolutions.[1] And I think you will be pleased when you see the despatch to Count Schouvaloff[2] which he is taking with him.

We are so very fond of Marie; she is so good, honest, kind-hearted, right-minded and unselfish with such a sense of duty. Always satisfied and so even tempered. Affie is indeed most fortunate. She is in excellent looks with so much colour and very strong.

From the Crown Princess

I will not discuss again about Bismarck as you do not like it, but only say that Fritz went to see him the day before yesterday and that he repeated most energetically, what I have always said. Therefore what has been told you has either been misunderstood or purposely put in his mouth. I most certainly have no object in defending him, but merely say what is my firm belief based on the best of reasons.

From the Crown Princess

I have painted a very large "Still life" which I have given to Charlotte and Bernard for their future dining-room! I fear I am naughty enough to wish it were yours and not theirs, because they understand nothing whatever about it; and Angeli thought it good—when I showed it to him at Berlin. Painting in oils is my happiness and delight and if only I had a proper *atelier* and good light—the right models at hand and regular lessons, I should in 2 or 3 years perhaps be able to do something tolerable. My eye has improved but my hand is still very awkward.

The Emperor spent the afternoon with us yesterday and seemed very well; I appealed to him whether he could not do something to shield the Empress from the shameful attacks which fill the press—and have also been directed on me. He will try and see what can be done, and was very nice—but also very calm about it! I am much pained to think the Empress should be exposed to such attacks.

We hear George of Meiningen and his wife are going to England, I

---

[1] The Resolutions broadly were that the British Crown should give no material or moral support to the Ottoman Empire until the safety of the subject peoples was secure, and reforms were started.

[2] The Russian Ambassador took this despatch to the Russian Government; it underlined the serious consequences of the Russian attack on Turkey which was a breach of former treaties.

hope dear Bertie will not see his wife, if she tries to be seen, or at any rate, only quite *en passant*. Alas! dear Uncle Ernest pays her visits—and shows her every civility in rather an ostentatious way, and as she is very ambitious and pushing it is better to be very reserved with her. It is a most awkward thing; George expects so much attention paid her—much more than he can fairly ask.[1]

I shall go once more to the theatre to see that grand actor Salvini;[2] we are all more or less a little cracked about him and certainly I never saw his equal not even Kean! What would dear old Skerett say? I wonder whether she saw his Othello in London. It is really perfection.

From the Queen

BALMORAL, JUNE 19, 1877

You say you hope we shall keep out of the war and God knows I hope and pray and think we shall—as to fighting. But I am sure you would not wish Great Britain to eat humble pie to these horrible, deceitful, cruel Russians? I will not be the Sovereign to submit to that! You say the poor Turks have not entirely a good cause; but what is their cause now? The defence of hearth and home and that they do defend bravely. You yourself told me that the Russians instigated the rebellion (and that is quite certain) for the Principalities don't wish to stand under Russia—and then they urged them[3] through Ignatief not to employ regular troops—and now because these very irregular troops committed horrors the Turks are to be crushed!!! I own my blood boils and I rejoice at every Russian defeat.

From the Crown Princess

NEUES PALAIS, JUNE 20, 1877

I hope dear Mama whenever you do see Henry you will make him talk English as he has almost forgotten it, and it wants polishing up a little, and if you could say something about his dreadful nails; he bit them down to the quick to my great distress and there is no stopping him. But if you said something to his Governor on the subject it might take the desired effect! Would you go on board the *Niobe* if she were in Cowes roads? How pleased they would be and how pleased Henry would be to show you his cabin.

---

[1] The father of Prince Bernard. After neglecting his second wife, Feodore, niece of Queen Victoria, he married morganatically the Baronne de Heldbourg.
[2] Tommasso Salvini (1829–1916). Played Othello, Hamlet, Macbeth and Lear.
[3] The Turks.

From the Queen

I send you here Willy's letter; I would of course be glad to see him for a few days but I could not see him for long and don't know if he is to go and see anything beyond Portsmouth—if he came. Only I do advise his not coming during the Regatta week—the company being so very bad at West Cowes—nor do I think he ought to go to London except for two or three days.

From the Queen

We have had very hot weather since I last wrote, and on Saturday when I went up to see Aunt Cambridge (who is suffering but alive to everything and delighted with Angeli who has painted an admirable head of her under great difficulties) and then the Emperor and Empress of Brazil at Claridge's—the heat was dreadful—thick, heavy, stifling air. The Emperor is really very eccentric—rushing about everywhere and seeing everything—from morning till night. But to come to the State Ball and Concert in a frock coat—with a black cravat and boots—is really quite incomprehensible and shocked people here very much also.

From the Queen

Before answering anything else let me say that the Paris,[1] who are in England for a short while, lunched here today and begged to enquire when you would be at Ostend as they are most anxious to see you and Fritz *de renouer les relations de famille*—so anxious that they would wait here in order not to miss you. Will you therefore tell me what I am to answer? I am sure you would willingly see them. This shows a desire to be well with Germany.

As regards dear William there will no difficulty. If he only comes for two or three days he can't be mixed up in anything and Leopold will be then ready and happy to be with him. Henry also. If Willy is with me he can't do anything without asking me. If he has good principles and right feelings he will keep straight as dear Arthur does. But that affectation of independence and "mystery" is quite intolerable and not

---

[1] Comte and Comtesse de Paris—head of the Orleans family.

at all right or kind.[1] Dear Bertie is the very last person who should take young people out or at least whom they should live with but he would never lead anyone willingly into mischief—that I am sure of—for he is so anxious about his own children.

We expect William of Hesse here tomorrow to announce Louis's accession and to bring back the Grand-Duke's ribbon. I send today at length the Raphael Catalogue which has been sixteen years finishing!!! It seems very good but you know I am not up in it at all.

From the Crown Princess

NEUES PALAIS, POTSDAM, JULY 7, 1877

It is indeed a little eccentric of the Emperor of Brazil to wear a black coat and cravat, at balls and concerts; he did so here too, to the horror of everybody—I wonder why no one has hinted to him that it does not do; he is such a remarkable and intelligent man, that one is sorry he should shock people with the little eccentricity, though it is not exactly a crime. Liszt is coming over here this afternoon to play to us, and I own I look forward to it greatly, it is so long since I have heard him.

We take little Louise of Fritz Carl's with us to Ostend, she is so pleased poor child, she is by far the nicest most sensible and nice of Marianne's girls, the only one who is intimate with our children (except the little boy) and quite brought up by an excellent English governess, a Miss Jackson, whose sister is governess to the Duchess of Buccleuch's daughters. Louise is a gentle timid shy girl, very lady-like in ways and appearance, but I do not think her pretty, although she has more grace and less heaviness than her elder sisters.

From the Queen

WINDSOR CASTLE, JULY 11, 1877

While the successes in Asia of the Turks have been very remarkable, in Europe they seem to be the very reverse and there is great fear that the exasperated Mussulmans may massacre the Christians.[2] I hear that Prince Reuss is active in a very Russian sense at Constantinople.[3] This really should not be. Altogether our task is terribly difficult and we have to work as it were in the dark. Affie, I am grieved to say, has become most imprudent in his language and I only hope he does not

---

[1] The Crown Princess had complained of this to the Queen.
[2] The Turks had recaptured Kars but the Russians, with a large force, were steadily advancing through Bulgaria.
[3] Prince Henry VII, German Ambassador at Constantinople.

make mischief. It is very awkward with this Russian relationship just now. This is what I always feared and dreaded. Lord Beaconsfield is well again and the mainstay of everything.

From the Queen

I will now answer your letter of the eleventh relative to Egypt the proposal about which (coming from you) has indeed surprised me very much, and seems to me to be entirely Bismarck's view. Neither Turkey or Egypt have done anything to offend us. Why should we make a wanton aggression such as the taking of Egypt would be? It is not our custom to annex countries (as it is in some others) unless we are obliged and forced to do so as in the case of the Transvaal Republic. Prince Bismarck would probably like us to seize Egypt as it would be giving a great slap in the face of France, and be taking a mean advantage of her inability to protest. It would be a most greedy action. I own I can't for a moment understand your suggesting it. What we intend to do— we shall do without Prince Bismarck's permission (for he has repeatedly mentioned it to Lord Odo Russell). Buying the Suez shares is quite another thing. That was more or less a commercial transaction. How can we protest against Russia's doings if we do the same ourselves? You say you are "perverse enough to feel for the Turks". I am sure it is only right you should and the monstrous atrocities committed by, or encouraged and instigated by the Russians, are such as to throw the so-called "Bulgarian atrocities"in the shade!

I feel so strongly that I can hardly bear to write upon it at all. I trust the Russians will be severely punished in one way or another— by [for] beginning this horrible war. You say you feel for the Turks "against your better reason"? Therefore you think the worst, most tyrannical and far more corrupt and untruthful government that exists is to regenerate Turkey which has now got a parliament which expresses its opinion very freely?

If the Turks are no Christians they at least believe most sincerely in a God—while the so-called Christians of the Principalities are said to be the most superstitious, horrible creatures possible. I heard this again only two days ago from an impartial person who had seen a gentleman who had lately travelled through these countries.

From the Crown Princess

How differently the younger generation expects to be treated from what we were. Fancy that Charlotte never tells me when she writes to Bernard or when he writes to her—they correspond daily almost, I believe, but he would be quite furious if I were only to ask, and she consider herself highly offended and very indignant if her letters were interfered with. Fritz thinks this all right for a German engaged couple and says it ought to be so, but considering how young and how immature she is, I have my little doubts sometimes, and find it rather difficult to know what to do. They resent the slightest restraint put upon them and Bernard thinks they ought to do just as they like—so I am obliged to let it all alone. I am sure you would not have allowed me half so much independence as they get, and I think I was not so queer as Charlotte is: but however young people will be very headstrong and one cannot keep one's influence if one stands too much on one's authority and in Germany certainly the ideas are different.

From the Queen

The horrible Russian cruelties which are corroborated by numbers and numbers. It is dreadful for people professing to fight for Christianity —as if there was any difference between Turks and Christians—especially such dreadful Christians.

I cannot help smiling at your complaints about Charlotte. I—and dear Papa even if possible more than me—so very much disapproved of that system of complete intimacy before marriage, and in that respect I am bound to say that you never gave us the slightest trouble or annoyance, but Fritz did, and made me very impatient. You were in other ways very difficult to manage, but not in that. I think there is a great want of propriety and delicacy as well as dutifulness in at once treating your bridegroom as though (except in one point) he were your husband. Papa felt this so strongly and it applies still more strongly to very long engagements like yours, your sisters' and Charlotte's. You, as time goes on, I am sure will change your great passion for marriage— and will understand the great change it is to a mother especially, though to a father too! Here now they have lost all modesty for not only do they go about driving, walking, and visiting—everywhere alone, they have also now taken to go out everywhere together in society—which till a year or so no young lady just engaged, ever did, and make a regular show of themselves—and are laughed at and stared at! In short young people are getting very American, I fear in their views and ways.

From the Crown Princess

PAVILLON D'OSTENDE, JULY 25, 1877

You will be alarmed at his [Willy's] appetite! What disappears at breakfast and dinner is surprising—and quite beats his Papa at whom you used to be astonished in former days!

From the Queen

OSBORNE, AUGUST 4, 1877

I think you will like to have a few lines since Henry's arrival on Wednesday afternoon. The dear child is unaltered though improved in looks and with such nice manners but always the same dear little fellow which makes him a general favourite. He and Willy drove out with Baby, Leopold and me on the first day, dined with me (of course) as well as their two amiable gentlemen. Captain V. Seckendorff is a peculiarly pleasing and amiable as well as good-looking man—and seems admirably suited to be with a boy of dear Henry's age. Yesterday the dear boys went to Portsmouth and came back in the evening in time to drive with Baby and me to Ryde. Dear Willy took leave last night as he left already at eight this morning which would have been too early for me to have been dressed. He is a dear and sensible, well-conditioned boy, anxious to do all that is right. Poor young Jacobi seems a most good-humoured youth—with a mouth going from ear to ear—but his eyes and nose are not bad and his face is so good-natured and beaming that I can't help liking it—and everyone liked him.

From the Crown Princess

PAVILLON D'OSTENDE, AUGUST 5, 1877

How kind of you to see old Goltz, I have no reason to like him, he is very ill-natured and *mauvaise langue*, has been very ungrateful to the Empress (though she hardly knows it) and has always behaved very ill to me, and abused me whenever he could behind my back, which I think most ungrateful considering all my kindness to his boys for poor Marie's sake. He is a man one cannot respect. His poor brother was a staunch friend of ours and a clever man, whereas this one is nothing but a vain spoilt old gossip! I am sure he will have been delighted that you allowed him to come to dinner.

From the Crown Princess

We have Bernard here now, and he would very much like to pay his respects to you. If you are not going to Scotland before the 19th perhaps he might go over on the 18th pay his visit to you and return the day after, at any rate he is anxious you should know his wish to present himself so that you may at least have seen him before he marries, as he is hardly likely to be able to go over to England at any other time between this and then. If, as I am quite prepared for, his visit is inconvenient to you, we can just tell him—and the matter is at an end, and at least you will know that he has not been remiss in offering to take the journey.

From the Queen

OSBORNE, AUGUST 11, 1877

Now let me answer about Bernard. I would naturally like very much to see him and know him before he marries dear Charlotte. But I own I fear (much as it really vexes and grieves me to say it) that I cannot manage it now. I am overwhelmed with business just now! Next week—my last here—I have a Council—an Investiture—Colonel Wellesley[1] (whose accounts are most interesting and who goes on Wednesday straight back again) and Ministers to see, and am not feeling very well and I fear I shall knock up entirely if I have any additional visitors. Perhaps the winter there might still be a chance?

From the Crown Princess

PAVILLON D'OSTENDE, AUGUST 13, 1877

I am very sorry indeed that a little visit from Bernard would not suit you, as there will be no opportunity in the winter. The thought of Charlotte's marrying someone you do not know, is painful to me. However, it is as you wish. Adolphus's wife will have been more fortunate! She is good and pretty but very insignificant, as you would find on nearer acquaintance![2]

---

[1] Frederick Arthur Wellesley, Colonel, Coldstream Guards 1844-1931, 3rd son of 1st Lord Cowley. At this time Military Attaché at the headquarters of the Czar. Colonel Wellesley pleased the Queen by telling her that the Czar was pacific but that he had been forced into the war by his advisers, the Empress and Mr. Gladstone (see *Letters*, Second Series, Vol. II, p. 560).

[2] This was an unwise remark as the Queen had written that she was much pleased with her.

I saw poor dear Charlotte of Mexico a few days ago! Marie kindly took me to Tervueren which is a lovely place. Her intellect seems almost entirely gone, but she is quite unchanged in looks, indeed looks as she did when she was 14—or 15—but it is too melancholy a sight! They say she knew me, but I should not have perceived it! She let me kiss her and take her hand, and gave one or two very low answers in a whisper but turned her head away and shut her eyes. Poor thing, what a life! She seems surrounded by kind and devoted creatures all cheerful and nice and the greatest possible care taken of her, and they say she is never unhappy—but placid and quiet, though often troublesome in a childish way. She had a dressing gown on; she has left off wearing dresses, and her hair is cut short like a little boy's—but her face is quite her own dear self!

From the Queen

OSBORNE, AUGUST 18, 1877

To make Bernard's acquaintance is a pleasure and he seems very amiable and intelligent—reminding me much of his grandmother's family. But I must say I was astonished and annoyed at the way in which you received my expression of deep regret at being unable on account of the overwhelming work I have had to do—the endless visits (my house is a regular (*tauben* full) here)[1] and it was only in order to show my affection for you and Charlotte that I made the proposal to Bertie to bring him here. But I must protest against these visits in future at the very end of my stay here when I want a little rest. I can't enjoy seeing them and can't receive them as I should wish. So pray dear child let this be understood in future. I was very pleased to see Bernard and to receive him with all affection.

From the Crown Princess

NEUES PALAIS, AUGUST 23, 1877

I am very very glad that our dear Bernard pleased you. It is also a great pleasure to us that you should have so kindly received him and that he should no longer be a stranger to you! I am very sorry indeed that my words gave such offence. I know quite well that visits are an annoyance to you; but is not this one quite an exception? And as such was I not justified in begging you would for this once make the sacrifice,

---

[1] *Taubenschlag* meaning 'dovecot' is used to indicate a place where there is constant coming and going. The Queen has omitted *schlag* but the meaning is clear.

for which the thought of how much pleasure you gave and what good it did in many ways must I am sure repay you. I hope you will forgive me, and not resent my having pressed my wish. I do not see how you could be inconvenienced again in a like manner, at any rate, not be us.[1]

I regret so much that Mr. Layard and Prince Reuss cannot get on at all, it is a great pity, I fear they write each other down wherever and whenever they can! Evidently the Reusses distrust and dislike Mr. Layard very much, and vice versa, which is most disagreeable at this moment. Reuss is very ambitious and of an intriguing disposition though not clever, but I believe is doing his duty very well. Having the Russian affairs to attend to it must make him look more Russian than he is.

From the Queen

BALMORAL, AUGUST 25, 1877

The cruelties of the Turks (that is the Irregulars not the Regulars) is confined chiefly to the men—but the horrors to the poor women and children committed by the Bulgarians and Cossacks are too revolting. It is really very shameful—as they do abroad in many places—to put the whole blame on the unfortunate Turks. That the war is most savage and one of "extermination", as Lord Beaconsfield calls it most truly, is alas! only too evident.

From the Crown Princess

NEUES PALAIS, AUGUST 29, 1877

In answer to your kind question about Willy I will only say that he twisted his knee while bathing in the Havel. It is all right again. It was not a bad sprain but we have begged him to take care of it which I trust he is doing but unless I go every day to see him, he does not trouble himself to come and see me, though it is only a drive of 10 minutes and a walk of 25 minutes from his door to ours.[2] I have not seen him since Sunday, and considering that I am going away to the Rhine, and shall not see much of him in the next few weeks and he is going off to Bonn in October, I think he might just drop in for one minute some time or other between 7 in the morning and 10 at night, just to say how do you do, and ask after his Mama, when his Papa is

---

[1] The Queen did not accept this explanation, and said that she disliked visitors being forced upon her "at a time most inconvenient to me. Osborne in the summer is really most fatiguing". August 28.

[2] He was serving with the 2ND Regiment of Landwehr Guards.

away, but that is a thought which never strikes him and I am not spoilt by marks of attention. But I suppose one must resign oneself to that, and not expect one's children to wish to see one, as one would like to be seeing them, i.e. as much as possible.

I have a deal to do about the trousseau which I want to be as nice and as useful as possible. How well I remember all the trouble you took about mine and how it touched me that you should see into each little detail yourself.

From the Queen

BALMORAL, SEPTEMBER 4, 1877

I will not enter into the discussion about Turks and Russians except to say that as regards Turkish regulars you are misinformed![1] I at once continue my letter but rather not on politics.

What you say about Willy grieves me and is not right. I can't help smiling sometimes, though I am truly sorry too for you, that you should have such experiences—that you should now learn what I—without a dear husband to share all—have had and have to go through. But excepting Affie who is very wanting in attention and consideration and Leopold occasionally, I have not had to suffer in the way you speak of. Bertie and dear Arthur are always most attentive. It is really a thing to be most carefully watched in education viz the neglect of parents—the total want of gratitude and thought for their feelings—and how much one feels it—how it cuts one to the heart you can now understand. But you have done so much and worked so hard for W.'s education that it is wrong and neglectful in him not to think of every little attention he can show his mother. Oh the ingratitude and the thoughtlessness of children does pain one so deeply. Henry I own I think far more affectionate and lovable and B.V. Seckendorff is sure to promote this.

Respecting the trousseau, I who have had four to look after, know what it is. Would you not perhaps order some few trifling things from your own old home? It would (as you draw your entire income from here) have such a good effect. For instance a dress or some chemises etc. from the School of Art—perhaps some white embroidery from Ireland where they do it so beautifully and cheaply. I have got a dozen Irish pocket handkerchiefs for Charlotte and any chemises or cheminettes would be very nice and most beautifully done. I am having some fine English lace made for her—and get poplins and shall add Scotch

---

[1] In reply to the Queen's letter of 25 August the Crown Princess asserted that the worst atrocities were committed by the Turks. August 29.

velvets etc. But if you would order just a few things from the British Isles it would do great good and have a good effect.

From the Queen

We leave this for 6 days or a week early tomorrow morning for Talladale—Loch Maree in Ross-shire where we have taken a small hotel in order to see the country which is very beautiful and little known. Only Beatrice—the Duchess of Roxburghe, General Ponsonby and Sir William Jenner go with us.

The dreadful, wicked, savage war engrosses everyone constantly.

From the Crown Princess

In this place I think so much of you and your visit [in] 1845![1] The people in the Schloss can still tell all about it! I sleep in the large bed which was made for you at that time and which no doubt was a very great rarity.

We heard yesterday that the Russians have had a great success at Plevna.[2]

It is so odd that my father-in-law maintains, that the Turkish successes are all due to the English officers that lead the Turks and exist in great numbers! I told the Emperor I did not think there were more Englishmen in the Turkish Army than German in the Russian but he did not believe it. There are so many Prussian officers who have been obliged to leave the service by some fault of theirs who now flock to the Russian Army, adventurers, etc.

During the Parade[3] my horse suddenly took it into his head to lie down and roll with me in the saddle, so that I was under him, and someone pulled me out, I succeeded in getting my legs free of him, I don't know how, and escaped unhurt with my legs only a trifle bruised, which was both a great mercy and a great marvel as he might have crushed me—being an immense animal! It was not a pleasant

---

[1] At Bonn where King Frederick William IV was her host. A concert was given in the Schloss with 60 regimental bands playing. Built in the early 18th century for the Archbishop of Cologne and restored by the King of Prussia in 1842 it is now the setting for official receptions by the Federal Government.

[2] Plevna, till then almost unknown, was in Bulgaria just south of the Danube. The Turkish defence was remarkable and the Russian attack at this time met with a disastrous loss of life.

[3] "The Kaiser Week" in celebration of the Emperor's 80th birthday which was held at Dusseldorf culminating in a Parade outside the city.

moment! But I was on again in a moment and I am happy to say it did not much disturb the Parade. Such a thing has never happened to me! The horse did it all in one minute without any warning so that one had no chance of pulling him up. It made me feel very foolish. The Emperor stands all the fatigues wonderfully well and is looking as bright and fresh as possible. I have not been here in the house since the year 1861; and am always struck with the richness of decoration and architecture especially of the staircase.

From the Queen

The Empress praised Charlotte very much. Her[1] poor arm is a great trouble and I am anxious about her. The Odo Russells tell me how monstrously the bad man B. behaves towards her. Now you should mark this to him, for no children should tolerate abuse and insult towards their honoured parents and it is really the least you can do, to show that you resent such monstrous behaviour. Do you think any of my children would be friends with or tolerate anyone who had spoken of me with insult?

I am so shocked at dear Willy's want of attention towards you. None of my sons would do that, though Affie and Leopold have at times been very wanting in kindness but still nothing like this.

I will not speak about the horrible, bloody, ferocious war—you hear only one side I think. If only it could be stopped but no one will join with us to stop it.

From the Queen

This horrible war makes one miserable and if the other Powers would act straightforwardly and as they ought—and joined with us— we might stop it. But I fear they don't care for the loss of life. You may think the Turks are in much greater need of help—and so no doubt they were, and without the generous help from England with doctors etc. they would have suffered far more, but I am sorry to say that now the sufferings of the poor Russian soldiers (whom I do so pity as they don't care for the war) are awful. I saw a letter from a well-informed English officer and I copy out the following as it is to be relied on and really too dreadful "the lightness with which the loss of life are regarded by those

---

[2] The Empress's.

who are responsible is said to be most extraordinary. The negligence and the want of arrangement (for the wounded) is quite astounding. One day at Plevna three thousand Russians, wounded in the head and arms and chest had to march twenty miles to the rear as there were only bullock carts for those who could not stand! An American surgeon of eminence, when he visited all the field hospitals, described the brutality of the Russian surgeons to the wounded as finding no parallel in any country. He repeatedly saw operators kick and strike their patients for crying out under painful operations." This is the evidence of a distinguished American surgeon who had come with strong Russian feelings which naturally are much modified.[1]

From the Crown Princess

I do not know why you should think I hear only one side of the war, I hear both, and as I have often said before, there are many of our newspapers that take the Turkish side with vehemence. Marie telegraphed to me to send her things for the wounded, and I sent her all I could get together, because it would have been unkind to refuse, and a wounded man be he friend or foe always rouses the same pity in one's heart. Here I believe people look upon me as very Turkish in my sympathies—much too much so. I cannot conceal a certain pleasure in hearing of a Turkish victory, and disappointment when I hear of a Russian one! Yesterday I heard that an official (highly placed) in the Foreign Office at Berlin, declared that the Turks gave no quarter whatever and made no prisoners whatever, i.e. kept none because they killed them all! This was official information received but I do not know whether to believe it—in spite of the high authority. If such is the case it must be known in England just as well! But even if it is, the Turks are not Christians and carry on war in their own fashion without intending to be specially barbarous I am sure; and as their ways are known, why did the Russians make war upon them knowing what they had to expect?

---

[1] At this time, as Lord Blake points out in his biography of Disraeli, the feelings of English people were divided as deeply and violently as they were to be over Munich or Suez. It will be appreciated that many people expressed themselves quite as strongly as did the Queen on one side or as did Mr. Gladstone on the other. But the constitutional propriety of partisanship by the Queen is a different matter. (See Frank Hardie, *Political Influence of Queen Victoria*, Oxford, 1935.)

From the Crown Princess

It is curious here, how many people who are against the Russians are also against the Turks. Master Willy talks great nonsense on the subject, and cannot understand how I can give the preference to Mussulmans over Christians. If a Peace is made, I am always afraid that Europe will feel bound not to let Turkey enjoy the benefits of its success which would be very unfair! On the other hand that Montenegro, Roumania and Serbia, and a part of Bulgaria should be independent seems desirable also, if it is not all to begin again! How great is my dislike of Roumania I am ashamed to say! I always thought it so foolish of Charles of Hohenzollern to go there. The Montenegrins are a savage cruel set, and one cannot feel an interest in the Serbs. If the Turkish Government could but be reformed and become modern and civilised and Christian in its principles who could wish ill to Turkey? But is this possible? That is the great question.

I venture to send you today the work of a very old Quaker lady who wants to sell it for £4 or £5 for the Seamen's Home; she had but one wish in her old age, that the Queen should look at her work! How touched and delighted she would be if you were to buy it. She is an aunt of a Mrs. Charles Ashley of Cambria House, Staines, about whom I know! Her work is a little quilt for the feet. We have sent £100 to the Indian famine fund, it is not as much as I should wish, but it is something! Really all the suffering in the world is so awful and so distressing that it makes one utterly miserable. If one could only relieve even a portion one would feel comforted! How cruel and how wanton the war seems!

From the Queen

Poor Marie A.[1] is totally deceived. She writes she hears no news but a great victory in Asia—which happens to be a great defeat. I believe they hear nothing and that none of the relations hear anything of their relatives, and that people are longing for peace in Russia and very angry at this war which I hear never was popular in the army. The filth of the Russians, the total want of all sanitary arrangements, the thousands of unburied people and animals, not to speak of other smells which I hear surround even the Emperor's dwelling are too bad, too

---

[1] Marie Alexandrovna, the Duchess of Edinburgh.

dreadful. I must say I think our Red Cross Society and other voluntary subscriptions and help are really worthy of every admiration.

I never perceived Willy's anti-Turkish feeling when he was in England.

From the Crown Princess

NEUES PALAIS, OCTOBER 9, 1877

I return the interesting letter today with many thanks.[1] I have shown it to a few people, but there are some who wish the Russians success and will only look at things from a Russian point of view. We hear for certain, but it is not to be spoken of, and I beg not to be mentioned, that the Russians have just ordered 1100 guns from Krupp, field pieces—and for forts also!! Oh dear this does not look as if the war were to end and as if all mischief and horrors were at an end!

From the Crown Princess

NEUES PALAIS, OCTOBER 11, 1877

How very kind of you to ask about the lace again, I think made up on a gown would be charming for Charlotte on pink or yellow or green or grey. She has grown very stout; now and then her figure reminds me of what Lenchen's was—only much much shorter! She is a good bit shorter than I am, and has quite done growing, but she has an immense bust and arms—a long waist and neck, and looks like a big person when she is sitting—and when she gets up she has no legs almost. Unfortunately she is most ungraceful when she moves and walks, sticks out her elbows and trundles about—in spite of drilling and dancing lessons. Her profile looking from right to left is really pretty, and Angeli is doing that view of her face, which is decidedly the most advantageous.

She has alas her Papa's hands and feet which for a young girl is most unfortunate.

I fancy I had better not let it be known how much I have ordered for the trousseau in England, as that is such a sore point here, and people are so very jealous—and think a Princess of Prussia ought not to have a "pin" from elsewhere than Berlin.

---

[1] From Admiral Sir Edward Commerell—the Second in command at Besika Bay—"a most distinguished as well as amiable man—covered with medals—a V.C. and dreadfully wounded at Ashanti having still a ball in his lungs". Letter from the Queen, October 2.

From the Crown Princess

I am quite in low spirits having just heard that the Russians have won a great battle and that Plevna will have to surrender as Osman Pasha is cut off![1] I am so sorry! The valiant Turks deserved a better fate, and the conceited Russians not so good a one. Their triumph and boasting will be sickening to hear, and I am afraid they will regain their military prestige! It is melancholy to think that the poor Turks have made those enormous exertions and sacrifices for nothing! I should not be surprised if the Russians, elated with victory, and more stuck up and impertinent than ever, were to carry out their first programme and push on, if not to Constantinople still to Adrianople. England's position seems almost more difficult than at the outset, for how can the war be stopped now? One may expect the Greeks to move also now I suppose.

I am sorry for Serge Leuchtenberg though he had become an awfully *mauvais sujet*, and was as wild as possible. Such a pity, he was charming when he was between 15 and 17! There is no mother to mourn his loss, it is well the poor Grand-Duchess Marie is spared the pain of losing a son in such a manner.

From the Queen

As regards the Layards let me tell you exactly the truth. Mrs. L. (who is a very superior, clever woman, daughter of Lady C. Schreiber former Lady Guest) wrote to Lady Ely that she liked Princess R. very much indeed and that she was helping in the good work.—But she thought them or at least him very Russian—and I know from Mr. L.'s letters that he (Prince R.) is so offensive about England that he (Mr. L.) tries to avoid seeing him as he cannot calmly hear his cynical and very russified remarks. Is this not very injudicious? The Empress is the very reverse of Russian.

I continue my letter which I could not finish. That Marie A. should be so happy and blooming with thousands and thousands of her poor countrymen sacrificed and cruelly neglected (only she don't know that) is too, too extraordinary. I think they are brought up with a notion of

---

[1] On October 13 and 14 the Turks met with defeat in Armenia. Two days before the Crown Princess wrote the Russians were able to close one of the roads to Plevna, but at heavy cost to themselves. Prince Serge Leuchtenberg, nephew of the Czar, was among the casualties.

human beings very different to ours so that in her (much as I love her) there is not much depth of feeling though great good feeling and sense of duty. Dear me when I think what a state I was in at the time of the Crimean war, what you and Alice felt during your very victorious German war—and what Alix suffered during the Danish one I can't understand it and it grieves me. She has never drunk the cup of sorrow or been mixed up with it as we have been. She knows not those events which make "all the world kin".

As regards the marriage itself I feel for you truly, deeply—for I think a daughter's marriage dreadful, repulsive; yours was far less so as my own darling husband was there to share all—and you have yours; but I can't say how kind and delicate the dear Empress was to me that evening! And I am sure she will be the same to you. Your being so fond of Bernard and he is so good and steady is a great help—but still it is a dreadful gulf, and one which please God I should never have to go through again.

From the Queen

BALMORAL, NOVEMBER 6, 1877

As for dear Alix her kindness, her devotion to her poor friend has made everyone but possibly some old-fashioned, stuck-up people, full of etiquette, admire and love her more than ever. Her unselfishness is indeed beautiful and will find its real reward! Her simplicity and humble-mindedness are truly admirable so unspoilt by the wicked, frivolous, flattering, pleasure-seeking world.[1]

From the Queen

GLASSALT SHIEL, LOCH MUICH, NOVEMBER 21, 1877

We are here quite away from everything in the dear, warm, cosy, quiet little house, and the complete rest and freedom from interruptions does me good. The morning was fair but it snowed the whole afternoon which it had not done since five weeks. Such a wild spot which makes the comfortable snug little house with our small party of people—only Baby, Jane C. and me—feel the cosiness, peace and comfort of it even more. The absence of all interruptions makes it the only place in the world where I can have complete rest.

---

[1] Charlotte Knollys was ill with typhoid fever at Birkhall.

From the Crown Princess

WIESBADEN, DECEMBER 8, 1877

Would you dearest Mama, be so very kind as to send me a note written in your own dear hand and dated and signed, on the weather, or some such important subject? It is for a Hanoverian gentleman here, who has a most splendid autograph collection, but who does not collect names alone, but little letters of persons celebrated in History! This gentleman is quite a fit person to receive such a precious present, or I would not venture to ask. Can I also have a little letter from Lord Beaconsfield for the same purpose, and one from Beatrice? I should like if possible before we leave here, and we go on the 17th. Perhaps you possess some indifferent little note from Bertie and Alix which I could also have?

From the Crown Princess

WIESBADEN, DECEMBER 14, 1877

Our thoughts are only with you today, and Alice and I sitting together and talking of all that is past, of all your sufferings and your bereavement shed many a tear! The memory of those days, and of the blessed and happy times before them can never be effaced from our hearts that are ever full of tenderest love and gratitude. It was a comfort to both of us to be together today! The 3rd volume of dear Papa's **Life** arriving today seemed a strange but comforting coincidence. I have read all the articles about it with the greatest interest, and they all seem in a very satisfactory tone and strain. Our 11 children gathered round the table today make us feel all the more what we have lost, and what they have lost, and we cannot help thinking that all the fresh and smiling young faces would have rejoiced beloved Papa's kind heart— and that he would have found among all his many grandchildren some who would have caused him pleasure, and given him hopes that all his labour of love and bright example were not quite in vain, though none I fancy will ever attain anything like his perfection.

From the Queen

WINDSOR CASTLE, DECEMBER 17, 1877

The fall of Plevna[1] was a bitter pill, a true grief to me who feels too

---

[1] On December 9 the Turkish Commander, Osman Nuri Pasha, and his army unconditionally surrendered.

strongly to speak of it! I cannot express in words my indignation! But please God we shall assert our feelings and position.

From the Queen

I remain here for Christmas, a measure rendered necessary by the very critical state of affairs which obliged me to see Lord Beaconsfield and to communicate rapidly with him. So we only go on the twenty-eighth D.V.—a disappointment. Parliament is to assemble on the seventeenth and energetic and at the same time a pacific line to be taken. The Country is roused to the real interests of our Empire and to our position. I can't say more now.

I am so sorry though not surprised to hear in one of your letters that George of Meiningen is so disagreeable—but I have for many years thought him hard and disagreeable and since he behaved so shamefully to poor dear Feo, and outraged her memory by his present marriage, I have thought the very worst of him, and I will never see him.

Our visit to Hughenden was very interesting and successful.[1] The country is lovely with hills and dales and much wooded and the house full of interesting portraits and books. I had been in High Wycombe forty-five years ago—as a child with Grandmama when we changed horses there coming from Lord Abingdon's near Oxford.

From the Queen

I received your dear and most interesting and important letter of the nineteenth yesterday.[2] I agree in every word and will not burn it—and have extracted the most important parts for Lord B.—who is full of energy and youth but who has untold difficulties.

---

[1] "The Queen going ostentatiously to eat with Disraeli in his ghetto." The distinguished historian Freeman quoted in Blake's *Disraeli*.

[2] The original of this letter is missing but a part of it is printed in *Letters of Queen Victoria*, Second Series, Vol. I, pp. 578–80.

The Crown Princess urged that England should assert herself and not allow Russia and Turkey to settle things among themselves. "How I do long for one good roar of the British Lion." She goes on that her experience and observation of politics on the Continent had convinced her that England was the only really humane country and far in advance of all other countries in the scale of civilisation and progress. "If Russia be allowed she will become the bane of the world. Germany can never or ought never to grow out of her own confines."

From the Crown Princess

BERLIN, DECEMBER 22, 1877

It is good news to me that Parliament is going to assemble and that England's voice will be heard! For my part her voice should never be raised but to command.

From the Crown Princess

BERLIN, DECEMBER 24, 1877

I am indeed pleased and relieved that my letter did not give offence, as after it was gone, I reproached myself with having spoken too openly —but I could not resist it! and I have heard much more those last four days which only confirms more and more the opinion I there ventured to express so freely.

From the Queen

WINDSOR CASTLE, DECEMBER 26, 1877

That letter of yours to me is most valuable and extracts from it, may help to open the eyes of many who quite bear out the humiliating and offensive opinion of England (Great Britain) but I must tell you that you are quite mistaken if you think that Lord Beaconsfield's age makes business "irksome to him".[1] If he had been able to do what he and I thought right months ago—you would have been satisfied;—but Lord Derby would do nothing one way or the other and some others had rather extraordinary religious views—and others again were alarmed— and Mr. Gladstone and some of his mad admirers did all they could to poison the minds of the nation! Thank God however the Country at large is roused to the danger of Russian aggression and ambition—and supported by me, and by most of his colleagues (the Lord Chancellor, Duke of Richmond, Mr. Hardy, Lord John Manners) and following them all the others—he has taken the reins firmly in his hands and Lord Derby and those who were foolish have submitted entirely and we are now ready to act in the right sense. Lord Beaconsfield will not loosen the reins again and I work very hard in writing to him and cyphering to him almost daily—sometimes. In strictest confidence I may tell you (but please tell no one) what the three points are which were triumphantly

---

[1] But the Crown Princess was well informed. "If it were not for the Fairy [Queen Victoria] I would at once retire." Disraeli to Lady Bradford, 25 October. But his health improved after he changed his doctor and was treated by a homoeopath. See Blake's *Disraeli*, Chapter xxvii.

carried by Lord B.—1. The calling together of Parliament as early as possible. 2. Asking for a large increase of forces. 3. Direct mediation on our part. Don't speak of this but this is what is agreed on and settled and to show publicly my support of Lord Beaconsfield's policy I went over to luncheon at Hughenden.

1878

From the Queen

I was so vexed I could not write yesterday but I never have been so overwhelmed with writing and work. The peculiar difficulties of the situation which I described to you—and which annoy me so much—and which seem to me so incredible for true English (British) people, give me so much constant writing. Lord Beaconsfield and I are always at work, and so many telegrams arrive that one gets quite bewildered and so tired.

I can't quite understand you saying "one can't understand" or "quite agree with" *The Times*!!! Surely you must have known long ago, that *The Times* is a mere tool in the hands of Russia, takes its inspiration from Count Schouvaloff, is, I believe, even bribed—and its reports from the seat of war are utterly unreliable, as Colonel Mansfield writes, having been written only with one object, viz for Russia?!!! You should read *The Telegraph* and *Pall Mall* which are excellent. Is it not almost treasonable to behave as *The Times* does? Then see that disgraceful speech of that absurd (though in some respects clever) little Lord Carnarvon—calculated to weaken all our efforts for peace—and to make our sincerity doubted. I had not seen him for long—nor had I yet read this speech—though I had heard by cypher that it had been strongly censured in the Cabinet, and when I met him yesterday I pitched into him with a vehemence and indignation—which was at any rate inspired by the British Lion—and he remained shrinking but still craven-hearted! wishing to say to the world we could not act!!! Oh! that Englishmen were now what they were!! But we shall yet assert our rights—our position—and "Britons never will be slaves" will yet be our motto. I own I never spoke with such vehemence as I did last night.[1] Somebody asked me, if there was any danger that, should we have to assist Turkey, Germany would attack us! I suppose I was right in saying neither the Emperor or Fritz would ever allow that—or Bismarck dream of it?

---

[1] The 4th Earl of Carnarvon (1831–90). At this time he was Colonial Secretary; receiving a deputation of South African merchants at Highclere on January 2 he said that "nobody in this country was insane enough to desire a repetition of the Crimean War". Disraeli described him as "living in his castle in the country, surrounded by literary parasites, chiefly contributors to the Liberal Press". The Queen had sent him the Crown Princess's letter of December 19.

From the Queen

I understand what you mean about Egypt and Candia but don't think anything can be done about it now. We are doing our best—but really two or three of the ministers are mad, like that foolish, misguided (and yet in his own department very able) little Lord Carnarvon! His speech was dreadful—but I gave him such a dressing—and told him what you said about the feeling abroad which they will not believe! And Mr. Forster has made a dreadful speech too.[1] Oh! how wrong how wicked to try and play England into the hands of Russia. It is really quite distracting. Were it not for this perfect craze everything would be easy.

Tomorrow the Crown Prince of Austria and Arthur come, the former for two nights.

From the Queen

I am, as you may imagine, much grieved at poor King V.E.'s sudden and untimely death. I always had a feeling for him—though not in '59—when I thought he behaved treacherously and shamefully and when dear Papa, who never liked him, was furious with him.[2] But he was always very friendly and kind to me, and latterly especially and he is a great loss for Italy.

Still I own I can't understand Fritz's going to the funeral. He is no relation, was no ally (as he was to us) and was not of a respectable character!

If I died—Fritz could do no more! It must be some political, Bismarckian view!

---

[1] At Bradford. He said that Bismarck had said that no Pomeranian ploughman should risk his life in the quarrel between Russia and Turkey and added "no Bradford artisan or Dorsetshire labourer" should be put at risk; "It could not be the duty of England to defeat Russia that we might make ourselves responsible once more for Turkish tyranny".

William Forster (1818–86). Liberal statesman; responsible for Education Act of 1871.

[2] Commanding the Sardinian forces and supported by the French under Napoleon III, Victor Emmanuel was in part responsible for the expulsion of Austria from north Italy. He was established as King of Italy at the end of the year (1859).

From the Queen

Many thanks for your two dear letters of the 12th, which crossed mine of the fourteenth—so I will not say any more about Fritz's going to Rome as you know my views. All you say about the poor King Victor Emmanuel's great qualities—in spite of great failings which are partly to be excused on account of his education and very peculiar temperament is very true. And he was most uniformly kind to me always, and what you say only confirms what I heard elsewhere. He sent me lovely horses and such kind affectionate telegrams not more than a year and a half ago! But I remember the day when Fritz could not bear him. And I also remember that dear Papa said in '59 that your father-in-law would never do what the King of Italy had done. Alas '66 belied that!

I am very vexed at Henry of Hesse's marriage which really is too annoying for Alice just now.[1]

We liked the young Crown Prince of Austria very much. He is so simple and unaffected and yet so well informed and with such charming manners.

Dear Arthur who has been here since the 10th has left us this morning—and now I come with a favour. You have given him a most charming Dackel and he tells me you have a breed of them—red and black. Now would you (as I have given you sheep and a Collie) give me one or two for the breed? A male and a female or one even? If possible after having had the distemper? My Dackels have gone down very much—and our own pet's children all died and were miserable things. I have some—but not very successful ones and I should be very grateful for one or two.

From the Crown Princess

I have read the speech with great interest, I only fear it will satisfy the Opposition and Peace Party more than it does me![2] It is very mild and moderate, but I fear will not stop the Russians from carrying out their plans to the very end, and sounds like handing over Turkey to Russia. But perhaps I ought not to say this. When the Russians mean

---

[1] Princess Alice's brother-in-law who married morganatically the Baroness Nidda.

[2] The Queen's speech, at the Opening of Parliament on January 17, referred to the Czar's earnest desire for peace but asked that this country should adopt "measures of precaution".

Princess Charlotte of Prussia, January 1878. *Reproduced by gracious permission of Her Majesty Queen Elizabeth II*

Family group of the Duchess of Connaught and her sisters taken in Potsdam in 1878. The Duke and Duchess are on the left, Princess Henry of the Netherlands and Prince Henry in the centre and the hereditary Grand Duchess of Oldenburg and her husband on the right. *Reproduced by gracious permission of Her Majesty Queen Elizabeth II*

peacefully I do not know, but who could ever believe what they say—as the utmost duplicity is their system, and has alas! hitherto been successful. I happen to know that they have ordered an immense number of guns from Krupp within the last few days! How should the poor Turks be able to go on!! They represent 16 millions and the others represent 80 millions.

About the dogs I went immediately to Bornstadt yesterday and chose a dear little pair, old enough to travel and I think will be very pretty. They have not had the distemper. None of our Dackels have ever had it, and our foreman says that it is not likely they will have it; if they do, it will be so slight as not to matter! The little creatures will leave by the messenger today. I suppose you will have them taken to Windsor or Osborne. They are still babies. Of course they are brother and sister—therefore it might be advisable to have one from Uncle Ernest, as a cross, or they might get too small in the coming generations. Our breed are particularly clever. The one we have in the house is really almost like a human being he is so intelligent. The dog that will be sent is called "Scherz" after Waldemar's poor little pet that was driven over, and the little lady is called "Duchess" after Aunt Alexandrine's dog. The little Dackels are very fond of running after ill-dressed or dirty looking people who they think ought not to be about the place, they jump and then bark and tear their clothes; but to their own friends and masters they are most gentle and amiable and affectionate. They are capital watch-dogs.

From the Queen

OSBORNE, JANUARY 21, 1878

One hurried line before going to bed to thank you so very, very much for the darling little Dackels. I could not believe it, when on coming in this afternoon Brown came in and said "here are two dackels come—bonnie dogs" and I at once guessed who sent them and we are so delighted with the sweet dackel babies. You know how I adore doggies and these are two darlings. How old are they? And how nearly related to Arthur's and to Waldy's poor little pet and what are their parents called and where do they come from? I hope you will not object to my changing their names—but the German names would be murdered here and we have a black and tan dackel—Duchess—so I have called them Prince and Princess. I have a few black and tans of my own breed—and one Count Münster gave me—quite black with only two spots of tan over the eyes.

From the Queen

Let me thank you very much for your last dear and interesting letter of the 25th. Before answering anything I think I had best tell you how distressingly the Government and I are situated else you will never understand it. It is the Opposition who causes it—whose conduct is really disastrous for they have (and I think it most shameful and disloyal towards me) entirely changed the old, right policy of this country—which had they been in office they could not have done, and wish Russia to take what she likes, for instance see Mr. Forster's amendment[1] to the all important vote (which however will be carried by a large majority), I truly grieve to say merely out of factious opposition. I have tried indirectly to appeal to their sense of patriotism but all in vain. Lord Clarendon's saying to me—a year or two before he died—when we lamented over this—is but too true; "self, then party and last Sovereign and Country". Oh is it not too sad! But to return to what has happened. Lord Carnarvon and Lord Derby had both resigned (and the former has behaved very ill and is a good riddance, though he is able in his way) and Lord Derby was to have gone when —two days after I accepted his resignation, Lord Beaconsfield in really the greatest distress and Sir S. Northcote also told me that all Lancashire and other important votes would probably be lost, if Lord Derby resigned, and that we must in order to secure this vote retain him!! Of course, what could be done but retain him, though I think he won't stay long. But this is the explanation of what passed last week— and why, for miserable Party objects, and a total misconception of Lord Derby's character, we can't do all we wish. But any further step of Russia strengthens the Government's hands for action. Pray tell this to the Empress whom I can't write to today and send this letter to Alice to see. What I—and poor Lord Beaconsfield too and many others suffer no one can tell. It makes me quite ill. The duplicity of the Russians is awful—and they will pay dearly for their monstrous conduct.

From the Queen

Things are greatly improving here. The very strong meeting in Sheffield, the City etc. have done immense good as also the letter of

---

[1] That there were "no reasons for adding to the burdens of the people" by voting increased supplies for armaments.

Lord Fortescue and the speech of Lord Fitzwilliam.[1] I hope you will read the debates. Mr. Gladstone's speech at Oxford[2] shocked everyone and I hear from impartial people that he is hooted and hissed in the streets and theatres, whereas Lord Beaconsfield is cheered wherever he goes!

From the Crown Princess

BERLIN, FEBRUARY 8, 1878

I read the debate and thought Mr. Gladstone's speech very weak and incoherent and not to the purpose.[3] If the 6 millions are voted, and war is no longer necessary I hope and trust they will be devoted to improving and increasing the Army. There was such an excellent article in the *Nineteenth Century* a fortnight ago on the Army! How I wish you would read it. Now is the time to reform and reorganise the British Army on the most simple, inexpensive, modern and probate[4] principles! And as beloved Papa is no longer there to fight for that, and insist upon the greatest perfection and efficiency being obtained, who is there to do that but you yourself? Are not the British officers and men the finest, strongest and bravest in the whole world? Whenever the English nation thoroughly sets to work to put a thing on the highest possible footing that end is obtained more surely than anywhere else as all the national energy, common-sense and practical knowledge is put in force. I am sure you think so too! Our Army as it cannot be a large one, ought to be the best in organisation as it is the best in material. It would always be a match for the Russians then! I think one cannot devote too much attention to the subject. Fritz is so anxious about it and I have heard the same opinion from the warmest lovers of England and also from old Moltke. Forgive my saying all this but I have my country's greatness and welfare so much at heart that, though thoroughly as liberal and progressive as any cotton spinner, yet I know what dangers are ahead which the manu-

---

[1] They were both Liberals.
[2] On January 24 the Mediterranean fleet was ordered to Constantinople through the Dardenelles. At Oxford on January 30 Gladstone described this as "an act of war", a breach of international law. *Gladstone* by Sir Philip Magnus, p. 249.
[3] He said that it was a mistake to usher in a conference with a clash of arms; he would lament if the Government went to the conference representing a divided nation and suggested that the vote for additional arms should be postponed. (The Armistice between the Russians and the Turks had been signed on January 31 and it was generally realised—though not as yet arranged—that the Armistice would be followed by a Conference of the Powers.)
[4] A confusion of language. German *probat* meaning excellent.

facturing population of England has perhaps no time or means to see and observe.

Everyone is puzzling here to know what Bismarck intends to do! Of course I can only form conjectures, but I fancy I am right. He wishes to curtail Russia's successes and disappoint her ambition as much as he can! But he does not wish to have the odium in the eyes of Russia and (rightly) does not wish to excite Russia against Germany. Therefore the objections which will have to be raised against all the Russians' demands in the Treaty of Peace Bismarck would prefer to see come from Austria which he would then support. I fancy he greatly builds on Austria and England offering all possible resistance which he would then gladly join, without seeming to the Russians to be the one to move first in the question. This seems to me to be a sensible course for him to take, and his reasons are good, as though he is as little a friend of Russia's as the Emperor is an unqualified one, yet he is so placed that he must not offend Russia, or appear otherwise than friendly though reserved! I am sure you see this also at a glance.

The poor old Pope is dead![1] He was so amiable, kind and friendly to me years ago that I have a tenderness for his memory—he was a dear old man, in spite of having been an ignorant and innocent instrument of great political evil and mischief and the representative of a bad cause. I am afraid the death-bed of a Pope is as sad and uncomfortable and lonely as possible—without family or friends.

From the Queen

OSBORNE, FEBRUARY 11, 1878

Never could I keep my promise of writing fully to you—for the amount of telegrams—cyphers—received and often sent—the keeping them together, referring to them etc., the debate etc. has been such that I have been quite unable to write for I felt my head and brain quite overtaxed—a very painful feeling—making all thinking, writing, etc., very trying and making me so tired. On Friday this was very bad and on Saturday and even today I feel so tired and nervous. But I will not omit later writing what I wish to about the Liberals—who really do not deserve the name as they really support and excuse and advocate Russia's conduct continually. However the Country is thoroughly roused—and the monstrous perfidy, treachery and lying of the Russians in all this affair of the armistice has enraged all patriotic

---

[1] Pius IX.

people. I hope you can read at least the abstracts of the debate on Thursday and Friday.

Many thanks for your dear letter of the fifth. Clever as Lord Odo R. is, I don't think he would do as well for the conference as Lord Lyons who is wonderfully clever—wise and wary and he is more a thorough diplomatist than charming Lord Odo.

From the Crown Princess

BERLIN, FEBRUARY 12, 1878

Waldy poor little man—in his uniform seemed rather uncomfortable! The Emperor insisted on appointing a military Governor to my utter despair. You know what a disagreeable and unnecessary thing it is, besides most embarrassing for us who are quite satisfied with Waldemar's tutor! However we succeeded in obtaining from the Emperor that Colonel Mischke, Fritz's former Aide de Camp and now head of the Staff, was the person appointed, and he will not interfere with the education so it will not be so bad in practice as in theory, and will only last till Waldemar goes to school which alas will be in a couple of years! Still the interference with one's children is a thing most hard and irritating to bear.

From the Queen

OSBORNE, FEBRUARY 13, 1878

My head will not allow yet of my answering the business, important parts in your letters which I am very anxious to do. But I will just say this—that I don't understand what you mean by reforming the Army. An immense deal was done after the Crimean War and Lord Cardwell reformed and altered to that extent that he did a terrible deal of mischief—and all those who understand it most and best say the harm he did while he was in office was very serious. It is however now in a really very efficient state excepting as to numbers, which will rapidly increase, and of course many of the men are very young, but the material is excellent.

Poor Marie is at Malta, and avoids I hear all politics with her people and reads the *Daily News*!!¹ Family alliances with great nations are of no use—in these days, indeed I think they are a great misfortune. You will have I hope read Mr. Cowen's speeches.² He is a great radical,

---

¹ The champion of the Liberal Party and of the Emancipation of the Bulgarians.
² Member of Parliament for Newcastle-upon-Tyne. He was rich but wore in the House

but an honest man and patriotic which I am shocked and grieved to say the Opposition as a body are not. The harm they have done their country is irreparable and I can never forget it.

From the Queen

OSBORNE, FEBRUARY 15, 1878

Mr. Gladstone goes on like a madman. I never saw anything to equal the want of patriotism and the want of proper decency in Members of Parliament. It is a miserable thing to be a constitutional Queen and to be unable to do what is right. I would gladly throw all up and retire into quiet.

From the Crown Princess

BERLIN, FEBRUARY 19, 1878

At 4 in the afternoon the dressing began. As I dressed Charlotte while I was dressing myself—it was rather a long and rambling business. She really looked very pretty—in the silver moiré train, the lace—the orange and myrtle and the veil (dangerous innovations for here)—but they were all very well taken by the Emperor and Empress! For the "*mariage civile*" which took place in our drawing-room there were *heaps* of people, such as did not wish to go to the Schloss. Herr von Scheinitz's address to the young couple was very fine, touching and impressive. After this the signing was done and they were *married*. Charlotte said she felt quite light and happy—now it was over—and would not mind the rest of the ceremonies at the Schloss! I then led her downstairs—and drove off with her—in a carriage with 8 horses and all the grooms carrying torches! At the Schloss all the ceremonies went off according to the Programme you have seen! It was *very very* long—*very* hot, *very* tiring, and almost too serious, solemn and heavy for a wedding, but so it always is here. After the *fackeltanz*[1] I took her to her room. After the crown had been taken off, I helped her to undress and get ready for going to bed, and with an *aching* heart left her, *no* more *mine* now—to care for and watch and take care of but another's and that is a hard *wrench* for a *mother*. With pangs of pain we bring them into the world, with bitter pain, we resign them to others— to life to independence—and to shift for themselves—we bore the one for their sakes with pleasure—and so must we the *other*. Forgive my

---

of Commons the Sunday clothes of a Northumberland miner. Gladstone complained that his speech "smelled too much of the lamp".
[1] A dance, with torches, in which only those of the highest rank took part.

paper being so blotted, but I cannot help shedding a few tears. When I came back last night and looked into her little empty room and empty bed where every night I have kissed her before lying down myself ever since she has been born (when I was at home) I felt very miserable. However it must be so, and she looks very happy and shed not a tear yesterday and Bernard dotes upon her.

I have thought *more* of *you*—than ever in my life and more than of every one else! Mothers do *not* lose their daughters if all love their Mothers as much as I do *you*.

From the Queen

WINDSOR CASTLE, FEBRUARY 20, 1878

Affairs are very bad. You Germans might have prevented it all—but the Great Man hopes to see everyone engaged and quarrelling. However I have no apprehension that the right thing will be done and that the British Lion will bite, now that he is roused and the so-called Liberals, who wish Russia to be protected and trusted (several including Mr. Gladstone have said this) begin to be really alarmed at what they, out of party feeling, have chiefly brought about—and to wish to support their country. Party is a great evil when it is carried too far—as the present Opposition do—or rather for two years only.[1]

From the Crown Princess

BERLIN, FEBRUARY 22, 1878

Things look very bad indeed in politics; alas! the Russians think themselves a match for the English twice over, but not for England and an ally and to get this ally seems to me so important! Whether the Austrians are to be relied on is so doubtful—and difficult to know! Prince Bismarck has however no wish whatever to see "everyone quarrelling" as you say—on the contrary. He must not quarrel with Russia, but can only regret anything that strengthens her or weakens England's power—this is self-evident and needs no explanation. He were a madman to wish anything else.

I fancy he is of opinion that it is the worst moment for England to go to war—and that the time is past, when it would have been useful and likely to lead to a result—i.e. to stop Russia's proceedings, which Austria and England might have done some time ago!

---

1 Difficult to read, but meaning as the Opposition have done for the two years since the Eastern crisis flared up.

From the Crown Princess

BERLIN, MARCH 1, 1878

Waldy and Fritz Leopold walked first, hand in hand, and then Vicky behind them with Sophie and Mossy on each side.[1] They were in blue satin slips with the Isle of Wight lace you gave them, and looked very dear each with a nosegay, and their fair hair hanging down their backs. They all behaved very well indeed, and Vicky showed the most touching tact all through those days—and now. She has tact and discretion far beyond her years, I am often astonished at the true, tender-hearted little woman she is in feeling. She has such a sweet disposition. I shall never feel anxious on her account, if she is but spared! One could trust her anywhere.

From the Queen

WINDSOR CASTLE, MARCH 6, 1878

As regards politics (oh! how I hate that word!) I wish to say that you seem to take as a matter of course that Russia is to have her own way; whereas we here consider the peace between her and Turkey, whatever it may be, an arrangement which we are prepared to dispute so long as it is inconsistent with existing treaties and our own interests and those of Europe. You are under a misapprehension that so far as England is concerned, all is finished in this business. In my view of the case (which is Lord Beaconsfield's) it has hardly begun!

From the Queen

WINDSOR CASTLE, MARCH 9, 1878

Let me also thank you for your long political letter of the sixth received yesterday. It is impossible for me to enter into arguments or to make you even understand all the reasons and necessities for our conduct. But that we shall stand on our own feet you may be sure of.

From the Queen

WINDSOR CASTLE, MARCH 12, 1878

I don't want to lose any time by waiting till tomorrow, and therefore write at once today to thank you for your long and interesting

---

[1] Princess Victoria's confirmation.

letter about Louise[1] as well as for the other short one which I sent to Arthur—both of the 9th. I did not—as I wrote—expect such a denouement nor do I like it—I must honestly say, as I have seen no real good spring from these alliances (though no doubt and please God! it is never likely that England and Germany should quarrel as England and Russia I fear always will). Besides I dislike the House [Fritz Carl's] she comes from, and I think the Prussian Royal family (the Emperor and Empress excepted) are particularly proud and overbearing which does not do here least of all nowadays. But if Louise is what you describe her to be—if she is so unhappy at home and so fond of England and so sweet tempered and if she clings to me and to her husband, asks me for advice etc. I shall become reconciled to it and do all to be kind to her and I have no doubt be very fond of her. I wish she were prettier! Nose and mouth being ugly is sad and Arthur said—bad teeth. Now however comes two all important points which I shall likewise mention to the Empress but which I hope you and Fritz will be firm upon. The first is that the marriage must take place here. Louise is not the Emperor's only daughter as Marie A. was, but only his great-niece and the third daughter. Arthur is my son and I am a woman, unable to travel any distance for festivities like those at your Court which I could not ever go through. Of course I would, like at Bertie's marriage, have the parents and some of the relations though you know how comparatively little room we have here.

The second and just as important point, in fact more so for the future happiness of the girl herself is that she—like dear Alix, who was just the same age as Louise—should come and stay for a short while alone with us before she marries. Alix came the beginning of November and stayed three weeks. Her father brought her and left her after a day —and came to fetch her again. Alix and I both think that to that stay is due much of the happy footing on which she was at once with us all. Now please try and arrange this in the interests of those you love so much, somehow or other.

From the Queen

WINDSOR CASTLE, MARCH 12, 1878

I said I would add a few words—and so I do—first as regards the Cambridges. I am sure Uncle George will be all kindness, but I am doubtful of the others, certainly of poor old Aunt—who is so suffering,

---

[1] The Duke of Connaught's engagement to Princess Louise—the youngest daughter of Fritz Carl.

and obstinate in her views. Mary I think would be kind. Moreover as the parents are not likely to come over often—or Arthur's home to be a centre of Prussians, Louise will become one of us and as such will certainly be loved if she be all you describe her to be. Alix won't like it I fear, as she wished Thyra which for many reasons I never did. Indeed Arthur is so good and steady I had just as soon he had not married at all; and all marriages are such terrible uncertainties that I am very doubtful about them and would never advocate any which I know is the reverse with you who think that marriages are one object! How is it that Louise should become in a few days so attached to Arthur? Did you and Charlotte not beforehand sing his praises to her? What I regret is that no one gave me a hint of this as I had so particularly wished Arthur to see others before he engaged himself to anyone. However there it is and the only thing is to do everything we can to make all work well and comfortably in the family. It would be a great thing if (as Arthur said was the case) she did not much care for going out;—it would have the best effect.

From the Queen

BUCKINGHAM PALACE, MARCH 21, 1878

Alas! you will share my sorrow and indignation when you hear that Affie has got into a sad scrape—which will I fear injure his future prospects in his profession. It is very terrible to have no sense of duty, no tact and I must add no sense of honour, but he never had. It was only yesterday that I heard the distressing circumstances, of which I will tell you more in a day or two![1]

What does a Prussian Princess receive? Is not old Prince Charles very rich and could he not give his grand-daughter something?

From the Queen

WINDSOR CASTLE, MARCH 27, 1878

This awful misfortune of the poor *Eurydice*—which you will see full descriptions of in the papers—will fill you with horror and give you a turn and perhaps a little damp your (to me) incredible passion for that most perfidious and dangerous element. That very way dear Henry encountered a heavy sea. But three hundred and fifty lives lost in one instant in sight of home is too awful![2]

---

[1] The details have not survived, but were probably political.
[2] The *Eurydice*, a training ship, sailing back from a cruise to the West Indies, was struck by a freak squall, preceding a snowstorm, on March 24 off Ventnor.

From the Crown Princess

Perhaps it might interest you to have a perfectly unofficial view of Prince Bismarck when he was only discussing different eventualities with Fritz last night. He said: "If England is bent upon war, she can carry it out with patience, without a Plevna or an Adrianople, by starving out the Russians, closing their ports, and stopping their commerce." Moltke said the same thing.

What a shame of the Russians to make that unfortunate Sultan give his order to the Russian Generals; I think it horrible! And Ignatief's visit to Vienna!! I am so afraid that the Emperor of Austria is inclined to give way to the Russians. Andrassy certainly is not![1] If only England and Austria and Italy and all the wronged and disappointed states, who were supposed to be liberated and regenerated by Russia, could act together, and the little ones shake off the Russian yoke under the protection of England and Austria. Perhaps my views (only those of an outsider) will make you laugh.

England can always afford to take up a good cause and do what is right and useful, in the right way! Whereas Russia only acts from ambition and carries out her plans by craft and cunning; that is not a policy which bears lasting fruit or which is successful in the long run. They have played the very worst part throughout and I can only hope that the matter may be wrested out of their hands—and turned into the very reverse of what they want, i.e. by England, whose prestige ought to rise, and not fall by comparison with a power whose chief aim seems to be to trick and dupe everyone! But still I hope by arming to the teeth and showing the utmost determination—a war may still possibly be avoided.

From the Queen

You will I hope have read and admired the very able and clear circular of Lord Salisbury (aided by Lord Beaconsfield) which is universally admired by everyone—though the Opposition will not have the courage to say so.[2] "Bent on war" God knows we certainly

---

[1] Count Gynka Andrassy (1823–90) Austrian Foreign Minister.
[2] By the Treaty of San Stefano signed between Russia and Turkey at the end of March, Bulgaria was greatly enlarged with ports on the Aegean. The British Government called out the Reserve and Lord Salisbury, who had succeeded Lord Derby as Foreign Secretary, issued a Circular to the Powers demanding that the Treaty should be submitted to the judgment of Europe.

are not—or we should not have tried every means to avoid it; but we are determined to assert our rights and to defend the rights and morality of Europe by being armed and prepared to maintain our views which I am sure you will agree in. Lord Derby was *rayonnant* when he gave up the Seals yesterday and Lord Salisbury will make an excellent Foreign Secretary. He is very able and very energetic. Mr. Hardy will do admirably for India and so will Colonel Stanley for War. He has all the qualities which his elder and far more praised but not really cleverer brother has not.

From the Queen

OSBORNE, APRIL 10, 1878

I must write in a great hurry to save the messenger. Many affectionate thanks for your dear and interesting letter of the 5th.[1] I have let Lord Salisbury know what you said as well as Lord Beaconsfield as I know how pleased they would be and how encouraged. But you will be shocked at Lord Derby's and Mr. Gladstone's speeches on Thursday. The former is (though possibly unintentionally on his part and most likely pushed on by his half crazy wife[2]) quite treacherous and most indiscreet.

From the Queen

WINDSOR CASTLE, Undated, probably MAY 19, 1878

The dear three weeks' visit is over like everything pleasant and everything evil in this uncertain world. I enjoyed it much, found you so sympathetic and improved, and understanding and sharing the load of anxiety which weighs on me especially about that wayward,

---

[1] "Since Lord Derby's resignation and Lord Salisbury's Circular one can hold up one's head again. . . . Now we know that England has a policy, and that it is a clear and right one, and this has already changed the aspect of the whole question." Crown Princess, April 5. The Russo–Turkish conflict now grows less prominent in the correspondence, principally because the Crown Princess was in England for several weeks. The Queen was at Balmoral in early summer and noticed on June 18 that 1100 telegrams were sent and received during the four weeks she had been there—principally concerned with the Eastern Question. The Congress of Berlin opened on June 13 and lasted for a calendar month. Lord Beaconsfield and Lord Salisbury were the British representatives and with the help of Prussia and Austria they secured terms which were satisfactory (though not triumphant) and successfully destroyed the Treaty of San Stefano without war. Lord Beaconsfield was rapturously received in London on the July 16. "I sent General Ponsonby with a letter and nosegay for him." The Queen, July 23.

[2] Daughter of the 5th Lord De La Warr and step-mother of Lord Salisbury.

undutiful Leopold![1] I enclose what I have written to him—which I would wish you to let Louise, Arthur and Bertie and Alix see. Let Louise also see the shameful letter and then please return them both. I mean to take no notice whatever of him—but what Bertie owes to me (and you all do) is not to let him find that though his "intense aversion" to be with me in Scotland has succeeded in keeping him away—he is not invited to dinner parties, plays, balls and above all to Epsom or Ascot. He must be made to feel that such conduct to a mother and a Sovereign cannot be tolerated. What would Bertie think (and Alix I know will feel it) if his sons were to treat him and her in such a way? If I am not supported by Bertie he will be letting down the authority of the Sovereign and the Throne.

None of my Uncles[2] would have permitted such conduct from their brothers—nephews and nieces—not to speak of their children. Only speak to Lenchen and Christian and hear what they think and feel.

I have just received your dear, loving, affectionate letter which has touched me much and given me the greatest pleasure. I know your warm, loving heart and I know that you can enter into my terrible trials and anxieties. I fear Bertie will be talked over by the strong-willed and wrong-headed boy, he having no experience of what it is to have grown-up sons—setting their parents at defiance and forgetting what they owe to them. If he stays a short time in London (for which he must ask my permission) we think he ought to go to Buckingham Palace to his own rooms upstairs—where he cannot so easily get in and out. Your sisters and Alix can do more with him than Bertie—as poor B. does not always set the right example. Arguing with him is useless—but what I do expect Bertie to help me in, is in not letting him (after three months perpetual amusement) think he has carried the day and put me down, and now he will go to Bertie's house and amuse himself as he likes! If Bertie does not do as I ask, I am entirely powerless, and ingratitude, undutifulness and disloyalty will be triumphant!! I am dreadfully annoyed and worried about it.

---

[1] Prince Leopold found intolerable the long sojourns at Balmoral. He was by no means alone in this. At Balmoral one of the Queen's ladies said that when people are temporarily unhappy they sometimes kill themselves. The Queen's private secretary replied "In that case suicide might be common here". In fairness to the Queen we have to remember that Prince Leopold was not really strong enough to live on his own. Part of the explanation for the Queen's vehemence is that she knew perfectly well that her elder children were privately critical of her long spells in seclusion at Balmoral. The Crown Princess was still in England.

[2] Meaning King George IV and King William IV.

From the Queen

I have thought so much of you and felt very sad that we could not talk so nicely together, or have our nice drives in the beautiful spring weather. I felt so much every affectionate word you wrote! Knowing what dear Papa was to you—how much more in many things your and his tastes accorded I feel myself always inadequate for you—you and I leading different lives and your not being (from the very different position I am in) able to understand feelings, resources and comforts which suit me. But on the other hand the older you grow—the older your children grow, the more our feelings will be in harmony for you are as anxious as I am for the welfare and success of our children, and we both have the same feeling of the trials and difficulties which they entail and of the frivolity and wickedness of the world. And this makes it a mutual comfort to be together and to be able to speak on all these subjects. I admire your knowledge and great talents and your great energy and perseverance but I would venture to warn against too great intimacy with artists as it is very seductive and a little dangerous. You are wonderfully modest of your great gifts and powers. All you say of my darling Beatrice pleases and touches me, but it is only the truth, for she is like a sunbeam in the house and also like a dove, an angel of peace who brings it wherever she goes and who is my greatest comfort.

From the Crown Princess

I spoke to my dear Alix about Leopold and she feels as we do, but also says he is very difficult to manage, and will not believe what his peculiar constitution is. Louise thinks the same about him and if we see him, we shall all tell him the same, I trust it may make an impression and that he will be a little more sensible.

I will send back the letter tomorrow. How can I thank you enough for your kind words in your dear letter, they are so very precious to me! Indeed I can understand what a burden of business, anxiety, responsibility of every kind you have to bear, and sympathise with you with all my heart, though I cannot but feel that "the back is suited to the burthen" and that with your long training and experience &c. none could bear it better, and thankful do I feel to Heaven, that all the sorrows and trials you have gone through have not crushed your mind and your spirits.

It was so cold yesterday more like February than May. I saw the old drawings in the Burlington Fine Arts Club, which interested me immensely.[1] How very pretty Lowther Lodge is; I admired the architecture and the size of the rooms, &c.[2] There was a bazaar there for a charitable society, and I saw a great many people whom I had not seen for ages, but many of them did not know me (i.e. the Duchess of Beaufort, Lady Barrington, and a few others) but afterwards they recognised me and were most kind.

From the Crown Princess

I have just received your dear and kind letter, and kiss your dear hands for it. It touches me most deeply! Indeed you cannot think how precious to me the understanding with you is! What can ever replace a mother to a daughter especially to one who has gone through a good deal, has growing children, and knows what the world is. I am sure that in many many things our views are quite the same, and that where there may be a difference (for no two people and no two minds are ever alike) it is not such as to prevent us from understanding each other.

About Leopold I have found the brothers and sisters *d'accord*, the only thing will be—how to bring him himself to understand what is required of him and what is for his good. He is no doubt very sensitive, and what another would see in one minute his irritability blinds him to. An older person with him, and a journey to the Colonies would be certain to great work changes! You have forgiven him so often and had patience with him so often, as mothers do, that he ought to feel it easy now to own he has been in the wrong and to feel the confidence, that it is not harshness that directs your wishes for his conduct, but simply his good and safety you have in view! I am sure he has not the slightest idea that he is wanting in respect and duty, and ingratitude, and this (should I see him) I will try and make him see, and so will Alix, Louise and Lenchen, and I am certain Bertie will do nothing which could look like encouraging him to pursue a course in opposition with your wishes,— still I should be very glad if you could once more say (exactly) what you do not wish to be done, and what he may do when in London, and that all the brothers and sisters should know this also! To prevent his going out entirely if he is here, would seem almost impossible, therefore it would have been better for him not to come at all to London. Will you say once more what you especially wish avoided?

---

[1] By the Dutch Masters.
[2] Designed by Norman Shaw. Now the home of the Royal Geographical Society.

From the Crown Princess

I wrote to Beatrice yesterday about the Hampton Court pictures. How I wish you could have a commission of artists with dear old Mr. Redgrave (who is getting a little weak of sight) at the head and with Mr. Bell who understands pictures, their history and their preservation so well, as one of the members, just to look after them—hang them in a better light, give them their right names, do up some of the frames, put other pictures under glass, and weed some out which are altogether unworthy of being hung up where they are much seen. I am sure that both in the interests of the Crown whose property they are, of the nation to whom they are precious—and of all lovers of art, a great thing could be achieved! I hope I am not wrong in mentioning the matter! But if dear Papa lived I should not hesitate to say so to him! One room he arranged and that is the only one that looks well and where the pictures are seen to advantage.

There are 2 Tintorettos which I feel sure would be far better at the National Gallery (as your property)—but still far better seen and cared for there than at Hampton Court. Also "The Procession" of Mantegna's.

From the Queen

He must go away for a time from Berlin and not drive in such a low open carriage.[1] I never was allowed to in a *calèche* or barouche after the blow I received in '50—and never in a low phaeton after Oxford's attempt in '40. These socialist atheists are awful! Believe me where there is no respect for God—no belief in futurity—there can be no respect or loyalty to the highest in the land. Authority of some kind does come from Above, and if that is trampled under foot and if the clergy—narrow-minded though they be—are ridiculed and abused everything will go down!

---

[1] The Emperor was severely wounded by Charles Nobiling, who shot at him in the Unter den Linden on June 2. Nobiling was described in the Annual Register as belonging to one of "the darker socialist sects". This is doubtful but Bismarck took advantage of his deed to dissolve the Reichstag. A previous though futile attempt had been made against the Emperor in the previous May. On that occasion Bismarck wrote "Should we not take occasion to propose a bill immediately against the Socialists and their Press?" As Miss Agatha Ramm correctly says in her book *Germany 1789–1919* public opinion was effectively excited against the whole Left. Watching by the Emperor's sick-bed the Crown Princess wrote to her mother "What may his thoughts be!!" implying that Bismarck's policy had provoked both attacks.

Philosophy without religion will bring the nation down, and it cannot, will not prosper. Believe my words, belief—even if exaggerated —should be encouraged not held up to be doubted and explained away by philosophy and science! Dear Papa always said "Science and Philosophy can only go a certain distance; then faith begins!" Do remember that.

From the Queen

What you say about Philosophy and Religion contains much that I agree in and to develop all that is good, humane, charitable, unselfish and humble-minded in man ought certainly to be one's first object. But to do this, you require the recognition and adoration of God who is Himself love and goodness and to recognise him as the ruler of everything. A mere abstract idea of goodness which is very much what philosophers profess and advocate is not desirable, nor does it lead to the very perfection which it pretends to do. It is only by trusting in God's all merciful goodness and in following the precepts of His beloved Son, that one can go through the trials, sorrows and difficulties of this life. Without this conviction sorrows and trials will lead to feelings of despair and bitterness, whereas if you can say "Thy will not mine be done" and "God's ways are not our ways" you will feel a peace and contentment as well as courage far different to the courage and sense of duty of Socrates. It is this alone which makes life and our future hopes a reality.

It is therefore, I think, not the right way to try and increase the dislike of and contempt for the clergy, amongst the masses. For what real good does it do them (I mean the masses) to disbelieve all they hear and to set up their own individual notions of abstract good or know-ledge, making *that* the sole aim? Science is greatly to be admired and encouraged, but if it is to take the place of our Creator, and if philo-sophers and students try to explain everything and to disbelieve what-ever they cannot prove, I call it a great evil instead of a great blessing. The belief in eternal punishment has almost entirely disappeared and certainly in its old form was perfectly absurd and monstrous. To im-prove and enlighten the clergy without encouraging those dangerous views would be by far the best means of bringing back the masses to true religion; not by ridiculing and pulling them down. The want of reverence for parents, older people and those in authority must exist if there is no reverence or trust in our Heavenly Father.

You say that you do not think there is any danger in shaking a "belief which had a wholesome influence in restraining bad passions" but I do not agree there, for I think that a simple earnest belief is far more important than that knowledge which teaches you to begin to doubt the truth of many things which you have learnt to believe and respect. Shake this in the masses, and you shake the foundation of everything. An Empire without religion is like a house built upon sand.[1]

This letter makes a moving finish to the correspondence between the Queen and her daughter of which this book forms the fourth volume of extracts covering two decades. In passing we may notice that this letter gives the clearest expression which we have of the Queen's religious opinions. These owed nothing to the fashionable Tractarian and Catholic drift of many of the devout in the nineteenth century, little to the influence of the clergy or indeed to the formalities of the Church of England but rest on her own simple faith and belief—her comfort and companion in sorrow. That her daughter could not share this solace was a grief to the Queen. Her great friend the German Empress once remarked of another daughter of the Queen's that "like all English Princesses she was a complete atheist." That remark was not made to Queen Victoria and it was certainly not true but it was sufficiently coloured by truth to have been remembered and recorded. The triumph of Bismarck's policy, which was marked, just as this letter was written, by the Congress of Berlin over which the German statesman presided, explains why the Queen included the last sentence which also reflects some of the Empress's feelings against the materialistic and anti-Church policy of Bismarck's government. Indeed this particular letter emphasises the completely different outlook of mother and daughter. For her part the Crown Princess would have felt that something more than religion was needed to combat what she once called "the poisonous spirit spreading so widely in Germany". Shortly after the Crown Prince's death she wrote to a member of the Reichstag explaining why she and her husband had been in opposition to Bismarck. "We wanted to see the greatness of the Fatherland linked with freedom, culture and the independence of the individual."[2]

---

[1] Unfortunately the letter from the Crown Princess, to which this is an answer, has not survived. But the general sense of what she must have said is clear from the Queen's comments. See also Dearest Mama pages 194–5 where the Crown Princess writes "Science and learning are slowly preparing the ground for a new reformation".
[2] Ludwig Bamberger edited by Dr. Ernst Feder. Frankfurt 1932.

INDEX

This index gives a brief description of only those people who are not already identified in the text, the footnotes, or the list of familiar names.

Martin, Mr., afterwards Sir Theodore (1816–1909), 142, 143, 167, 243
Maxwell, Sir William Stirling, 9th Baronet (1818–78), 234
Mayo, 8th Earl (1822–72), Viceroy of India, 27, 34
Mecklenburg, Princess of, 110
Mecklenburg-Schwerin, Grand-Duchess of, sister of the Emperor, 165, 187
Mecklenburg-Schwerin, Duke William of (1827–79), son of the above, m. Princess Alexandrine of Prussia, 165, 187, 236
Mecklenburg-Strelitz, Prince Adolphus of (1848–1914), 134, 236, 248, 259
Mecklenburg-Strelitz, Grand-Duchess Augusta of (1822–1916), daughter of the 1st Duke of Cambridge, 97, 248
Member for Paris, 27
Mensdorff-Pouilly, Count Alphonse, son of the Queen's aunt, Sophie of Saxe-Coburg, 90
Metternich, Prince Richard, 70
Mexico, Empress Charlotte of, daughter of King Leopold I, 260
Michelson, Professor, 107
Midhat Pasha, 241
Minghetti, Marco, Italian statesman and scholar, 91
Mischke, Colonel, 281
The Mistletoe, 190, 206
Molkte, Count Helmuth von (1800–91), Prussian Field-Marshal, 249, 279, 287
Montague, Captain Oliver, 199
The Moonstone, 41
Muller, Professor, Friedrich Max, 54
Münster, Count, afterwards Prince (1820–1902), 82, 83, 85, 86, 87, 88, 89, 99, 100, 167, 205, 277
Münster, Marie, daughter of above, 153, 205
Murray, Grenville, 127

NACHTIGALL, DR. GUSTAV (1834–85), German explorer, 182
Napier, 1st Baron (1810–90), Field-Marshal, 228
Napoleon III, Emperor, 17, 74, 77, 275
Napoleon, Prince (1822–91), son of Jerome Bonaparte, 78
Nemours, Duchess of, 214
Normann, M. de, 76
Northbrook, 1st Earl (1826–1904), successor to Lord Mayo as Viceroy of India, 34
Northcote, Sir S., afterwards Lord Iddesleigh (1818–87), 220, 222, 278

O'CONNOR, ARTHUR, 34, 38
Oldenburg, Duchess of, 246
Oldenburg, Princess of, 58
Oliphant, Mrs., 41
Orange, Prince of (1840–79), 218, 220, 230
Osman Nuri Pasha, Turkish commander, 268, 270

Otto of Bavaria, Prince (1848–1913), later King under a Regency, 48, 49

PAGET, SIR JAMES, 145
Palmerston, 3rd Viscount, 53, 54, 130, 248
Paris, Comte and Comtesse de, 254
Paris Exhibition, 1878, 226
Pasini, Alberto, 180
Patteson, Bishop, murdered at Santa Cruz, 198
Peel, Sir Robert (1788–1850), Prime Minister, 128
Peiniger, Herr, 170
Persia, the Shah of, Nasr-Ed-Din (1831–1896), 93–5, 95–8, 100
Pius IX, Pope, 280
Plevna, Bulgaria, 263, 265, 270
Ponsonby, Sir Henry (1825–95), the Queen's private secretary, 35, 169, 205, 263, 288
Portugal, Prince Augustus of, 188–9
Prince Imperial, son of Napoleon III (1856–79), 77, 79, 133
Prussia, Prince Albert of (Abbat), 58, 61, 62, 87, 120
Prussia, Prince Albrecht of, 2, 61, 63, 64, 67, 94, 139
Prussia, Princess Alexandrine of (Addy), m. Duke William of Mecklenburg-Schwerin, 41, 120, 139, 165, 187, 203, 209, 210, 236, 277
Prussia, the Empress Augusta of (1811–90), 5, 28, 38, 39, 56, 82, 109, 116, 142, 143, 149, 158, 166, 177, 181, 183, 225, 236, 237, 239, 246, 250, 251, 264, 278
Prussia, Prince Augustus of, 55
Prussia, Prince Charles of, 235, 236, 238, 239
Prussia, Princess Charles of, wife of above, 235, 236, 237, 238, 239
Prussia, Princess Charlotte of, 139–9, 149, 163, 196, 201, 235, 241, 245, 246, 250, 252, 257, 262, 264, 267, 282–3, 286
Prussia, the Dowager Queen of, widow of King Frederick William IV, her death, 119, 120, 122, 131
Prussia, Prince Frederick Charles of (Fritz Carl) (1828–85), 38, 48, 50, 285
Prussia, Crown Prince Frederick William of (Fritz) (1831–88), 36, 37, 38, 56, 70, 78, 81, 82, 85, 89, 106, 126, 149, 164, 173, 183, 195, 199, 214, 215, 218, 227, 236, 237, 274, 287
Prussia, Fritz Leopold of, son of Prince Charles, 216, 284
Prussia, Prince Henry of, 2nd son of Crown Princess, 57, 73, 139, 149, 151, 152, 165, 174, 201, 203, 215, 231, 237, 245, 253, 258, 282
Prussia, Princess Louise of, daughter of Prince Fritz Carl, afterwards Duchess of Connaught, 255, 285, 286

and all it has to offer, 135–6; has a poor opinion of German doctors, 138; writes about the progress of her children, 138–9; meeting with Princess Marianne of the Netherlands, divorced wife of Prince Albrecht of Prussia, 140; compares the rigid regime laid down by the Prussian Emperor for the education of their children with the liberty and independence enjoyed by the Prince and Princess of Wales for their children, 141–2; describes a narrow escape at a railway level crossing, 142; visit to England and Osborne, 144–5; which she leaves with regret, 146; refers again to their conflict with the Emperor regarding the education of Prince William, 148; sends an account of Prince William's confirmation, 149–50 and praises the part played by the Prince of Wales, 150; overcomes the Emperor's plans for Prince William, who is to go to school for three years, 150; visit to Hanover and to the school at Cassel which her sons will attend, 152; is angry at German newspaper reports about the Prince of Wales' debts, 153; and complains that the German press feeds on scandal, 154; gives news of the arrest of Count Arnim, 155, 156; has fresh difficulties with the Emperor over her sons' education, 155–6; re-asserts her belief in religious tolerance, 157; and regrets the warfare between the Catholics and the Civil Authorities in Germany, 161; congratulates the Queen on Britain acquiring the Fiji Islands, 161; asks the Queen's permission to buy three sheep and three pigs from the Windsor farm in order to improve their German breeds, 162; complains again about the Emperor's lack of understanding and obsolete ideas concerning the education of children, 164, 232; reports on the progress of Prince William and Prince Henry at school, 165; thinks that the trial of Count Arnim is disgraceful, 166

1875:
Is angered at ill-natured Russian reports of the English Court and Prince Alfred, 169; attends a performance of Handel's 'Hercules' under Joachim's direction, 169; wonders if Prince Bismarck is about to resign, 172; but this report is denied by the Emperor, 173–4; expresses sympathy for the Empress who is distressed by the friction between the government and the Catholic church, 177; visit to Italy, 178, 180; answers the Queen's questions about Pasini's style of painting, 180; is with the Queen of Sweden during a 3-day visit, 181–2; comments on the abuse of England in

the German press, 182; in which she sees the hand of Bismarck, 184; visits the Royal Observatory, 184; is delighted with the portrait of the Queen by Angeli, 187; receives a legacy of a collection of antiques, 193; visits the Letterhaus institution which she helped to found, 194; praises the English climate, 197; speaks of the sensation caused by a pamphlet written by Count Arnim, 198; congratulates the British government on acquiring half shares in the Suez Canal, 199–200.

1876:
Hopes to persuade the German government to send exhibits to the Exhibition of Scientific Instruments at the Kensington Museum, 202; expresses a wish to see her mother when the Queen visits Coburg, 203–4; approves of the Queen being named Empress of India, 207; comments on the loyalty of the English people to the Crown, 211; fears that England and Germany may become estranged over the Bulgarian–Turkish affair, 213; but later reports that Bismarck hoped England would take the lead in settling the issue, 214, 218–19; blames the Russians for fomenting the unrest in the Balkans, 221, 223, 225, 226; but considers that a strong Russia is a better ally for Germany than a weak England, 228; feels that Germany is encircled by enemies, 233; is sad at the illness of Princess Charles, and the grief of Prince Charles, 235–6; sends a tactful refusal to the Queen regarding the proposed bestowal of the Grand Cross of the Bath on Prince William on his coming of age, 237; thanks the Queen warmly for investing Prince William (through the Crown Prince) with the Order of the Garter, 239; feels that the peace of Europe can only be maintained by England standing between France and Germany, 241; gives an account of a meeting with General Ignatiev, whom she found vain and patronising, 244; stresses that Bismarck distrusts Russia and is a sincere friend of England, 248, 252; complains of the uncivil behaviour of the Grand-Duchess of Mecklenburg-Strelitz, 248–9; describes a visit from the Emperor of Brazil, 249; complains of attacks against herself and the Empress in the German press, 250; and appeals to the Emperor to take steps to shield his wife, 252; visits the theatre to see the actor Tommasso Salvini, 253; is distressed at the resentment shown by the younger generation to any form of restraint, 257; tells of a visit to Charlotte, Empress of Mexico, 260; is very glad

Prussia, Crown Princess Frederick William of—contd.
that the Queen received and liked Prince Bernard, 261; complains of the indifference to his parents shown by Prince William, 261–2; speaks of a Russian success at Plevna, 263; attends a parade in celebration of the Emperor's 80th birthday and is rolled on by her horse, 263–4; admits that her sympathies lie with the Turks, 265; and fears that in the event of peace the European powers will not allow Turkey to benefit in any way, 266; is downcast at the news of Russian successes in Armenia, 268; asks the Queen for a signed letter to add to the autograph collection of a friend, 270; writes affectionately to the Queen on the anniversary of the Prince Consort's death, 270.
1878:
Refers to the Queen's speech on the Opening of Parliament, which she fears will not deter Russian aggression, 276; sends the Queen a pair of Dackel dogs, which she describes as 'capital watch dogs', 277; urges the Queen to support the re-equipment and reorganisation of the British army, which she regards as the best in the world, 279; discusses Bismarck's policy in opposing Russian demands in the Treaty of Peace, 280; attends the wedding of Princess Charlotte to Prince Bernard of Saxe-Meiningen, 282–3; is doubtful whether Austria would be a reliable ally for Britain against Russia, 283; describes the confirmation of Princess Victoria, 284; once again expresses her longing for a united stand against Russia, 287; shares the Queen's anxiety about Prince Leopold, and wonders how he can be made to realise his physical disability, 275; is concerned about the pictures at Hampton Court, which are not displayed to advantage, 292.
Prussia, Princess Victoria of, 2nd daughter of the Crown Princess, 149, 210, 284
Prussia, Prince Waldemar, 3rd son of the Crown Princess, 139, 152, 216, 277, 281, 284
Prussia, the Emperor William I of (1797–1888), 17, 28, 67, 113, 114, 115, 116, 118, 141, 143, 148, 149, 167, 174, 176, 182, 183, 232, 242, 246, 248, 263, 264, 274, 292
Prussia, Prince William of, later Kaiser William II (1859–1941), 5, 56, 57, 73, 83, 85, 86, 88, 89, 139, 148, 151, 152, 160, 165, 166, 174, 199, 201, 203, 209, 215, 231, 237, 238–9, 242, 254, 258, 261, 262, 264, 266

Queen Mary by Lord Tennyson, 188
RAINER, Archduchess, Marie Caroline, grand-daughter of Leopold II and Marie Louise of Spain, 91
Rawlinson, Sir Henry (1810–95), Assyriologist and Persian scholar, 101
Redern, Count William, 223, 224, 243
Redern, Countess, 187
Rendano, Alfonso, 81
Reuss, Prince Henry VII of, 204, 255, 261, 268
Hélène Reuter, reputedly daughter of Ernest II, Duke of Saxe-Coburg, 47
Richmond, 6th Duke of (1818–1903), 129, 160, 272
Richmond, Duchess of, wife of above and niece of Charles Greville, 158
Richter, Gustav (1823–84), 123, 170
Ripon, Marquis of (1827–1909), 151
Ross, Sir William, 63
Rossmore, Lord (1851–74), 134
Rothschild, Sir A. de (1810–76), created baronet 1847, 147
Rousselet, M., 171
Roxburghe, Duchess of, wife of the 6th Duke and Lady of the Bedchamber to the Queen, 30, 263
Royal Titles Bill, 208
Royal Vault, Windsor, 93
Rubinstein, Anton, 173
Rudolf, Crown Prince. See Austria
Ruland, W., Librarian to the Prince Consort, 77
Russell, Lady Emily, daughter of the 4th Earl of Clarendon, wife of Lord Odo, 154, 218
Russell, Lord Odo, British Ambassador in Berlin, 16, 46, 83, 89, 99, 154, 155, 217, 218, 229, 230, 238, 239, 247, 248, 256, 262, 281
Russia, Emperor Alexander II of (1818–81), 58, 60, 66, 68, 102, 126, 129, 137, 183, 215, 221, 225, 226, 230, 248
Russia, Cesarevitch Alexander (afterwards Emperor Alexander III), 95, 96, 100, 105
Russia, Grand-Duke Constantine, 137
Russia, Dagmar, wife of Cesarevitch Alexander, 68, 85, 102, 103, 112, 126
Russia, Empress Marie of, wife of Emperor Alexander II, 127, 129, 137, 163
Russia, Grand-Duchess Marie of, daughter of Czar Alexander II, married H.R.H. Prince Alfred, 4, 22, 76, 88, 89, 102–3, 112, 118, 119, 122, 126, 131, 135, 152, 171, 265, 266, 268, 281, 285
Russia, Grand-Duke Nicholas Constantine (1850–1918), 137
Russia, Grand-Duke Nicholas (Nicolaievitch) (1856–1929), 246
SALISBURY, 3rd Marquess, statesman, 205, 231, succeeded Lord Derby as Foreign Secretary, 286, 287

Victoria, H.M.—*contd.*
the Government and Mr. Gladstone, 29, 30; attends Thanksgiving Service for the Prince of Wales at St. Paul's, 30; expresses great gratification for the loyal reception received in the streets and describes the procession and service, 31–2; writes of proposed visit to Baden, 32; is attacked by Arthur O'Connor, who is disarmed by John Brown, 33; awards John Brown a 'Victoria Devoted Service Medal', 34; visit to Baden, 36–7; is displeased at the light sentence passed on O'Connor, 38; but is pleased with the good relations between her daughter and the Empress, 39; who visits Windsor, 40; decorates the Empress with the Victorian Order, 40; approves of the names of the Crown Princess's new baby, 41; is anxious concerning the health of Prince Leopold, and reflects on the ingratitude of children towards their parents, 42; defends her strict treatment of Prince Leopold, 45; dwells upon the difficulty of being both Queen and mother, 47; laments the death of the Rev. Norman McLeod, 48, 49; and accuses the Crown Princess of lack of feeling, 49–50; visits the Agricultural Show in the Home Park, 51; her sympathy with the working classes, disapproval of religious intolerance, and belief in education for women, 51; inspects the completed Albert Memorial, 52; is dismayed at Baron Ernest Stockmar's life of his father, 53–4; which she reads with mixed feelings, 56; proposed marriage of Prince Alfred to Grand-Duchess Marie of Russia cancelled, 57; visit to Scotland—lays Memorial Stone to Harriet, Duchess of Sutherland, 60; meets the explorer Stanley, 60; sends good wishes to Prince Albert (Abbat) on his engagement; and later reproves the Crown Princess for her unfriendly silence on this subject, 62; wishes her sons to have freedom of choice in regard to marriage, 65; writes about Prince Alfred and his marriage plans, 68–9; is grieved at the disunity in her own family, and praises the example of the Danish Royal Family, 69; sends birthday greetings to the Crown Princess (November 16), 69; has further misgivings about Prince Alfred, 71; but defends his omission of paying the Crown Princess a visit when in Germany, 72.
1873:
Reports death of the Emperor Napoleon III at Chislehurst (January 9), 74; plans for marriage of Prince Albert to Grand-Duchess Marie of Russia renewed, 74–5;

hopes that the Crown Princess will visit England in May, 75; describes her visit to Chislehurst and the lying-in-state of the Emperor Napoleon, 77–8; receives a visit from Lord Tennyson and the Prince Imperial, 79; Ministerial crisis caused by the Irish University Bill, and resignation of Mr. Gladstone, 80; which does not, however, take effect, 81; discounts any suggestion of a French–English alliance or any war of aggression on the part of the French, 81–2; is shocked at the morganatic marriage of George of Saxe-Meiningen, 82, 83; Prince Alfred invited to meet the Russian Royal Family at Sorrento, 85; approves of the appointment of Count Münster as Prussian Ambassador to London, 86–7; presents the Colours to the 79th Regiment Cameron Highlanders, 87; is worried at the uncertainty of Prince Alfred's marriage prospects, 92; is shocked at the death of Princess Alice's second son, 92; describes her visit to the Royal Vault at Windsor, 93; entertains the Shah of Persia on a three-day visit, who receives the Order of the Garter and attends a Review in Windsor Park, and later meets an enthusiastic welcome in Liverpool and Manchester, 95–8; regrets the impossibility of attending Prince William's confirmation in Berlin in a private capacity, 98; complains of tiredness and overwork, 99; refutes the accusations of cruelty levelled against the Shah, 101; announces the engagement of Prince Alfred to Grand-Duchess Marie, 102; does not agree with the Crown Princess's religious ideas, and declares her staunch adherence to Protestantism, 104; reports Ministerial changes in the Government, 106; is pleased at the gift of a snuff-box formerly belonging to Queen Caroline of Denmark, 107; spends a week at Inverlochry, 108; refers with disfavour to the King of Italy's method of obtaining the union of Italy, and likens it to the similar attainment of German unity at the expense of lesser royalty, 111; expresses her distaste for the acquisition of India, 111; speaks of Princess Beatrice's confirmation, and her determination to keep her as her constant companion, 112; emphasises the importance of good relations between Germany, Austria, Italy and Russia, 113; supports the German Emperor's reply to the Pope's protest against the measures taken towards Catholicism in Germany, 114; returns to the subject, and supports Protestant opposition to Roman Catholicism, 115,

156; is indignant at the quarantine of the Crown Princess's dogs, 115; is hurt that the Crown Princess should think her lacking in discretion, 116, 117; illness of Prince Leopold, 116; is grieved at the death of the Queen Dowager of Prussia, 119; sends Prince Alfred words of good advice regarding his behaviour in his future married life, 121; and voices her fears to the Crown Princess, 122.

1874:
Describes the confirmation of Princess Beatrice, 124; is gratified that the Liberal Government is replaced by the Conservative Party with a large majority, 127–9; and considers Gladstone to have been a very unsatisfactory Premier, 130; is pleased with the enthusiastic welcome given to Prince Alfred and his bride on arrival at Windsor, 132; does not agree with the Crown Princess's suggestion for the mutual destruction of their correspondence, except for letters of no importance, 132–3; finds the Duchess of Edinburgh easy to live with, 134; reviews troops returning from the Ashanti War, 134; asks the Crown Princess if she is interested in obtaining any of Landseer's work, to be sold by auction at Christie's, 135; enquires about a scandal and Grand-Duke Nicholas Constantine of Russia, 137; approves of the Crown Princess's meeting with Princess Marianne, 140; speaks of the difficulty in preventing 'little Princes' from becoming spoiled, 140–1; and sympathises with the Crown Princess's difficulties regarding the education of their children, 142; asks the Crown Princess her opinion of Mr. Martin's biography of the Prince Consort, 146; contrasts the love of parents with the ingratitude of children, 147; is anxious about the Prince of Wales' gambling debts, 147; sends her blessings for Prince William on the occasion of his confirmation, 148–9; believes that Prince Waldemar would be more suitable for the navy than Prince Henry, 152–3; sends the Crown Princess a short paragraph contradicting the reports of the Prince of Wales' debts, 153; and decides that abuse of Royalty has its roots in jealousy, 155; asks the Crown Princess if she should intervene in the matter of her boys' education, 157; is shocked at the Queen of Bavaria's conversion to Catholicism, 157; is indignant at the article in The Times, 156; which attributes the Prince of Wales' expenses to his duties as representative of the Queen, 158; first child born to the Duchess of Edinburgh, 159; is angered by a book of Memoirs written by Charles Greville, 160–1; refers to Mr. Gladstone's pamphlet criticising Papal Infallability, 162; christening of Prince Alfred's son at Windsor, 163; presents the Crown Princess with the pigs and sheep she wished to have as a Christmas present, 163; feels that girls should not regard marriage as the only object in life, 165; attaches great importance to civility towards others, 166.

1875:
Reproaches the Crown Princess for not commenting on the biography of the Prince Consort, 169; disregards reports of Russian abuse of the English Court, 170; mourns the death of Charles Kingsley, 171; queries the wisdom of a proposed visit to England by the Crown Princess and her large family, 171–2; feels that Bismarck has gone too far in his quarrel with the Catholics, 173; reports progress of portraits by Angeli of herself and Princess Beatrice, 174; with which she is very pleased, 175; compares the work of Angeli with that of Winterhalter, 175–6; agrees that the persecution of the Catholics in Germany is a great mistake, 178; is distressed at the death of Lady Caroline Barrington, 179; visit of Princess Alice and family, 180; enquires about the style of Pasini's painting, 180; spends her birthday at Balmoral, 181; speaks of preparations for the Prince of Wales' tour of India, 185; sends her portrait by Angeli to Berlin to be photographed, 186; is indignant at the assault of a young lady by Colonel V. Baker, 189; receives a present of 4 horses and 2 ponies from the King of Italy, 189; the Royal yacht Alberta collides with the schooner Mistletoe, 190; feels that the inquest on the accident will be prejudiced, 191; and that the ordering of a Naval Inquiry is a mistake, 192; refuses the Crown Princess's request to come and visit her in November, but assures that she is not 'unwelcome', 192; visit to Inverary, 194; suggests remedies for the Crown Princess's neuralgia, 196–7; attends the funeral of John Brown's father at Balmoral, 197; sends New Year greetings to all, and criticises her grandsons' handwriting, 201; reproves the Crown Princess for thinking that she takes no interest in her grandchildren, 202; and returns to the subject of the waywardness of children, 203; refers to the progress of the Prince of Wales in India, 204; complains that she finds receiving visitors very fatiguing, 204; and lists the

aware of the Russian threat, 280; and
does not agree that the British army
needs reforming, 281; is of the opinion
that Party government is a great evil
when carried too far, 283; is not pleased
with Prince Arthur's engagement to
Princess Louise of Prussia, and insists that
the marriage shall take place in England,
285; fears opposition to the marriage
from the Duke and Duchess of Cambridge, 285; is interested in Princess
Louise's marriage dowry, 286; approves
Lord Salisbury's Circular to the Powers,
demanding European judgement of the
Treaty of San Stefano, 287; which was
subsequently destroyed at the Congress
of Berlin, 288; is annoyed at the behaviour of Prince Leopold who resents
the guarded and secluded life his mother
expects him to lead, 289; writes the
Crown Princess an affectionate letter
comparing their similar outlook and
mutual care for the welfare of their
children, 290; is of the strong opinion
that religious belief must not be explained away by philosophy and science,
292–3; and that a simple earnest belief
in God gives the courage to sustain the
trials, sorrows and difficulties of this
life, 294
Victoria, Princess of Hesse-Darmstadt,
eldest daughter of Princess Alice, 180, 181
'Victoria Devoted Service Medal', 34
Von Angeli, M. (1840–1925), 123, 125,
139, 170, 174, 183, 185, 199, 247, 251,
267
Von Ense Rahel (1771–1833), 193
Von Werner, H., 180

WAINWRIGHT, JACOB, 157
Waldeck, Princess, daughter of the Duke
of Nassau, 182
Waldemar, Prince, youngest son of the
Crown Princess. See Prussia

Walderburg, Fraulein von, 55
Wales, Alexandra, Princess of, 20, 85, 86,
93, 96, 100, 111, 124, 125, 126, 141, 144,
145, 167, 180, 188, 200, 219, 269, 270,
285, 286, 289, 291
Wales, H.R.H. Albert Edward, Prince of
(1841–1910), illness of, 19–24; Thanksgiving Service at St. Paul's for his recovery, 30–2, 33; visit to Paris, 46; 47,
63; attends lying-in-state of the Emperor
Napoleon III, 74; 85, 86, 87, 88; acts as
adviser to the English exhibition at the
Vienna Exhibition, 91; 92, 96, 100, 111,
117; attends the confirmation of Princess Beatrice, 124; 125, 128, 140, 141,
144; rumours about his gambling debts,
147, 148, 150, 151, 153, 154, 156, 158; is
present at the confirmation of Prince
William in Berlin, 149; visits France,
158, 159; death and funeral of Major
Grey, a member of his household, 166–
167; 180, 186, 188, 193; leaves for the
tour of India, 196; 200, 204, 209;
enthusiastic welcome on arrival home,
211; 212, 219, 223; invites Prince of
Orange to Sandringham, 230; 253, 255,
260, 262, 270, 289, 291
Wallace, Sir Richard (1818–90), be-
queathed Wallace Collection to nation,
247
Wegner, Dr., physician to the Crown
Princess, 70, 138, 249
Weiss, Amalie, wife of Joseph Joachim,
170
Welch, Captain, 192, 206, 218
Wellesley, Colonel Frederick Arthur,
259
Westminster, 1st Duke of (1825–99), 207
Wiasemsky, Princess, 132
Winterhalter, Franz, 102, 111, 170
Wolseley, Sir Garnet, 205
Wrangl, Field Marshal (1784–1877), 183

ZANZIBAR, Sultan of, 101